PIMLICO

841

CHRISTOPHER LLOYD

Stephen Anderton is a gardening writer whose books include *Rejuvenating a Garden*, *Urban Sanctuaries* and *Discovering Welsh Gardens*. He is gardening correspondent of *The Times* and formerly National Gardens Manager for English Heritage, having begun life as a professional gardener after graduating in Drama and Classics. It has been said that his wicked cabaret songs 'are to gardening what *Private Eye* is to politics'. Married with three daughters, he now lives in the Black Mountains of Wales, where he is making a garden of 20 acres.

Stephen Anderton knew Christo well for 20 years and had first-hand experience of his love of back-and-forth letter writing, as well as the social life at Dixter. Yet from a distance after Christo's death he can see, warts and all, the complete picture of this complex character and the way the private man and the public persona fit together.

Christo himself had asked Stephen Anderton to write his biography, and this was endorsed after his death by the Trustees of Great Dixter who have made available for the first time Christo's chaotic, 100-year archive of bundled, dusty papers relating to the house, garden and family – letters, diaries, cuttings, photographs, treasure troves which were found stuffed into drawer after drawer in room after room at Dixter.

Also by Stephen Anderton

Discovering Welsh Gardens
Urban Sanctuaries
Rejuvenating a Garden

CHRISTOPHER LLOYD

His Life at Great Dixter

———

STEPHEN ANDERTON

PIMLICO

Published by Pimlico 2011

2 4 6 8 10 9 7 5 3 1

Copyright © Stephen Anderton 2010

Stephen Anderton has asserted his right under the Copyright, Designs
and Patents Act 1988 to be identified as the author of this work

This book is sold subject to the condition that it shall not,
by way of trade or otherwise, be lent, resold, hired out,
or otherwise circulated without the publisher's prior
consent in any form of binding or cover other than that
in which it is published and without a similar condition,
including this condition, being imposed on the subsequent purchaser

First published in Great Britain in 2010 by
Chatto & Windus

Pimlico
Random House, 20 Vauxhall Bridge Road,
London SW1V 2SA

www.rbooks.co.uk

Addresses for companies within The Random House Group Limited can be found at:
www.randomhouse.co.uk/offices.htm

The Random House Group Limited Reg. No. 954009

A CIP catalogue record for this book
is available from the British Library

ISBN 9781845950965

The Random House Group Limited supports The Forest Stewardship Council (FSC),
the leading international forest certification organisation. All our titles that are
printed on Greenpeace approved FSC certified paper carry the FSC logo.
Our paper procurement policy can be found at www.rbooks.co.uk/environment

Printed and bound in Great Britain by
Clays Ltd, St Ives PLC

Contents

List of Illustrations

Section of black and white illustrations

Dixter, September 1911: workmen on the roof of the kitchen in Lutyens' new wing.

Dixter, February 1956: the Topiary Garden under snow. Photographed by Col. Evans.

The Yeoman's Hall, brought to Dixter as a dismantled timber frame.

1923: in full Puritan dress, Daisy Lloyd sails from her bedroom into the garden. Not for nothing was she known as The Management.

Daisy and Les Six in 1930: Back row: Oliver and Selwyn; Christo, Quentin and Letitia in the middle; and Pat in front with Bunch the spaniel.

Christo, aged 9, with Daisy in Nathaniel's new Sunk Garden.

Ken Stubbs. Photographed at Dixter by Nathaniel Lloyd in 1928.

'Saturday, September the 9th, 1933. Christo & his Cacti.'

1934: Christo in his typically shy stance, firmly clamped to Daisy who is holding a spaniel puppy.

'Taken at the Students' Camp, Weissensee, Saturday, August the 21st, 1937.'

'Taken Monday, May the 2nd, 1938. Trio in the Parlour.'

Christo in uniform during the War. With Daisy.

Christo after the War. With Daisy.

Christo in the potting shed.

Selwyn, aged about 18. Oliver, 21. Patrick, 19. Quentin, 16. Letitia, 17.

1970: an open day at Dixter. Daisy, in her nineties sitting as ever in front of the porch with her dog.

Romke van de Kaa. In the vinehouses at Lismore Castle, 1979.

Anna Pavord and Fergus Garrett tulip-hunting in Turkey, May 1993.

Pip Morrison, in the Solar.

Section of colour illustrations

Daisy Lloyd, with one of her sons, probably Oliver, c 1913.

Daisy and Nathaniel Lloyd.

Dixter: stencil work on plaster, in Lutyens' new wing. *Country Life*

Christo's arrangement of oriental poppies in the Great Hall. Photographed by Pamla Toler.

Lutyens' staircase, with banister details by Nathaniel Lloyd. *Country Life*.

Dining room table and suede-upholstered chairs by Rupert Williamson. Studio shot. *By kind permission of Rupert Williamson.*

Olivia Speer (née Lind) in the kitchen, Christmas 1986.

Holders of the Royal Horticultural Society's Victoria Medal of Honour, 1997. Christo sits alongside luminaries of the British gardening establishment.

Back row, left to right: John G. Hillier, Fred Whitsey, Alan Hardy, Lady Anne Berry, Kath Dryden, David McClintock, Peter Cox, Dr Max Walters, Lawrence Banks, The Hon. Alasdair Morrison, Robin Compton, John Bond, Raymond Evison, Dr James Smart, Louis Russell, George Lockie, Penelope Hobhouse.

Centre, left to right: Charles Notcutt, John Simmons, Carolyn Hardy, Dr Jack Elliot, Mary Shirville, Sheila Macqueen, Prof. Leonard Broadbent, Dr Alfred Evans, Prof. Douglas Henderson, George Sheard, Helen Robinson, Clive Innes, Derrick Fuller, John Sales, John Mattock, Brian Mathew, Adrian Bloom, Roy Lancaster.

Front, left to right: Stuart Ogg, Martin Robinson, Martin Slocock, Charles Puddle, Edward Kemp, Prof. William Stearn, Julia Clements (Lady Seton), Lord Aberconway, Robin Herbert, Lady Loder, Sir Giles Loder, Bt, Graham Stuart Thomas, Valerie Finnis (Lady Scott), Christopher Lloyd, Prof. John Hudson.

Not pictured: Joyce Wethered (Lady Heathcoat Amory), Alan Bloom, Christopher Brickell, Beth Chatto, Dame Sylvia Crowe, Jack Drake, Prof. Adrian Posnette, Frederick Roach, the Hon. Miriam Rothschild, Anthony Schilling, HM Queen Elizabeth the Queen Mother. *Country Life*

The Meadow Garden with camassias. The porch in the background. *Jonathan Buckley*

The porch in 2003, with displays of potted plants. Christo with Anne Wambach.

The enclosed Rose Garden in the early 1980s. Photographed by Pamla Toler.

The Exotic Garden in the 1990s. *Jonathan Buckley.*

Christo and Fergus Garrett. They uprooted in the roses in order to plant exotic perennials. *Jonathan Buckley.*

Coffee after lunch, by the Horse Pond, July 1985.

Friends in the Yeoman's Hall, 1991.

Still gardening in his 80s. Christo at work with Fergus in the Long Border. *Jonathan Buckley.*

Unless otherwise stated, all illustrations are from the Great Dixter Archive.

The author and publishers have made every effort to trace holders of copyright in both text and illustrations. Any inadvertent omissions or mistakes can be corrected in future editions. The reproduction of family photographs and the quotations from family papers including the writings of Daisy and Christopher Lloyd are by kind permission of the Trustees of the Great Dixter Charitable Trust. The correspondence of John Hills is reproduced by kind permission of Bradfield College. The map of Dixter garden was drawn by Reginald Piggott.

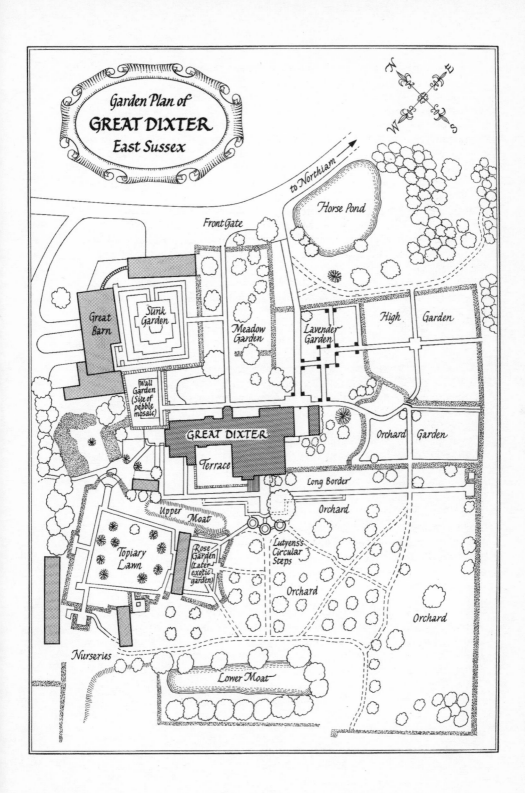

Preface

In January 2006, a month after Christopher Lloyd suggested that I might like to write his biography, he died unexpectedly. We had time for just one discussion about the project, sitting in front of a blazing log fire in the Great Hall at Dixter, he in a wheelchair with a blanket over his knees. This book, therefore, is not the one either of us expected it to be, but perhaps it has some advantages of its own. I was unable to quiz him much about his childhood, his private life, his personal satisfactions. But on the other hand, as his friend, I already knew him intimately, from the inside; and as his biographer, I was freed to inter-pret the copious Dixter documents, including letters, diaries, note-books and photographs, and to form, from the outside, a considered and dispassionate opinion of the complex subject of this book.

I first met Christo in 1986. I was then head gardener at Belsay Hall in Northumberland, and Bob Seeley, an old friend of Christo's, brought him to see the garden, having arranged for me to show him round. Christo and I clicked. Before he left, out came the shabby black calendar, bound by its rubber band, and he fixed a weekend for me to go down to Dixter. Bob Seeley said afterwards that I should be very pleased: it was not everyone who was invited to 'the best small hotel in Sussex'.

That visit began an energetic and delightful correspondence, which lasted for twenty years. Receiving a letter from Christo was like opening a bottle of champagne – bubbly and intoxicating and, in our case, full of music, plants and people. The urge to reply at once was embarrassing. Our correspondence led to friendship and many a happy visit to Dixter. It was my pleasure to accompany Christo on trips round Britain and abroad, and many times to hear opera at Glyndebourne. An abiding memory is of a Glyndebourne picnic, Christo lying on a rug on one elbow, in his burgundy dinner jacket and cummerbund, soft belly bulging against his shirt. The group of us (the evening was warm) crossed the lawn, like Mr Lloyd's horticulture class, to a clump of dictamnus. Christo asked the smoker among us to hold a lighter above the seedheads (the evening was still and the plant generous of its volatile oils) and there was a flash of flame above the plant as the oils ignited. People stared. Some muttered, 'That's Christopher Lloyd!'

The first time I went to Dixter after Christo's death, the Cornish composer Russell Pascoe was staying there. He and an American garden designer, Anne Wambach, had been due to go to Glyndebourne with Christo that weekend – the tickets were a gift, as always – and they had travelled long distances to be there, to honour his memory and his invitation. It was Russell's twenty-fifth consecutive visit to Glyndebourne, courtesy of Christo and, before that, of Christo's brother Oliver.

Russell is an old friend of mine and, since I was slightly squeamish about starting to dig through all the secret corners of Dixter where so much of Christo's life story lay hidden, I asked him to come with me to Christo's bedroom over the porch. It was as good a place as any to start. We pulled out drawers to find hoards of family letters from the 1930s and wads of rolled-up half-finished embroidery. One cupboard held a chocolate-brown, drawstring velvet bag, containing what felt like a tall sweet jar. Curious, I opened the strings and there on the container's lid was written *Christopher Lloyd*. It was his ashes, and the beginning of this exploration of his life.

There followed months of wading through yellowed family correspondence from every decade of the last century, most of it filthy with age. Sometimes, I would leave the little attic room where I worked simply to wash my hands. At other times, I would leave simply to suck in a lungful of clean air and forget this dysfunctional family, the Lloyds of Great Dixter, and its troubled, troubling matriarch, Daisy Lloyd.

The reading was not easy. I was familiar with Christo's octogenarian scrawl, but less so with his younger style. His mother's minute script – 3mm upper-case, 2mm lower-case – was endless and impossible to speed-read.

I talked to his family and friends, reread his books and his journalism, and came to the conclusion, gradually and reluctantly, that Christo had lived two lives: one before and one after his mother's death. No biography of Christo would be of any value without the story of his mother.

Preface

I toyed with the idea of calling the book *Christopher Lloyd: Two Lives*, as it seemed to me it covered both *his* two and *their* two lives. My editor at Chatto & Windus thought it not wholly accurate. This is a book, after all, about Christo and Great Dixter. But there is no escaping the fact that Christo and Daisy and Dixter and all the Lloyds are bound together, tight as the twisted strands of a hawser. You must take all of them, or none.

Stephen Anderton, Wales, October 2009.

Introduction

'Come on, faster, faster!' he barks at me from the passenger seat as we career southwards with the windscreen wipers on double speed. He hops from one buttock to the other, as if he's ready to grab the wheel or demand an emergency stop and swap seats to drive himself. This is Christo. Christopher Lloyd, the grand old man of English gardening, at eighty.

Even out of a car there is a whiff of Mr Toad about him. Unruly white hair cut short to his head in a wiry cap. White toothbrush moustache. Jowly. The everyday shabby tweed jacket with leather elbow patches and cuffs, baggy grey-green gabardine trousers (turn-ups, of course) and the shoes. He and the shoes go back a long way; they are Clarks, broad as bulldogs and cracked as the face of a *National Geographic* peasant. The sole of one shoe flaps disconnectedly at the front like a benign shark.

The car is Christo's and I am driving him back from his annual foray to stay with friends and see gardens and landscapes in Scotland. It's an ancient Volvo with no frills: hard fascia, filthy, collapsed seats reeking of dog. It moves fast, but its well-worn suspension thrusts us forward with a kind of circular motion, as if it were trying to drill its way through the mist and spray. Like owner, like car, they say. We are going back to his home at Dixter in East Sussex – Great Dixter – an extraordinary place.

Dixter was one of the most charming marriages of house and garden in Britain, and the garden second to none in the quality and energy and innovation of its planting. But when Christopher Lloyd died, on 27th January 2006, Dixter ceased to be that same living family home

1

and garden. All the national newspapers carried long obituaries. His death was seen as the end of an era. Would the garden survive, and would the gardening world be the same without Lloyd's maverick presence? Friends said that the Dixter they had come to love had died with Christo; some said they would never go back.

After the great storms of 1987, which flattened so many great English gardens, people had been equally pessimistic, declaring them irrevocably lost. This was said with a certain superiority, as if they had enjoyed something that others could not; as if they shared a sophisticated taste no longer available to anyone else. Christo himself was uncomfortable with this kind of horticultural sentimentality. He saw the storm damage more as an opportunity than a loss, and had no patience with the 'end of an era' brigade. Those who genuinely cared for those wrecked gardens must get busy and make something new. And Dixter may no longer have the guiding presence of Christo, but of course it continues and must become something new.

For himself, Christo always saw Dixter as a ground plan upon which he was privileged to experiment during his lifetime; but true to form, when he came to handling its future, he was his usual unsentimental, not to say careless, self. He announced loud and often that he had no desire to see the garden set in stone exactly as he had left it. Nor did he want Dixter to 'fall into the hands of English Heritage or the National Trust', whose approach to gardens he felt was too conservative, mealy-mouthed and impersonal. But in his very last years Christo began to feel that it was important, when he was gone, to keep the place together, so that it could be somebody else's ground plan; and to that end he arranged, with resignation and reluctance and a good deal of relief, for the setting up of the Great Dixter Charitable Trust to manage Dixter after his death.

So today the garden is able to race along as fast as ever, in the hands of Fergus Garrett, Christo's last head gardener and closest friend. Christo's dachshunds still toddle around like unconvincing pantomime horses, now more generously fed than in Christo's day and less prone to snapping at children. Dixter is open to the public more than ever before, and people continue to come from all over the world to admire Christopher Lloyd's garden. Inevitably the atmosphere is not the same. Its hub – that impatient, generous, witty, repressed, irascible old man with his loud shirts and shabby jacket, the man who through his lectures and books and journalism and nursery made Dixter one of the best-known and most highly respected gardens in the world – is gone. But what made him, and what he made Dixter, and his influence on a fast-moving century of gardening, is a fascinating story.

It is a commonplace English habit to use the name of a house to stand for the garden alone, even when the house is also open to the public. *Dixter, the garden*. And yet at Dixter it is impossible to separate the two. The house and garden were largely created for Christo's parents by Edwin Lutyens in 1910, and Christo's father Nathaniel Lloyd, himself an architect, continued to refine the structure for several years.

Nathaniel was fourteen years older than Christo's mother Daisy and, when he died in 1933, he and Lutyens between them had left a powerful framework of borders, paths, hedges and open spaces upon which Daisy could garden for another thirty-nine years. This she did with the constant help and companionship of her youngest son Christopher, and the two of them worked on it together until her death at the age of ninety-one in 1972. Christo was then fifty-one. For the next thirty-four years the garden was his alone; and almost half of that he spent with Fergus Garrett.

During Christo's lifetime gardening changed in many different ways, passing from the grand Edwardian manner and the passion for rock gardening, through the final demise of the great public parks, through the compartmented inter-war gardens of Vita Sackville-West and Lawrence Johnston, through the polite, pastel period à la Rosemary Verey, through the boom in consumer gardening that came with increasing home ownership and television gardening, through the fashionable, ecologically correct grasses-and-perennials movement, and finally to the fields in which Christo was a passionate pioneer – meadow gardening and the revival of exotic, subtropical gardening.

Sometimes he was ahead of the game, sometimes merely its best practitioner, but always he was a part of what was new, a busy, genial spider at the centre of gardening's evolving web. Why should he not take part in that game? He had a wonderful garden to play with, a modest private income, and relative leisure in which to experiment. He had been a serious student of gardening since he was a young child and was introduced to the great Gertrude Jekyll, that massively influential gardener, colourist and writer, who blessed him, patted him on the head and said, 'I hope you will grow up to be a great gardener.' Apart from school, university and his time in the army, Christo never lived away from Dixter. He travelled, he taught horticulture, he ran his own specialist nursery from the 1950s onwards, he advised on horticultural commit-tees (although he was anything but clubbable). His eye was constantly on the lookout for inventive, polished, plantsman's gardening. He had little interest in, or even awareness of, professional and civic garden management or large-scale commercial horticulture. His world was the world of private gardens and the people who made them.

Latterly, and to his happy bemusement, he became a minor celebrity. Television loved to wheel him out as an arbiter of taste, the wise old man of anarchic colour; the dahlia dude with the crazy cardigans. He became familiar to the millions who were not hands-on gardeners, but watched television coverage of the Chelsea Flower Show for its colour and spectacle. Christo's fashionable Exotic Garden (a relatively late development at Dixter) became his accepted trademark and proclaimed him young at heart. Glossy magazines throughout the English-speaking world courted Christo to write for them or to be interviewed. Lecturing took him across the globe.

Books flowed from him until the day he died. His early ones, such as *The Well-Tempered Garden* and *Foliage Plants*, straight away became bibles for serious gardeners young and old. Some books such as *Clematis* and *Gardening on Chalk and Lime* were specialised, others such as *Dear Friend and Gardener* and *Other People's Gardens* were ruminative. In his later years he returned to books on constrained subjects such as *Meadows* and *Succession Planting*, perhaps the two greatest preoccupations of his gardening life at Dixter. The seminal books stayed in print, some of the pot-boilers faded away.

His weekly column 'In My Garden' appeared in *Country Life* for forty-two years, an extraordinary achievement in gardening or any other subject. He wrote columns for *The Observer* and *The Guardian*, and contributed regularly to the glossies and several of the more serious American magazines. His output was simply prodigious.

Christo ran Dixter like the captain of a sailing ship, admired and respected by his staff, and always treating them (those that did not become friends) with an appropriate degree of old-school aloofness learned from his mother. At the garden's peak after 2000, Dixter had a sizeable crew: adoring guides who took the public on tours of the house; nursery and tea-shop staff; and of course several gardeners, one or two of whom might be students, there for experience's sake and billeted on the top floor of the house.

His journalistic work, fed by direct experience, was something he could produce quickly and concisely, writing by hand or on a primitive laptop computer, taking an hour on his own in the Parlour, a dark ground-floor room remarkably like a captain's cabin with its low ceiling supported by a central post. In effect the Parlour was his office. Around its timber-framed walls were ranged bookcases, chests of drawers stuffed with nursery catalogues and transparencies, a black Bösendorfer upright piano, and watercolours by his beloved music master at Rugby. In one corner was a huge fireplace beside which stood an embroidered wing chair bearing the initials of its embroiderers, DL and PL, his mother Daisy and brother Patrick, and there in the centre of the room was a new, blonde, sinuous Cinderella of a desk by Rupert Williamson, a furniture designer whose work he admired.

The real office was behind the Parlour, and it was here that the computers and telephones and tangles of modern wires lay. Christo rarely spent time in the office; it was not his world, and he felt the need not to waste effort on administrative matters that he did not wish to understand. He expended only the necessary minimum of thought and energy on such tedious concerns as the Dixter estate, legal matters and money. Perhaps it was in recognition of his absence from the office that he had Rupert Williamson make for it a beautiful new door, of oak slashed with long strips of aquamarine stained glass. Out of sight, but not *quite* out of mind.

Christo was regularly to be seen on his knees in the garden. Most visitors would ask the usual questions – how many staff, how long does it take to clip the hedges, isn't it a lot of work? – and the questions had more to do with speaking to the owner than seriously wanting information. If Christo thought a question worthwhile, he would answer it tantalisingly well. If he thought it was a lazy question, he would snap, whence his reputation for being as bad-tempered as his dachshunds.

After Christo's mother's death in 1972, Dixter changed. Faced with the prospect of rattling around in the house, Christo began to ask people to stay. Strings of weekends would go by in summer when there were at least four or five guests, some old friends, some new. Dixter became an international transit lounge for people throughout the world of gardening.

Christo learned to cook (but not to wash up – there were people for that). After the garden and classical music, his great love became entertaining, which he did on a scale that was lavish not because he threw silly money at it, but because of the energy he put into it, as cook and host. He had neither wife nor children and took virtually no foreign holidays except as part of lecture tours. His day-to-day clothes were notoriously even more ancient than his car. And so to spend generously on excellent meat and fish and wine, accompanied by fresh fruit and vegetables from the garden, and to have a big laundry bill, could hardly be seen as extravagant. Yet to a visitor it felt like luxury. Christo gave the best of everything without ceremony, as if Dixter were 'the smallest and most select of hotels', as well as a place where one could meet interesting, like-minded guests.

His greatest extravagance was to buy £5,000–6,000 worth of tickets every year for Glyndebourne. He gave many of them to his guests, organising parties of those who would most like to hear a particular opera or composer, and arranging splendid picnics.

Most generously of all, he took up young people who were as keen on gardening as he was and gave them a fast track into the gardening world, introducing them to good living, and to interesting and useful people. Some might be outgoing, others might be as shy as he once was. Call it philanthropy or call it keeping himself occupied after his mother's death, but Christo was forever busy and forever big-hearted. He was Prospero, pulling the strings in a magical world, making opportunities for his protégés and seeing what they would make of them. No one could accuse him of not keeping Dixter alive. He once admitted, when pressed and only with reluctance, that he 'preferred people over plants'.

He slept in the little bedroom over the porch, where his mother had slept before him, and woke at six every morning to let out his smooth-haired dachshunds, variously Tulipa, Dahlia, Canna, Crocus and Yucca (there were always two). Breakfast was something that happened hours later.

At weekends, at about nine in the morning, Christo and guests would turn up to find tea, brown bread and stewed fruit from the garden with double cream. It was served in the old servants' hall off the kitchen, which he used as a dining room although located very much on the wrong side of the old green baize door. What a strange and intimate room that was, very small and so much the heart of Dixter: the Edwardian cast-iron range, the ancient carved court cupboard and oak chest stacked two feet deep in magazines, the Windsor chair where the dachshunds lay invisible under a foetid old blanket, a cheap plastic toaster and a chrome banana hanger (bananas were 'only ready to eat if they were brown' – surely a Daisy Lloyd injunction), the white but yellowed gloss-painted walls and ceiling; and down the middle of the room, the superb, sinuous, striped blond dining table and pink suede chairs by Rupert Williamson. And at the centre of it all, of course, Christo himself, Master of Ceremonies, in his official chair. His guests might be a couple he had stayed with in Canada or Australia, the curator of a Hungarian botanic garden and his wife, maybe an opera producer, a head gardener or garden designer, and perhaps a handsome student of gardening or of music.

Towards the end of breakfast on weekdays various members of staff would arrive to take orders for the day. Someone was going into Hastings, and did Christo want fish? People were staying on for lunch, and which vegetables did he want dug or picked? Fergus was there to go through the post with him, the great pile diminishing gradually as Fergus opened envelopes, summarised the contents out loud and, if they were of sufficient merit, passed them to Christo for closer scrutiny. 'I suppose we'll have to write to him about that' might be the reply, or 'I think we'll keep that letter, don't you?' It would go into a box somewhere, in some cupboard.

Sometimes he would write a piece for a magazine or newspaper before breakfast, consulting his ever-present black notebook as he did so. Occasionally he would write in the Sunk Garden, his old laptop balanced on a thin plywood board on his knees. Sometimes he would shut himself up in the Parlour and spend the morning writing for a book.

And at some stage – his greatest pleasure – he would make the tour of the garden with Fergie, planning, looking hard, their notebooks to hand, discussing what was happening and what should be done now and next month and next year. The two of them were so eye-to-eye on the manner of gardening at Dixter that what was in reality a process of great complexity and subtlety sounded like child's play in their mouths.

At weekends after breakfast Christo would take his friends round the garden before the public arrived, pausing to consider what was especially good just then. If guests were new, there might be an element of game to the tour. I once heard him ask a group what they thought of some piece of planting, which he had told me the day before was a ghastly mistake. He wanted to see who had the nerve or sense to suggest that; and cast me just the smallest of twinkles of the eye to make sure I'd noticed – his stance, as ever, a hunched chin on chest, hands behind back, looking down at the plants more than at his interlocutor.

Mid-morning his housekeeper might come in to wash up. Young William, one of the gardeners, might be seen stacking perfectly uniform, perfectly seasoned logs in the vast Solar fireplace, or there might be a delivery of tea – mango and Darjeeling, in large brown paper bags – from Christo's supplier in London.

Some guests might have gone out for the morning, to look round Rye or old Hastings or to see the garden at Sissinghurst, but woe betide them if they were not back in time for drinks before lunch. On the terrace behind the house, raised well out of sight of the public, a small, raddled, gate-legged table would be brought out and half a dozen white plastic chairs of the garage-forecourt variety. A wooden tray would emerge, carried by the guest most at home, bearing a modest champagne and a dish of olives, and the party would discuss what they had seen and done. Then people would go indoors to eat, perhaps a soufflé Christo had made, or salami or cheese, and a vast bowl of fresh, dressed salad. Some days a guest might be sent to fetch beer from the cellar, where the boiler seethed and the great lantern shone down over the billiard table beside wartime tins of flour and a pile of garden rakes to be sold in the shop.

On sunny days after lunch, the party would troop out to the horse pond to take coffee on the grass, lying on heavy woollen blankets. Someone would tread carefully out, past the lady house-guides mustering in the porch for afternoon opening, bearing another wooden tray, this time laden with cracked china coffee cups, the ancient grey enamel coffee pot, more cream and (long before they hit the supermarkets) Bendicks Bittermints. Christo would take place of honour, like an old otter, on his rug and receive a cup of coffee which, when emptied, he set down for the dogs to clean out. They loved it, and perhaps they enjoyed the high, for by now the public would have arrived in the garden and there might be a child or two to snap at (an activity with which their master was in perfect sympathy). Conversation about people and gardens and plants would quieten, the young men might slope off for some fun, and Christo would curl up on his side for twenty minutes, guarded by dragonflies.

At some stage in the afternoon he would start to cook. He roped in the odd guest to pick vegetables or fruit. This was another test that had to be passed, an initiation into Dixter ways: learning, usually without help, which was that obscure salad leaf he had mentioned, and whether you picked that particular fruit with or without the stalk, and which was which variety of his beloved artichokes.

Guests would reassemble after an afternoon of activity or siesta, and tea would happen, on the terrace once more, this time served in chunky, stained-and-crazed polychrome mugs. There would be cake – probably a guest's home-cooked contribution. Someone might arrive from the nursery with a roll of bank notes: the day's takings.

Later Christo would retire for his bath. Guests would chat, regroup, stroll around the garden yet again, until somehow it was time for drinks and the tray would appear in the Solar, the long first-floor sitting room, or in the Yeoman's Hall. Olives again, but this time with a spittoon for the stones (no stones in a Dixter hearth – thus had spoken Daisy Lloyd), cashews perhaps, Christo's favourite Syndicate whisky, foreign gins of one kind or another . . . Christo would eventually appear, carrying a ticking timer, and take up his official place on the sofa, and 'the girls' would snuggle up under a rug by his side. When the timer pinged, off he went to put the finishing touches to the meal. Everyone was to follow in five minutes.

First down would have to hand-peel potatoes (he had a thing about skinning Pink Fir Apples red-hot *after* boiling) and the loaded plates would proceed to the dining room, where candles were burning, silver was sparkling and French wine was standing on the old range. There would be a hefty pudding, cheese, and finally the party would process back to the Solar with another tray of coffee for more talk of gardens and music. People would chat and eventually Christo would fall asleep, chin on chest and dog on knee, and remain so until everyone was talked out and ready to retire for the night. Someone would wake him and he would heave himself to his ancient knees, delegating someone to put in place the fireguard. He would put out the dogs for a last leak, set the burglar alarm, and turn off every corridor and landing light before pulling to the door of his little bedroom over the porch, where bare boards rolled across the floor and beams hatched the walls, then climb alone into the four-poster bed where his mother had died. This was not a lonely man. But, as in *Peter Pan*, the window was always open.

Few people in their eighties could live and work at that pace, but Christo was driven to it; that was how life *had* to be lived, busily, to the full, with never a moment's idleness. Dull moments were for the dull. And if Christo had become the grand old man of British gardening, it was partly due to his industrious, precise and generous nature, and partly – massively – due to his mother: Daisy Lloyd, descendant of Oliver Cromwell, and known to all as The Management.

PART ONE
Life Under Daisy

Letitia found this drawing, to represent
Christo's family nickname: Lambikins.

Chapter 1

Tan and His Vixen, 1905–30

When I was 12 or 13 I conceived a secret ambition to be the best mother in the world (both morally and physically) and have the most beautiful children. If I hadn't married, I should have been a school marm. As it was, I had a class of six!

Daisy Lloyd

The story of the Lloyds of Great Dixter starts with the marriage of money and opportunity. On 20th May 1905, Daisy Field, of 14 Cambalt Road, Putney, married Nathaniel Lloyd, co-founder with his brother Robert Wylie Lloyd of Nathaniel Lloyd and Co., Lithographic Printers in Blackfriars. A rich man. He was thirty-seven and she was twenty-four. *Mine and Thine*, it said on the inside of the ring.

Daisy's family was well-to-do. Her father Basil Field was a London solicitor at Field, Roscoe and Co., and the family had a country house at Ramsbury in Wiltshire as well as the Putney house. Such were the Fields' many artistic and intellectual talents that Basil tossed off plays for fun, and Daisy and her sister Myrtle made the costumes as well as acting in the shows. By fifteen, both girls were passionate botanists and entomologists. Writing and plants were clearly in the Fields' blood. The family travelled a good deal, taking fishing holidays abroad, and Daisy herself was sent to Frankfurt in 1899 and to Missouri and Ontario in 1901 – her Grand Tour – to broaden her education. Her French and German were excellent, as was her command of European classical literature. 'I first fell in love with John Keats when I was 12,' she claimed, 'and used to wish I had been his mother, sister, wife – anything so that I might take care of him.'

Nathaniel was born in Lancashire, first son of John Lloyd, a bleacher at Horwich, and grandson of Nathaniel Lloyd, a calico printer and bleacher. His mother was a Wylie of Glasgow. While Nathaniel and his brother Robert were still children, their parents separated and the boys moved to Clapham with their mother.

Nathaniel first kissed Daisy at a family party when she was twelve, chastely no doubt, and at her request. She claimed to have fallen in love with him at thirteen (a year later than she fell for John Keats, but perhaps none the worse for that). Nathaniel, or Tan to his friends – it was Nat backwards – was a tall, thin, moustachioed Neville Chamberlain-like figure, serious and precise, a keen fisherman and golfer and, like his brother Robert, a good businessman with excellent prospects. It was in that year of the kiss that the brothers founded Nathaniel Lloyd and Co., Lithographic Printers, which was to make them so much money. Daisy's mother Amy cultivated the company of the promising Mr Lloyd at their house in Putney, and by 1903 Daisy and Tan were corresponding, even when they were on holiday.

Throughout her life Daisy set marriage, and her own marriage in particular, upon a pedestal; it was the proper goal of every woman worthy of the name; but *motherhood* – that was everything. Not surprisingly, her eldest, a son, Selwyn, promptly came along in 1908, the first of six children (she rather fancied the idea of twelve), and she dutifully produced another every two years: Oliver in 1911, Patrick in 1913, Quentin in 1915, followed by a brief pause for the war. The last two children, Letitia (1919) and Christopher (1921), she called her postwar credits. For Daisy, motherhood was a kind of war: 'I always broke my babies in,' she advised, 'to 1 bottle in the 24 hours at 3 months and 2 bottles at 4 months and then weaned them in 1 week at nine months.' Such was Daisy's energy for things domestic that even her mother would sometimes tire of her enthusiasms.

Daisy's greatest pride was that she was descended, if rather distantly, from Oliver Cromwell. At Dixter his portrait hung over her bed. The Cromwellian idea of trusting one's own authority over others' was essential to her character, but it did not make life easy for her. Her love of correctness made her lean towards the established, conservative side in most arguments, yet when the establishment's view clashed with her own independent view, then her loyalties could jump either way. Thus, the idea of the King as authority incarnate appealed to her, but living, fallible

14

members of the royal family never lived up to her moral expectations; and in any case her famous ancestor had had no time for royalty.

If Daisy could be both independent *and* correct, she was happy and satisfied; but when it came to religion, this presented her with problems. Her ancestry forbade her to have anything to do with the smells and bells of Roman Catholicism or High Church Anglicanism, let alone the doctrine of confession. One is tempted to think that, in her own opinion, she didn't sin. Yet, as someone who wished above all else to be a figure of respected authority, she found herself unable to warm to the alternative – a Low Church in which all men were equal. Daisy, and her family, stood way above the common herd; this she knew. Perhaps she was not so much an outright social snob as an intellectual snob who felt free to patronise the uneducated classes. And yet her devotion to the Cromwellian idea of the 'simple' life led her to outrageous eccentricities of dress: the Austrian dirndl for each- and everyday wear; the belted, grey Puritan dress instead of an evening gown for special occasions.

Also from her Cromwellian convictions came the belief that diligent work was a duty, both to oneself and to others, and she strove hard to bring up her children believing this. No moment was to be wasted, but rather spent in writing letters or with needle and canvas, or in any other of the honest crafts. She found contentment not in relaxation, but in the knowledge that she was doing her duty. More troubling is the implication that she found contentment in knowing that she was doing her duty when others were not.

A fourteen-year age gap between Nathaniel and Daisy may seem unusual today, but in an age of sensible, arranged marriages it was not uncommon, especially if one party had wealth. Many a young woman found herself, at a tender age and for better or worse, duty-bound in charge of a substantial household and its staff. These girls sank or swam, and Daisy Lloyd was determined and well able to swim. Behind that quietly drawn-back dark hair, that broad-arching brow and those low-lidded eyes, behind her perpetual intimation of a smile, there was power at work.

Independent of spirit and aware of the age difference between herself and Tan, she made it a condition of the marriage to be apart for a month each year, doing whatever each individual might want to do to find fulfilment. For him it was golf. For her, until the Second World

War, it meant a return to see her artistic friends in Europe (she had spent a year with the Hirsch family in Frankfurt, broadening her education during what today might be called a gap year). Sometimes it meant a holiday in Switzerland to look at wild flowers with Oliver and Christo, or to let her delicate son Quentin ski there in the healing mountain air. But she never allowed herself or the children to be out of touch with home, and to Tan she wrote assiduously. 'I used to say to Daddy, "Once a day isn't often to speak to your own Best Beloved, and when we're parted writing has to do instead."' The bemused and largely delighted Tan received her letters twice a day.

There is no doubt that Nathaniel was fond of his energetic young bride, and she claimed to the end that theirs was the most perfect, loving marriage, bound together by their great project, the children, Dixter and the garden. But in fact the marriage was far from a meeting of minds. Daisy's letters show an honest, likeable young woman enjoying life and her family, but she and Nathaniel were of different generations. She would call him 'Daddy Darling' or 'Dear old Dog Fox' (because of his moustache) and would refer to herself, perhaps with a sparkle in her eye, as 'Your own Vixen'. She corrected his spelling and ran his bath as she would for a child, and as, in fact, she did for Christo until he was fifty-one.

Nathaniel the Edwardian businessman did indeed expect her to be an efficient wife, and she obliged him by running a tight domestic ship and by taking proper, rigorous care of the children. Not a thing in the house or garden was wasted, nor was the potential largesse of the house ignored. In 1917, during the First World War, the Great Hall was used as a Red Cross convalescent hospital for the wounded, fresh back from the front (twenty-two beds), and Daisy organised concerts and played the pianola to the men. Nathaniel was awarded the OBE for Dixter's efforts in the war and for his work in recruiting.

When Tan was away golfing and beginning to take the older boys with him, Daisy would chase him up on appropriate domestic duties: 'Will you please cut my 1st baby's finger-nails on Monday? I daresay his toes will go a little longer. Tell me when you have done it,' she demanded. So much for his month apart. His replies to Daisy were scrawled, plain to the point of brusqueness, mere bullet points, and reaching a level of such obliqueness that she had to ask her, '1st baby', Selwyn, in her (also) daily letters to him, to tell her what Tan was doing.

16

But in coming to him through the children she never stepped below an appropriate parental solidarity: 'I hope you will be very good and sweet to our precious daddy, and never say "why" if he tells you to do anything.' This was Daisy's principal lesson in life to her children: she was (and so, at a push, was Daddy) always *right*.

She wrote screeds to Tan of the battle of her daily life at Dixter and how her days passed in teaching, exercising, whacking and playing with his current children and sewing fine seams 'for the one (or ones?) to come'. *She* was dealing with a house perpetually full of mosquitoes, *she* was storing apples, *she* was cheerfully bringing up hungry babies or having them in her bed when lightning cracked overhead. When he was at parties in London, she wished she were there too, but how *could* she? – she was too busy at Dixter and 'tired and depressed'. Actually she was far happier at Dixter, but Daisy always craved active appreciation, she had to be *told* what a wonderful mother she was. It was a form of emotional blackmail, which was to become one of her greatest skills, learned partly, no doubt, through handling dear, dry, old Tan during the twenty-eight years of their marriage. And the more she pestered him for attention, the more he retreated into his work. An Eliza Doolittle to his Henry Higgins, she wrote, 'Dear old Dog Fox, I do miss you so! And I love you very dearly, although I plague you at times, interrupting your reading the newspaper or typing those endless military documents.'

So successful had been Nathaniel's business that by 1909 he could afford to sell his share and retire, leaving in charge his brother Robert – 'Robin' – but retaining joint managing directorship with him of the Star Bleaching Co. Ltd, until it was sold in 1912. It was a parting of fortunes: Nathaniel to spend his, and lack for capital later; and Robin to invest his, and thereby to become the infinitely richer brother. Robin, the bachelor businessman, went on to become an esteemed art collector. He was also a serious mountaineer and collector of butterflies, and by seventeen was already a Fellow of the Royal Entomological Society, of which he later became a major benefactor. He and Tan both suffered from a Victorian sense of guilt at idleness, just like Daisy, and, for them, recreation could never mean relaxation. What more could Daisy have sought in a new family: fishing, plants, natural history, a consuming industriousness . . .

In 1910 the early-retired Nathaniel was now free to pursue his ambition to become an amateur architect; he could indulge his fascinations for old English timber and brickwork, for photography and for golf. In all these fields he became a respected and sometimes expert figure, although self-taught. His best project of all was to seek, with his fecund young wife, a suitable place in which to make a house according to their own tastes, and in 1910 he bought Dixter, the wreck of a timber and brick house with a small farm, on the edge of the village of Northiam in Sussex, eight miles to the north of Rye.

The old hall house was fifteenth-century, dating from 1450; from the outside it looked decidedly shaky on its feet, and the simple, spacious interior had been subdivided many times over the centuries. But Tan could see possibilities in the place and it satisfied his love for old English brickwork and oak-framed buildings. It sat on a sunny but exposed ridge, overlooking the pastoral countryside and, down below, the wet meadows of the Rother Valley and Bodiam Castle. There was no garden, only some ramshackle barns, a couple of orchards, a few ponds, a bay tree, a pear and a fig, and lots of nettles. It would mean the end of Daisy's allotment gardening in Rye; this was to be her 'first *serious* garden'.

For all Nathaniel's aspirations to be an architect, it was plain that the timber shell of Dixter would need an experienced professional to turn it into a house worthy of his ambitions, and he employed the Arts and Crafts architect Edwin Lutyens to do the job. Lutyens, then forty-one, had become known at the start of his career for building rural vernacular houses in Sussex, unpretentious buildings made of local tile and brick. He worked in collaboration with Gertrude Jekyll, he setting out the garden plans, she adding the decorative layer of planting; it was he who built Jekyll's own house at Munstead Wood. But not surprisingly Lutyens' interests changed over his career, and by 1910 he had moved on to a more classical style, shortly to start his most famous project, the Viceroy's house and the building of New Delhi in India. However, it was the earlier vernacular style that appealed to Nathaniel, and Lutyens was happy to return to it.

The Dixter estate (not then Great Dixter) cost £6,000, and Nathaniel initially asked the firm of Ernest George & Yeates to draft a plan for its remodelling in 1910. Their ideas did not suit him and it was then that he turned to Lutyens, because Lutyens was an architect who liked to 'make old houses sing' and whose draft plans looked promising. But when they were fully costed they far exceeded Nathaniel's proposed budget of £5,600 for alterations and additions, so a much less grand scheme was drawn up. The old house at Dixter was to be stripped of all its internal additions and returned to something like its original fifteenth-century condition. A ruined yeoman's hall house of 1500 was found at the village of Benenden nearby and bought as scrap for its timber value, at £75. It was then dismantled, its timbers numbered, and was re-erected at Dixter, the two buildings being joined together with a new service and bedroom wing designed by Lutyens. His wing was not in the least 'mock-Dixter', but rather an honest piece of contemporary building, although made with complete sympathy for its ancient partners. It shared the same materials, the same fenestration and the same predominance of roofscape. The whole house, old and new, had an extraordinary unity.

Nathaniel himself had considerable input into the stylistic details of the house, and the great brick fireplace in the basement billiard room was designed by him, receiving praise from Lutyens himself. Nathaniel also commissioned and had made the vast, stage-like oak bed in the Benenden Hall, long enough for any Lloyd and costing over £44; it was copied from a bed in a Florentine palazzo that he narrowly missed buying.

It was not to be a particularly large house. Under Lutyens' reworking, the older, Dixter house offered a grand, social space open to the roof – the Great Hall – and beyond it a more modest, cosy Parlour, a work room for Daisy, and on the first floor a long Solar or sitting room with windows only at both ends. The Lloyds' bedroom and its monstrous bed – Daisy's brood chamber – occupied almost all of the ground floor of the re-erected Benenden house.

In Lutyens' new wing, the kitchen, pantries, servants' hall and other offices were practical: there were high, heat-relieving windows operated on a pulley, coal-fired ranges, deep sinks, stone shelves, fly-screens at the pantry windows and swing doors for staff carrying trays. The family rooms in Lutyens' wing possessed the same leaded windows as the old house, capable of casting shafts of light across the dark, polished floors, oak timbers and unpainted, pale plaster. On all the doors were the same simple wooden latches. Single pendant lights hung from the ceilings. Inside the ancient, original porch, Lutyens' rather gloomy new entrance hall led up stairs to Day and Night Nurseries and half a dozen bedrooms on two floors (servants and daughters at the top), each floor with a bathroom. The pipes were lead, the taps monumental and the baths oceanic.

In those days Dixter had six indoor staff: a cook, a kitchen maid, a lady's maid for Daisy (usually French- or German-speaking), a parlour maid and a couple of house maids. In the lofty but still overheated kitchen, cockroaches swarmed over the floor at night: the children received a penny for every one they could trap (this scuttling population continued to inhabit the kitchen until the days of DDT).

There was central heating throughout, the radiators disguised as oak chests, and, after consultation, water closets rather than earth closets were installed. Dowsing was used to find a good water supply (it has served the garden ever since) and a reservoir tank was dug in the field.

By 1911 the work was well under way and Nathaniel, taking it upon himself to act virtually as a clerk of works, was badgering Lutyens to give more time to the project and bombarding him with examples of period designs for doors, screens and other details. Daisy always claimed that Lutyens and Nathaniel remained good friends, but Nathaniel must have been a nightmare client, too closely involved for either man's good. Lutyens himself was keen to start planting the garden as soon as possible, but Nathaniel wanted a plan, and once again found himself chasing the busy, fashionable architect. 'My wife is counting the minutes until she sees the garden plan,' he protested. 'It is so nice to think it won't be long now.' It finally arrived in August 1911 and Nathaniel at once began pegging the garden out.

Lutyens' plan showed a garden of formal compartments and axes, yet it could hardly be called a series of separately styled 'garden rooms' of the kind that were developed later at Hidcote Manor under Lawrence Johnston. It was full of straight lines certainly, yet it did not have much truck with symmetry. Instead it was a gentle progression through spaces of different size and character: the front lawn bisected by the path to the rickety front porch; the linear, Long Border facing onto open orchard; the High Garden for rows of fruit and vegetables; a broad, flagged terrace under the walls of the house; the hedged and fully paved Rose Garden with its matrix of little beds; a T-junction of a space surrounded by walls, where paths went off in three directions, known as the Wall Garden. There was a massive, U-shaped oak bench known as the 'family pew', set into a specially made recess in a hedge; and the whole garden subtly took into account the scattering of old farm buildings that lay across it – the low, tiled 'Hovel' (a cow shed) re-employed to make a dark loggia beside the Rose Garden, and raised, circular water tanks used as punctuation to close a vista or propose a change of direction. On plan and in practice, a walk through the garden would invariably circle the house, and it could be done without ever stepping off a well-made stone path.

Despite the garden's several divisions it had a simple layout, whose planting details could be coloured in by Daisy and Tan, their inclination always to soften the less formal areas and to add complexity to the formal ones. To some extent they cherry-picked from the finer details of Lutyens' design. On plan, many of Lutyens' open spaces had no purpose or detail indicated at all, so Nathaniel made a Topiary Garden of the lawn where the family pew stood, and planted topiary peacocks in a Lavender Garden on the way to the vegetable garden; Lutyens' wide, formal paths through the orchard were not constructed, but became a thin snake of brick through a waving, daffodil meadow; proposed new walls beside the front gate, separating the garden from the lane, became simple yew hedges more suited – in Lloydian eyes – to an ancient house. Indeed, young yew trees and York-stone paving were a major expense of the garden.

Much later still, Lutyens' plan was altered further. Nathaniel designed a Sunk Garden centred on a formal pool, in a walled enclosure by the barns where Lutyens had suggested a croquet lawn; Lutyens' plan had included no water in the garden other than the existing horse pond and moat pools. Lutyens' already-long border was stretched by one-third of its length to become Christo's Long Border, and the very Edwardian, labour-intensive strip of grass that ran alongside it was dug up to make room for an even deeper border. Young ash trees were planted west of the garden to keep out the wind at the expense of the view. Notoriously, Christo eventually turned over the Rose Garden to exotic plants.

Meanwhile, in 1911, Daisy got to work, filling up substantial borders in the Jekyllean mode with which she was familiar, and setting plants into the lawns and around the horse pond, in the manner that her hero William Robinson had advocated in *The Wild Garden* (1870). Robinson had been keen to experiment with garden plants placed sensitively in the tamer parts of an estate or countryside; Daisy, in her turn, brought native plants such as orchids into the garden's rough spaces, to grow alongside imported plants such as crocuses and camassias, the combination intended to seed and naturalise together. Dixter was a fresh, sunny creation, and all of it under open sky; no cooler, Robinsonian woodland gardening here, it was all intensive work even where a border was north-facing. But Daisy's flower-spangled 'Prima Vera' lawns were her signature.

For all the Lloyds' tweaking and planting of the garden, the design could never be taken for anyone's but Lutyens'. It had his well-loved arched doorways, detailed in brick and in tiles packed on edge, like hatching. The same combination was used in the paving, all crisply set when new, but with the promise of picturesque colonisation by ferns, mosses and Mexican daisies as the structures matured and softened. There were Lutyens' favourite radial steps and, beside the Long Border, steps comprising a series of radiating, satellite grass circles, which were to become an icon not just of Dixter but of Lutyens' work as a whole, as did his circular tanks at Hestercombe.

The principal stone paths were wide, for sure, and indeed all Lutyens' houses, in the *Country Life* articles where they were first published, have around them brand-new paths fit to be motorways. But Lutyens was a master of scale, and now that the paths are dressed with planting, they look absolutely, effortlessly right. What a gift was a Lutyens garden to a talented gardener. At Dixter he created one of his greatest house-and-garden marriages, not least because, from the garden, the house is never out of sight; the two are inextricably linked in physical reality, exactly as they were to become in the Lloyds' family life.

Set in this silver sea, the life of Great Dixter began.* Four-poster beds were found, dark, spindle-legged tables, bureaux, chests, and heavy, deep-hued carpets; pewter, majolica and clocks of all kinds. Routines developed. Bells for lunch and bells for dinner in the Great Hall. Nathaniel at work in the Solar, at his elegant, oak drawing board, surrounded by books. Tea in the upper moat, an oval pond below the terrace drained to create a dell of flower-spangled turf, down whose sides toddlers could roll. The maid took the mail to the post-box at the appointed hour. Against the walls, apricots, peaches and figs were

---

* The Lloyds rechristened it Great Dixter to distinguish it from the farmhouse, Little Dixter, just across the fields.

planted and, at the top of Lutyens' miraculous circular steps, two black mulberries stood ready to shed their luscious load. Sir George Thorold, of the old Lincolnshire family, drew up the first planting plans for the borders, and Daisy, with a copy of *The Wild Garden* in her hand, began to plant the meadows and orchards. Tubs of mounded, self-satisfied hydrangeas stood in pairs to mark the steps, and Nathaniel's beloved hedges and topiary began to define the garden. Vegetables grew. Water flowed.

When the weather was warm, Daisy and Tan dined out on the terrace every night, planning: he might shave the topiary lawn close enough for the boys to practise putting; he would collect enough bricks for his little boy architects to build scale models of the great European cathedrals. He and Daisy went out in the half-light together, searching for moths for Tan's collection. One morning, early, three airships flew slowly over Dixter low enough for them to see the men in the gondolas below, and the little boys danced around in their dressing gowns on the wet grass, waving. Daisy's dream family was launched.

Even the war, which was bad for Nathaniel's investments, could not dampen Daisy's spirits, and when Selwyn went off to Winchester College for the first time, aged nearly nine, she bore it bravely. She took him up to London and put him on the train from Marylebone along with dozens of other new boys, then went straight back to her hotel in Pall Mall, scrubbed the London smuts from her face and, in the manner of her father Basil Field, letter-writer extraordinaire, she began the first of thousands of letters to her absent children:

My own darling 1st Baby!
It is now 4.45 pm (about an hour and a half since we said goodbye to each other) and I feel I must have a little 'letter-talk' to you. If you can't actually speak with a person you love, the next best thing is to write to them – you will find that out some day. Keep my letters and Daddy's – they will be interesting to you when you grow up – but don't leave them lying around. I will take care of them for you.

And so she did, for all her children. She requisitioned and kept many of the letters she wrote to them, 'love-letters' as she called them, but kept very few of theirs to her. She was in love with love.

* * *

Little by little Dixter was becoming an institution. In January 1913 it had been featured in *Country Life*. Nathaniel took the photographs for the article, and showed it looking sparsely but elegantly furnished, as they liked it. He had a passion for photography and was gradually turning himself into an architectural historian. He developed a fine library of glass negatives of buildings and architectural details from all over the country, most useful for his book A *History of English Brickwork* (1925). He used them to give lectures, and they were hired to illustrate technical journals. His shots of Great Dixter itself were proudly made into postcards and became the family's icons and their calling cards: when Christo died in 2006 there was hardly a desk or a drawer that did not contain at least one of the cards.

All the children aspired to be photographers like their famous father, and Daisy was hugely proud of her old Dog Fox, writing in 1942:

I have just found the enclosed good print of *my* photograph of the front of the house [1915]. I got up at 5 o'clock every day for a fortnight, until the perfect morning appeared, with bright sun and no wind, when I roused Himself, and he took the photograph from a platform which [Sindy the maid] and I had erected on the far side of the wall between the Wall and the Sunk Gardens – so I have a right to call it mine! I always remember Daddy in his pyjamas, dressing gown and Panama hat, standing on top of the pantry table – I took a snapshot of him – he looked so echt!

In 1919 Daisy had Rudyard Kipling to tea and got her boys to recite poetry to him, including of course his own 'Glory of the Garden'. Pat, the future career soldier, twinkled and shone for the old man, like the wordsmith and performer he was, reminding Kipling of his only son at the same age, and now killed in the war. A tour of the house was made and Oliver pointed out the row of Kipling's books on the shelf in the North Bedroom. 'My boy, I didn't come seventeen miles to look at my books,' he cried to Daisy's delight, 'show me some more of your furniture.' And having seen the Charles II corner cupboard in the Night Nursery, Kipling suggested that he might come back quietly with a screwdriver. Daisy was thrilled, and her boys' behaviour had been exemplary.

Daisy and Tan had actively decided to have no more children during the 1914–18 war. Times were harder, investment income poorer for everybody, not least the Lloyds, and the world was an uncertain place; but with the war over, Daisy got back to business. Conceived in her great bed under the family's portrait of Cromwell, the first to arrive was Letitia, her first and only daughter, born in 1919. Christo followed on 3rd March 1921. She had wanted a second daughter. He was to be her last baby, and she was well aware that in a few years he would be her last child at home.

There is rapture in Maggie Smith's face when, in the film of *The Prime of Miss Jean Brodie* she proclaims, 'Give me a girl at an impressionable age and she is mine for life!' Sentiments Daisy Lloyd might have followed on the subject of her youngest son. More than all the others, Christo was the one she moulded in her own image. Her other children had been different. Selwyn, her best-beloved firstborn, was a delight, but cooler and less demonstrative than little Christo; Selwyn and Patrick were more serious characters, both influenced by their education at Winchester and not at all interested in the arts. Oliver was supremely capable, a polymath, but mercurial, nobody's creature. Like Christo, he was schooled at Rugby. Quentin was a merry soul, not physically strong but straightforward, and musical like Oliver and Letitia. Letitia was jolly, wilful, but a girl and therefore, as Daisy saw it, destined to play a supporting role in life.

For the first nine years of his life Christo remained at Dixter, where he had been born in the North Bedroom's fine four-poster bed. As an infant he crawled in the Day Nursery to the deep windowsill and watched the coal man heaving sacks into the boiler room below and the gardeners weeding the Long Border or pulling leeks in the High Garden; he listened to the kitchen staff, clattering pots and pans in the high-ceilinged room below, or to his mother's two cocker spaniels barking at a hedgehog. It was a good life. Under Daisy and Nathaniel's tutelage he was taught embroidery, how to identify birds and butterflies, to know the stars and when they appeared, and to begin to learn everything there was to know about plants and gardens. His brothers were delighted with their curious little brother with the wiry, curled hair permanently rolled to one side, a keen eye and prodigious memory. It was a happy place. All Christo had to do was be good and absorb to his very bones the peculiar essence of Dixter.

Chapter 2

Prep School, 1930–4

I do love my Mummy! I love her better than myself!
Christo, 14 March 1929, recorded in Daisy Lloyd's leather-
bound collection of her children's *bons mots*

Christo was nine when he left home in May 1930 to board at his prep
school, Wellesley House, near Broadstairs on the east-Kent coast. It was
not a large establishment, but it was Christo's first time away from Daisy
and it was her first time without him, a gruesome wrench for both of
them. Broadstairs may only have been fifty miles away on the other
side of Canterbury, near enough for her to drive down by the day to
see him, but it felt an unbearable distance. Christo was the last of her
brood, her 'littlest chick', and his departure left Dixter – and Daisy,
who prided herself on her powers as a mother – childless at last. She
was not going to let him go easily.

There was a tense departure on the school steps, Daisy proffering
her Dixterly brand of ostentatiously suppressed emotion, and the boy
doing his best to imitate her with a troubled, tight-chinned face that
seemed to follow him in photographs all through his childhood. That
dreadful day was etched in Christo's mind for the rest of his life and,
even in his eighties, he would frequently quote its anniversary.

Brother Quentin, six years Christo's senior, was already at Wellesley,
which helped Christo settle in, but Quentin belonged to Daisy's pre-
war babies, and the two boys were never particularly close. All the
schoolboys had to make a little garden, and at least the brothers were
paired for this, which made a double refuge for the plant-loving Christo
in his strange new world. Not surprisingly, this quiet, dreamy little soul
was bullied.

26

Daisy wrote to him assiduously, as she had to all her departing chicks. 'My darling Lambikins' she addressed him every time, signing herself 'Mother Sheep Ma-a-a-a-a-a-a', or more commonly just M-S. There was plenty of talk of obligation and duty, and she scolded the nine-year-old sarcastically for his spelling mistakes (Christo did the same to other people all his life, so heavy was Daisy's influence). His weekly high position in the class of fourteen was never good enough for her. She was always pushing him to improve, and cruelly threatening to cut him off without letters.

Daisy may have been a suffocating and possessive mother, but Christo knew he could pull her strings too. If she missed writing just one letter to him, he behaved like a brat, calling her 'VERY UNKIND, HORRID' and knowing he could get away with it because she needed her baby as much as he needed her. One thing in particular she had that Christo wanted: the garden at Dixter. Even by nine he was keenly observant of natural history, wild flowers and the stars. But his fascination with gardening was extraordinary, not to say troubling. He already spent unnaturally large amounts of time gardening, at an age when other children were out playing together and enjoying high-jinks. With his brothers so much older or away at school, Christo had spent hours alone with Daisy, learning with all her compelling discipline about gardening and the natural world. Abandoning Dixter for Wellesley House left him starved of his constant companion – the garden – and now Daisy was the only person who could give him regular reports on its progress. What was happening to his precious cacti? What was happening to his 'golden-rayed lily of Japan', with which he had been so proudly photographed at the age of six? His detailed observation of plants and their lifecycles and taxonomic relationships was brilliant, noticing not only the form and colour, but the precise time that plants would perform:

On Thursday my first dwarf iris came out and on Friday another one did. To-day two more came out, another was quarter out and another not quite as much. Are they ahead of those at home? We must go together at half term to Dixter wood and dig up some more orchis maculater, they will be in bloom then and so quite easy to see. Have the orchises we got from the downs near Lewis [Lewes] come out yet? When you send me my flowers do send me some of that pink apple blossom that grows by the oast house, also some of the double cherry blossom (if it is out) which grows only a little distance away. I should love some lilac and some of that saxifrage that grows by the horse pond. If you think it is worth sending wistaria do, and if there is any rhododendron I should like that, and lastly irises if there are any, perhaps there are by the lower moat. Of course I like having any other thing at all that you happen to send.

And then, at the end of the letter, off he goes to his little school garden to pick and arrange two colours of wallflowers and some forget-me-nots for the staffroom. But notice those Latin names amidst the subjunctives: clearly he knew exactly what *Orchis maculata* is, even if he couldn't spell it. And all the time Daisy was sending him great boxes of flowers:

double poet's narcissus, 1st yellow Dutch iris (in bud), columbines, Jacob's ladder (POLEMONIUM), BLUE AND WHITE, from Quentin's garden and yours, double Daisies (to remind you of your loving Mummy!) *and* Forgetmenots! Rosemary (that's for Remembrance!), the last dwarf Iris (two) that you love so much, also the last of the grape hyacinths, which have behaved so splendidly this year, then in a little bunch all tied together, the *first* rock pinks, Androsace, thrift (pale and dark) and that pale pink Alpine campion (Silene) that I grew from seed collected in Mrs Atkinson's garden. One spray of Guelder Rose (still very green), the first varie-gated Weigela (stolen from Wellesley *years* ago!), a few stocks, the first delphinium (rather a 'misery'), a bunch of Centaurea, to show S'audie [a member of the indoor staff] how nice they look with their heads together, and if you smell them with your eyes shut, you can imagine peaches on a hot wall! Anchusa, a small patter of lilac for you to smell, a tiny sprig of Deutzia in your garden, heuchera, geum, marigolds (soucis!), buttercups (because you love them), 1 paeony (in bud), the 1st Antirrhinum (a trap word – learn to spell it!) and the *last* of the Wallflowers (which are all being pulled up) for Mr Russell's desk. Right at the bottom of the box you will find a little parcel containing a '*Mummy* ruler' with **** Christopher Lloyd **** on one side and 'May 20 1930' on the other. **** are the kisses, and I have *really* kissed the places where they are – everyone else will think they are just ornaments, but *you* will know that they are Mummy Kisses – one for morning and one for night – bless you my little Lambikin! I put the date of our Silver Wedding on it because that makes it more interesting.

What an extraordinary mixture of high learning and threats along-side smothering, conspiratorial love. But Christo enjoyed this distant relationship with his garden through letter and by parcel. After the first term, his letters home contain remarkably little except plants and gardening. The other siblings humoured their baby brother in his all-absorbing interest. Mother Sheep would test him on the English equivalents of Latin names, as if Latin was the language for plant names that first sprang to his mind. Brother Patrick, then at Winchester, wrote sweetly advising Christo rather than his mother on new planting in the Long Border. Brother Oliver sent him seeds of annuals for his birthday. Family friend Ken Stubbs acquired for him offsets of a new lily intro-duced by the great collector Reginald Farrer. In the end even his father Nathaniel wrote to him about flowers. Who knows if this remarkable young child was glad when, for a change one week, instead of flowers Daisy sent him a crochet hook to make a blanket.

In effect Daisy was writing to Christo as one adult gardener writes to another; her lists could have appeared in Vita Sackville-West's gardening articles twenty-five years later. And Christo was sufficiently Daisy's confidant in the garden to put forward his own suggestions for new planting and to call Sands the gardener stupid, without any sense of overstepping the mark.

Daisy knew a great deal about wild flowers and wild gardening as well as conventional gardening, and her ideas had been pressed into Christo before he went to prep school. She wrote to tell him how she was letting the pyramidal orchids set seed before Sands was allowed to cut the long grass and how, in the grass beside Lutyens' circular steps, she had planted for her Christopher a 'C' of orchids. Christo was learning to love wild gardening and meadow gardening too, and approved of Quentin's idea to plant weeds in their school plot, so long as they were pretty and yellow. He was a mere child when the seed of meadow gardening was sown, something he would write about at length in his eighties.

Daisy drummed into all her children that they must write letters when they were away from home, but it was the writer-to-be Christo who best took up her injunction, and he particularly enjoyed correspondences that regularly batted backward and forward. Lloydian letters, as instituted by Daisy, were written to be read and reread, factually informative and intimate at the same time, and the prose carefully crafted. Throughout her lifetime she passed on the letters she received from one son to another, or to her friends, and she would copy out whole pages to pass on or to keep. They were her conference calls. She saved letters and filed them away, something that Christo also did as an adult, but whereas Daisy labelled her hoard, Christo stuffed his in a box. Hoarding letters was for him uncomfortably close to sentimentality, but he could not bear to throw away good or witty prose.

At prep school Christo did well. There was the usual round of juvenile ill health, mumps, and a trip to Harley Street to have his tonsils removed. He learned to shoot, an unlikely accomplishment for this unpractical child. It served him well later in the army and in popping off rabbits outside their holes in the woods. Music was one of the many disciplines Daisy thrust upon all her children, and Christo learned piano at school, passing his exams with Honourable Mention. His final school report called him 'a boy of simple and unruffled nature', so perhaps the child who had felt so cast adrift from all he loved on his first day at Wellesley had toughened a little.

In all the letters between Daisy and Christo, his father Nathaniel appeared as a distant patriarchal figure, cruising around the county in his big black car to indulge his passion for golf. It was *Nathaniel*, Daisy claimed, who refused to change his golfing plans to fit in with school exeats and could not spare the car so that she might take Christo and Quentin out for the day; 'Daddy' was much too busy *for boys*, being the man of the house, and was quite properly beyond her control and persuasion, an older man not to be refused.

Nathaniel, sixty-three when Christo went away to prep school, wrote to him only infrequently, on important occasions, to cheer him up if he was ill in bed or to congratulate him on good academic grades. But he simply did not know how to write comfortably to a sensitive nine-year-old. It was as if, having had so many sons already and lived through a terrible war, he had grown out of small children; he was now an author and architect and the owner of a substantial house. Selwyn and Oliver were old enough to take away with him on golfing forays to St Andrews;

to them he could write manly letters about sport. But Christo was different. 'Goodbye,' ends one letter to him, 'I am so glad you are a worker. Good man. Your Dad.' How different from Daisy's effusive farewells. Lacking Christo's deep passion for plants, Nathaniel wrote to him about the nearest thing he himself loved: golf-tee maintenance:

> We are playing on the new fourth green at Rye. The new 15th has been patched and we have taken away all the Poa annua turf . . . the new remedy from America for leather-jackets is LEAD ARSENATE and is a poison which acts slowly but surely . . . we now have a motor tractor which carts soil at a great pace and will pull a triple mower. This mows a swathe 9ft wide at about five miles an hour . . .

Perhaps it was this surfeit of turf culture that put Christo off lawns. In later life he delighted to ridicule the time that people waste on turf and, although he admired the lawns his father had made at Dixter, he was quite happy for his dachshunds to mark yellow constellations every night on the lawn outside the front door. Still, the boy must have derived some pleasure from Nathaniel's turf reports, because Nathaniel would sometimes take Christo to the golf club at Rye and park him with the grounds maintenance crew while he played his round.

Looking to restyle herself in a childless Dixter, Daisy took to wearing a dirndl skirt, which, bizarrely, became her daily costume and most conspicuous eccentricity for the rest of her life. She had taken in as a 'vice-daughter' a girl in her twenties named Dorothea ('Dodo') Emsworth; her brother Raymond was working at Nathaniel Lloyd and Co., and when their 'beautiful but stupid' mother left them to live abroad, Daisy clutched them to her bosom. Dorothea had been given a cheap tourist's dirndl brought back by Raymond from Bad Ischl, and she wore it once to Dixter. Daisy fell into raptures and instantly found a better one for herself, at a shop in London specialising in Austrian goods, and ever after she copied from it her own dirndls. The peasant costume, made with beautiful detail, appealed to her Cromwellian ideals of simplicity, even if it meant that she was occasionally taken for the maid (and, on one occasion, a maid kissed by Mr Lloyd).

The 1930s were not a good time for Daisy Lloyd. Dixter itself was then twenty years old and showing its age; the heating had to be over-hauled for the second time. The place needed money. Her three older boys were grown up and entering the world of work. Her fourth son Quentin was physically too delicate to follow brother Oliver to Rugby, and was sent for his health's sake to Canford School in Dorset. Letitia was boarding at Benenden a few miles away, and Christo was away at Wellesley. Daisy was desperate to have children in the house again.

1933 became her nightmare year. Christo was due to leave prep school the following year and his future schooling had to be arranged. Nathaniel had put his name down for Winchester, to follow Selwyn and Patrick, but Christo was refused a place. It was therefore proposed that he should follow Oliver to Rugby. In his letter of application Nathaniel announced to the headmaster 'I really think [Christo] will prove to be the pick of the brood, and we do want him to go to you.'

Daisy's third son Patrick, a physically fearless boy, was due to leave Winchester in the summer of 1933 and had decided to become a career soldier. Daisy dreaded losing him, too, from the family fold, but as ever she was determined that there should be no sentiment displayed; it was not for her to hang around and worry. Off she went to Frankfurt for her summer holiday, with Christo tucked under her arm, in order to visit her old friends, the Hirsches. Paul Hirsch was an industrialist who was developing an important collection of musical manuscripts, espe-cially works by Mozart (his collection later went to the British Museum). Daisy was in the habit of making the trip to Frankfurt to see Paul and his wife Olga, taking whichever of her children were free to accompany her. The Hirsches' was just the kind of household Daisy admired – one as keen on golf and skiing and music as her own, and sufficiently artistic that its regular guests included Richard Strauss, Wilhelm Furtwängler and Bruno Walter. As Jews, the Hirsches were having a difficult time in Germany, and Daisy was determined to show solidarity and make the visit. Nathaniel meanwhile took Selwyn, Patrick, Letitia and Quentin golfing, to the Grand Hotel in St Andrews.

Of course letters flowed between Frankfurt and Scotland, and between Daisy and every one of her children separately; many a letter covered all the same news, inevitably, but duty was satisfied. Daisy's letters would suddenly throw in a word or phrase in French or German, in the hope of making the children feel at home with foreign languages; Pat, ever the soldier at heart, told her plainly to stop it, since he did not understand them. Not surprisingly, Christo wrote to his father about the wealth of flowers to be seen growing in Frankfurt city, the *size* of the dahlias in the Palmengarten, the clematis nursery he had visited, the wild flowers on the Feldberg, how he had arranged flowers for the Hirsch household (fresh water and stems recut every day), and the wonderful cactus he had bought in a flower shop (he came back from Frankfurt with a haul of thirteen, determined to make a cactus garden in the old boiler-house garden). Nathaniel wrote drily back, saying there were only willowherb and harebells in St Andrews.

At St Andrews, life without Daisy's direct presence was easier. Golf came naturally to Pat and Quentin, and Nathaniel enjoyed teaching them and seeing their success. For the younger children and daredevil Pat, there were swimming and playing about on the rocks. Letitia wallowed in *Vanity Fair*; Quentin read up on his beloved mechanics and ogled the golfers' expensive cars. Even Nathaniel seems to have been in holiday mood and relieved not to be 'on duty', as he was at his own Rye golf club. There were other illicit temptations to be explored by the St Andrews group, such as a toe in the water of organised religion. Pat and Selwyn even went so far as to attend a Catholic service, the excuse being that mass would be sung, not spoken.

Nathaniel of course also sent regular letters to Frankfurt, but his were scrawled, brief as memoranda, never using a verb where one could be omitted. In return, Daisy badgered him to attend to the children's teeth and fingernails and generally act *in loco Daisis*. It was not for her to relax her duty of care, even when she was absent.

On 8th August 1933, soldier Pat received his marching orders from the War Office. He was to sail to Jhansi in northern India on 14th September, and his heavy luggage was to be on board the previous day.

Daisy and Nathaniel said goodbye to Pat, tall and glamorous in his uniform, under the porch at Great Dixter, each with their emotions once more under appropriately iron control, and never a tear shed. When his car had rolled away from the gate the couple coolly walked to the Barn Garden and 'after a little chat, dispersed to their separate occupations'. Daisy was in turmoil underneath; straight away she got hold of little Christo and marched him off to inspect his ducks and put in an afternoon's gardening.

Nathaniel, a man's man if ever there was, cool but lovable somewhere underneath, began to write voluminous letters to Pat as he never could to Christo, typed in business-like manner on sheets of flimsy paper (carbon-copied, one for his own file) and, in true Lloydian manner, he wrote them in numbered sequence in expectation of a long correspondence. He offered Pat genuine running prose, where Daisy received only blunt notes.

Pat was a mixture of his parents, a lover of mannish pursuits, brave, ambitious, forward-looking, kind, the peace-keeper of the family; but he also had Daisy's extraordinary belief in his family's specialness. What did he make of Nathaniel's emotionless letters to him in India? They were dull. No enquiry about Pat's life, no follow-up to Pat's own letters except to remark – when, after a few weeks, Pat moved to Rawalpindi – that he would be on the border of Kashmir and might expect some big-game hunting. But there were reams about golf matches and golf tees, and insurances and investments; and, very occasionally, an unconnected, explicitly smutty joke, relating the anecdote quite without polish or fun, but, presumably, feeling he was doing what a father should do towards a soldier son. It was as if Nathaniel and Daisy had divided up the children: the men and Letitia for Tan, Christo for Daisy.

In October 1933, Daisy's mother Grandma Field died, after being bedridden for four years at the Field family house in Putney. In Nathaniel's letters to Pat, her death merited only the briefest of mentions. Selwyn and Oliver had watched the old lady die, but for Nathaniel it was more compelling to tell Patrick about selling her house in Putney, about Selwyn and Oliver having to move out of it into a flat, of the £1,000 each grandchild could expect from her estate, of business meetings in London and a weekend's shooting at the house of his brother Robert – 'Wicked Uncle Robin' – Treago Castle in Herefordshire, in the company of bankers, generals and industrialists.

It is tempting to imagine that Nathaniel's increasingly generous amount of time spent away from Dixter was the cover for some *grande affaire*, but he was simply a man unpassionate about women, a man fleeing the emotionally charged atmosphere of Dixter, a man whose pleasures were intellectual more than physical (with the exception perhaps of golf), and whose numerous children were something procured for him by this wonderful young wife of his rather than something overwhelmingly desired by him. He was proud of his brood, no doubt, but by the time Christo was born he was a distant and quaint fifty-four-year-old figure, if very kind. Still, Daisy took every opportunity to tell society about her intelligent, successful husband and her enviable, fecund, deeply loving marriage. It was this doubtful status that she impressed upon the children with such determination, not the reality of the cool, remote Nathaniel and a woman more interested in her children's success than in her husband's deeply hidden feelings.

Selwyn was meanwhile doing very well working for Wicked Uncle Robin. Robin was a most astute businessman, drier even than Nathaniel, and worked himself and his employees very hard; by the time he died he had control of the store Wylie & Lochhead in Glasgow (later bought by House of Fraser), Druce's store in London's Baker Street, Christie's, the *Morning Post* (later to become the *Daily Telegraph*) and various bleaching enterprises, including Nathaniel Lloyd and Co. Amongst his most lucrative products were the tear-tape that parted the cellophane around packets of cigarettes, and the line of special foil that runs through bank notes. He was known for never wasting a penny and when, as chairman of the Bleachers' Association, he turned up to meetings in a moth-eaten forty-year-old bowler hat, his fellow directors offered to buy him a new one out of sheer embarrassment. Robin said no, he would take care of it, and went back to the same shop where he had bought the first hat forty years before and asked for a discount as a long-standing customer.

Robin worked Selwyn as hard as he worked himself, and Saturday mornings were part of his working week. One of his main concerns was the expanding of the business in Viscacelle, a competitor to Cellophane (cellophane eventually became a generic term for the product). So pleased was Robin with young Selwyn's efforts for the firm that he thought of him as his natural heir. Selwyn was by then engaged to Elaine Beck, daughter of the managing director of the construction firm Mowlem, but as a junior in Nathaniel Lloyd and Co. he could not yet afford to marry. Nathaniel took the chance of a shooting weekend at Robin's rented mansion in Herefordshire to raise the subject of Selwyn's promotion, but Robin, true to his reputation for meanness, said that Selwyn was already looking for a house, according to Elaine's father, and that promotion was not necessary.

Daisy was not pleased. As her first means of securing grandchildren, Selwyn's marriage was a pressing matter for her, and she was keen at least to slot Elaine into her proper place at Dixter. The girl was asked to visit on her own, while Selwyn was busy with the business in Birmingham, and she was introduced to the virtues of cross-stitch. When Elaine wrote to Daisy, her letters were forwarded to Selwyn for his approval and return; and when the girl made cakes for Selwyn, Daisy was genuinely jealous. Elaine may not have been Daisy's choice of daughter-in-law (*Low Church!*), but Selwyn loved her, and Daisy was determined to fit this square peg into a round hole even if she had to hammer it in.

The trickiest sticking point was indeed religion. Elaine felt she could not marry a man who was not a member of the Church of England, and Selwyn was an unbaptised free-thinker in the image of his mother. Elaine demanded that he must be christened. 'Bigoted and unreasonable' Daisy robustly called her family, the Becks, 'bears of Little Brain', and of Elaine herself, 'she's the sort of girl who wants beating, and I believe she'd enjoy it'. This from the woman who, most unusually for her time, had refused to swear to 'obey' her husband at the marriage ceremony. Elaine's brother, Buster Beck, met some of the worst face-to-face lashings from Daisy for daring to smoke inside Dixter (an injunction only ever relaxed for Vita Sackville-West, of whom Daisy was, for once, in awe). When, on a visit to Dixter, Buster's trousers were taken away for pressing by the maid, but not returned for the next morning, Buster, who was only 5'4", borrowed a pair of trousers belonging to Oliver (6'6") from the cupboard, labelled inside with his full name Oliver Cromwell Lloyd. Buster made a comical entrance at breakfast, saying that according to the label they belonged to Oliver Cromwell. Daisy was incandescent with outrage and indignation. Clearly the Becks were going to give her trouble.

In December of 1933 Nathaniel made one of his regular forays to the golf course at Rye, as usual depositing Christo, home for the weekend, with the greenkeepers. While they were there, Nathaniel had a dizzy spell and had to sit down to recover; he told Christo it must not be mentioned to his mother. Two days later, on 8th December, Nathaniel suffered a heart attack on the golf course at Rye and died shortly afterwards.

At Wellesley House, Christo was at once called before the headmaster and gently told the sad news. Daisy herself then drove over to collect him and Quentin, to take them home to Dixter.

Daisy was stopped in her tracks by the death of Nathaniel, the kingpin of her life's plan, the man she had fallen in love with at thirteen, but she maintained her self-control as ever. He was sixty-six and she was fifty-two. Her own mother was only three months dead. What a comfort it must have been to Daisy, then, to have her little Christo. He was just twelve. Letters of condolence arrived at Dixter, and Daisy replied fulsomely to them all, filing the letters and copies of her responses. To Nathaniel's friend Lord Leverhulme she wrote a few days later, with Cromwellian certainty, 'There are two things in this world, it seems to me, people make too much fuss about: Money and Death. This house has always been a particularly happy one, and I am determined that it shall continue so.'

Nathaniel left his estate in trust for his six children, as well as making provision for Daisy. But it was a difficult time economically in Britain, and Nathaniel's investments were not performing well; brother Robin was helping to pay for the boys' education. Daisy put Basildene, her mother's house in Putney, on the market, but it would not sell, remained empty and was burgled. Her lawyers then advised her to try for permission to convert it into maisonettes, so that it could be put to auction for a good price; this would at least bring Daisy some much-needed capital on which to gain interest. In 1939 it sold at last, and a good deal of the furniture came to Dixter.

Chapter 3

Rugby, 1934–9

Letter writing seems to have developed into a second life.
Christopher Lloyd's diary, 15th September 1992

In 1934, only months after Nathaniel's death, Christo left home for his first term at Rugby, trussed up in his 'horrible new clothes'. At Rugby, he was on the far side of London, and it was not easy for Daisy to visit. But in dealings with the school she was her usual tough and purposeful self; with Tan gone, she now had to be the man of the house. Christo's housemaster, A. R. Tatham, sent her the school's tactfully worded enquiry, issued to all parents, to discover whether the boy had received any sex education or whether the school need administer it at an 'appropriate time' (the alternative prospect of self-abuse hovers invisibly). Daisy replied very clearly that Christo lived in a modern liberal household and had learned at home all about sex in a happy marriage. And, yes, he had had all his necessary vaccinations too. She was equally robust about Christo's general abilities:

> I hope you will be fond of Christopher and make a man of him. He is not at all keen on games, but this must not be given way to. His virtues you will find out for yourself: his chief faults, as far as I can see, are an inclination to selfishness (which I *hate!*) and indolence in subjects in which he is not interested. I have always found him truthful and essentially kind, so I hope for the best. Tell your wife if she ever wants flowers arranged, she can safely leave it in his hands.

Christo arrived in September for Advent Term. The school ran on the house system. About fifty boys lived in each house, all within the vicinity of the main school buildings, and each was presided over by its own housemaster (there were no girls at Rugby then). Christo was put into Stanley House, a pale stucco, early-nineteenth-century building overlooking Barby Road, where he slept in a dormitory with three other boys and one sixth-former, who bore the responsibility of beating his charges if they misbehaved. On his bed Christo spread the counterpane Daisy had given him, embroidered in large letters with his father's name, Nathaniel Lloyd. From the window he could see the playing fields where the game of rugby was first invented, not that this meant much to the sport-hating, flat-footed Christo; of greater pleasure to him was to watch the great Spanish chestnut tree outside his window, as it came into leaf, put out its malodorous strands of flower and dropped its spiky fruits onto the grass beneath. It might not be the figs and apricots that grew under the windows at Dixter, but it was alive and it was not sport. At least he still had his weekly boxes of cut flowers from Daisy, and in her letters she continued to tell him, vase by vase, what she was bringing indoors at home that day:

> The most important thing of all is the dog-tooth violet (Erythronium Dens-canis – let us not be behind on our botanical names!), that we carried all over Switzerland and Austria last year – I having previously dug it up in Italy! The 'liliaceous bulbs' (according to friend Robinson [William Robinson]) have all come up, and there is one solitary precious bloom.

Life at Rugby, costing £81 per term, meant new and different rules: wearing his striped cap whenever he went outdoors, never walking with his hands in his pockets or his jacket unbuttoned, never taking shortcuts across the grass (that was for boys in the sports teams). Chapel was attended at least once a day. For Christo, the only right rules were the Dixter rules, and he felt unfairly bound by his new environment. For every house photograph he stood with that block of tight curls over his forehead like a lop-sided soufflé, narrow-shouldered and lonely, but perfectly self-possessed. Lloyds must never give in to pressure.

The new school meant new clothes. The official list of clothes required by pupils at Rugby was enormous by today's standards, and it has an aristocratic charm. Besides endless types and colours of socks, there were:

    10 soft collars
    4 Eton collars
    1 silver napkin ring
    1 Prayer Book
    1 Bible
    1 travelling rug
    1 nasal syringe
    1 duster

Christo had the lot, and on top of that Daisy happily indulged herself knitting socks and pyjamas for all her children with the pace and output of a small factory. 'I am a mother above all!' she proclaimed.

The tough world of Rugby intimidated Christo. His first school reports said, 'Usually knows the answer but too rarely volunteers it. Still solitary. Makes very little effort to join general conversation. Old enough to crack the shell.' A year later, at fourteen, he was 'Less reserved and shy. Young for his age', but also 'quietly confident'. When Christo was fifteen, the headmaster wrote grudgingly but certainly with a smile, 'Excellent progress: he will speak one day.'

And gradually Christo did. At sixteen, he was 'Still up in the clouds but coming on. More personality than of old, if not much more method.' At seventeen, he was 'learning to take his place'. Those virtues that Daisy had prophesied would make themselves plain began to show in his favourite subjects, especially English. It was Christo's first real chance to develop his skills as a writer, and his experience of letter-writing stood him in excellent stead. His heart was still as Dixter, and he chose to write extravagantly of natural history and the wild marshes beside the river Rother, where his beloved kingcups grew: 'They did not long stay bright, for night already held the land in her gentle embrace and the notes of a solitary thrush saw out the last glimmerings of daylight in the west.'

Sometimes he played with words and ideas: 'our Lord tells us that even Solomon in his glory was not arrayed like the simple lilies of the field (though I think it was careless of Him not to specify as to which lily He was talking about)'.

At other times the boy experimented with irony: 'My aunt [Daisy's sister Myrtle, whom Daisy hated absolutely] revelled in illness and although the good lady died long before I was born, I believe she brought the doctor's bills up to phenomenal heights. Fortunately she saved the family from ruination by eating a poisoned ice in Italy at the age of twenty-one, and dying from the effects.' This was a fact.

He tried his hand at fiction; and even knocked up a one-act play, just as his Grandfather Field had written farces.

His mother's ingrained conservatism came out in everything this most unusual teenager wrote. He disapproved of modern electric oast houses and praised the traditional, more picturesque kind found at Dixter; he lamented the state of the nation's woods, unmanaged since the First World War, and banged home the need for their proper management, while at the same time disapproving of the planting of the Lake District with 'black conifers' instead of English, rounded deciduous shapes. The jolly, unintellectual kind of music enjoyed by his wicked sister Letitia was put firmly in its place: 'I regard jazz as a modern invention to supply the needs of the totally uneducated: it appears to me to be music for those who haven't the intellect to appreciate classical music. Pardonable as such.'

As well as its sports, Rugby had a remarkable Natural History Society, comprising many different sections: Chemical and Physical, Ornithological, Wireless, Railway, Botanical, Meteorological and even a Pottery Section. Christo quickly joined the Botanical and Entomological Sections. Lectures to the society were given by outside academics and professionals on weighty matters, from quantum theory to architecture in steel and concrete, and of particular interest to Christo was Canon C. E. Raven* on 'Some Experiences in Bird Photography'. In 1938, when he was seventeen, Christo himself lectured on 'The Natural History of Skye', after an enjoyable family holiday there; for his age, he was an excellent field botanist, a skill learned with Daisy at home and on their Austrian skiing trips. No surprise, then, that he became secretary of the Botanical Section. It all suited Christo admirably, just as it had suited his brother Oliver, who went on to become a most able botanist and entomologist and remained so all his life. For Christo,

* Raven was father to John Raven, whom Christo later knew at Cambridge and who made such a remarkable garden at Docwra's Manor.

the school society was a means of making real all the things he loved and studied at home.

Some consolation to Daisy on losing her baby boy was that at Rugby he was under the influence of Kenneth Adair Stubbs, Honorary Associate of the Royal College of Music, Fellow of the Royal College of Organists and director of music at the school. Ken was a long-standing and regular guest at Dixter, a 'lame duck', clutched (like Dodo Emsworth) to Daisy's Puritan bosom, partly because she felt it was her duty to discover bright, socially disadvantaged young people like Ken and Dodo and encourage them to spend time at Dixter, and partly because it was useful to have an ally at the school attended by Oliver and Christo. Ken lived as a surrogate son to Daisy and as a brother to the Lloyd children. Even the cool Nathaniel was fond of him. But for Christo, Ken was a true soul-mate, though there were twenty-two years between them.

Ken's mother died shortly after his birth in Canada, and his father brought the boy to live in England, at Wells near Bath. He was sent to school in Bristol where, under the tutelage of the music teacher A. H. Peppin, he showed extraordinary ability. Ken became Peppin's ward and the two of them moved to Rugby in 1915 when Peppin took up the post of director of music there. Music became Ken's life. He won an organ scholarship to Worcester College, Oxford, and was briefly organist there before moving back to Rugby to be an assistant music master under Peppin, a job that he managed to combine with work for the Royal College of Music.

When Peppin retired to work in the Church, Ken was offered the post of director of music, organist and choirmaster at Rugby, where he presided with great energy over the setting up of the new music school, a modern, purpose-built music block complete with staff accommodation, chamber-music recital room and practice cubicles.

Boys already attended chapel at least once a day and the choir was a thriving institution, but Ken made music truly a major part of school life. In the large and acoustically superb Temple Speech Room, there were organ recitals and concerts by the City of Birmingham Orchestra, the London Senior Orchestra and the Boyd Neel Orchestra, as well as string quartets, trios and vocal recitals. The great pianist Solomon loved to come to Rugby. There was an excellent school orchestra and even an Officer Training Corps band. The music they played varied from contemporary composers such as Poulenc and Hindemith to composers of the recent repertoire such as Brahms and Dvořák, and as far back as the great masters Beethoven and Bach. Before each concert Ken offered lectures about the programme so that the pupils were always well prepared. There could not have been a more enthusiastic musical environment, and for a boy like Christo it was perfect. Under Ken's eye, he continued to learn piano, and at fourteen he took up the oboe. Unphysical child that he was, he struggled even with that because his fingers were feeble. But by sixteen he was first oboe in the school orchestra and was playing solos by Schumann and Mozart at school concerts. Ken fed him a diet of Bach and Dvořák and he acquired a lifelong passion for Brahms.

Ken and Christo were remarkably alike, both passionately interested not just in music but in birdlife, the stars, walking, wild flowers, embroidery and gardens; and both were sticklers for detail, whether in matters of music or natural history. Ken's one quality not shared by Christo was the ability to paint and draw; he was a skilled watercolourist (his paintings still hang in the parlour at Dixter). Ken lived just a few minutes' walk from the music department and Stanley House, at 16 Horton Crescent, a building that he shared with another music teacher, Alice Dukes, an aged, rather grand dowager known by all as 'the Duchess' and employed in 1916 as the school's first female teacher. 16 Horton Crescent was a dour three-storey villa of high Victorian gables, built of dark maroon and blue bricks with pale stone details. It stood on a corner plot looking onto a leafy square, with a garden surrounded by substantial brick walls. The garden was a delight to Ken, and having an enthusiastic young Christo to help him plant it was heaven. (The house came with a paid gardener to deal with non-botanical chores, as well as a maid.) Scattered across a lawn sheltered by tall robinias and a great blue cedar, Ken installed a maze of fussy Victorian rockeries, with little cascades, pools and bridges, and amongst these humps and bumps he and Christo would indulge their passion for alpines. Not content with the space around the house, Ken also annexed half an acre across the road for the planting of trees and this was soon known, in the Cambridge manner, as Stubbs' Piece. Every woody plant there was precisely labelled with bespoke cast-aluminium labels, and for the school it was the next best thing to a botanic garden. In Ken's greenhouse Christo was allowed to grow carnivorous stapelias, and the whole garden quickly became his laboratory.

In later life Christo would sail past beds of alpines in other people's gardens as if they simply did not exist, as he was by then, he claimed, more interested in the bigger picture and content not to grow things that could play only an insignificant part; but in those early days he was keen to learn about any and every plant, alpines included. He and Daisy always brought back seed of tiny alpines from their annual trips to the European Alps, and some of it always went to Ken.

Ken's large ground-floor study overlooking his garden at Horton Crescent was a well-known institution at Rugby. Here, on Sundays, he held gatherings of sympathetic boys – mostly sport-hating musical characters like Christo – to listen to music on his new gramophone, the very latest kind, with an auto-changer for 78s. To suit his unusual tastes, the walls were panelled with a dark-red wood and lit by semi-concealed pink fluorescent lights, which, to his annoyance, constantly hummed and crackled. On his own clavichord and the Duchess's Steinway, Ken played duets with the boys and accompanied pieces for oboe, violin or cello. Sweets and chocolate were laid on. For the boys, the price of indulgence was merely helping weed Ken's rockeries. The school was in favour of the arrangement, and for Christo it was ideal. He and Ken endlessly played duets, with Brahms always top of the bill, and the over-talented Oliver even knocked off a composition for them – an oboe sonata completed while he was on holiday in Italy, feeling bored because he was ill with sinusitis. With Ken's assistance, Christo learned to read a score as easily as a single vocal line, and his family bought him miniature scores of his favourite symphonies as birthday presents, in the same way that other parents buy their children board games or books.

At weekends Ken and Christo cycled off into the countryside around Rugby, noting which flowers grew where and precisely when they bloomed, and what birds there were to be seen or at least heard. Letters flew back and forth from both Ken and Christo to Daisy; in Ken she had found, and proceeded to cultivate, the perfect mentor for her son.

All the Lloyds benefited from Ken's hospitality and Horton Crescent became a hub through which every travelling Lloyd passed, using it as a staging post on journeys north and staying overnight or sometimes for a few days. Letitia went alone to stay with Ken, a not improper arrangement perhaps because the Duchess was always in attendance. In the holidays Ken regularly came to Dixter and claimed it was his real home. He called Daisy 'Mummy' or 'Mother D.', as did many of her young protégés (Ken had never known his own mother). To complete the web, the Duchess became a Dixter visitor, and the young Christo taught her how to do embroidery stitches and to play billiards on the big table in the basement.

Gradually the lone, but sociable, Ken came to crave the Lloyds' company. He would beg them to visit him at Rugby and, like Daisy, begged them to come *together*, in little satellite flarings of Lloyd family love far from the Dixter beacon. He felt a genuine part of the Lloyd gatherings, and in turn every one of the siblings regarded Ken as a brother. When he was at Dixter he was pulled into the daily routine of the house – weeding, picking apples, bottling plums, and making jams, marmalade and cakes. 'Nine batches of marmalade,' crowed Daisy, '310lb!'

On occasions Ken visited Dixter when all the children were away, and Daisy was glad of his company. The two of them settled to long sessions of embroidery, sometimes sitting indoors, often in the garden, she advising him on patterns and wools and frequently setting him off on a new piece that she had begun for him. Not a day went past when Daisy was not writing to the absent children about the minor goings-on at Dixter, and Ken would fill up the last half-page himself. 'I'm now off for a bath,' he scribbled to Christo, 'without you to give it to me! I miss your not being here *so* much. Mummy and I mention you about every five minutes.'

Socialising in the bathroom, it should be said, was a Lloydian foible. Daisy ran Christo's bath till the end of her life. When her third son Patrick was home on leave during the Second World War, he insisted on reading Saki to Daisy in her bath. 'And I, of course,' said Daisy, 'am expected to return the compliment.' She was then fifty-nine. Call this intimacy between the generations brave, natural and free-thinking, or call it childish, it must always have been unusual.

Daisy chose not to question the curiously intense relationship between Ken and the boy Christo, perhaps for the sake of convenience and perhaps because it made everybody happy. No love was ever more platonic. When Christo was at Rugby, Ken formed a link to Daisy and life at Dixter. The school was obviously not uncontent with Ken's pastoral care. Daisy's own close relationship with Ken enabled her to be ever more in contact with Christo and find a need to visit Rugby, sometimes by train, through London, or occasionally driven by her chauffeur Booth in the big Vauxhall. Lloydian relationships were, in any case, all intense. She herself was happy to tell Christo, her 'angel-baby and presh-presh', when he went back to school with Ken after the summer holidays, that she had slept in his bed to remind herself of him, while continuing to write to him twice a day.

The greatest pick-me-up for Daisy, after Nathaniel's death, was recognition of Dixter by a visit from Queen Mary in March 1935. Daisy had been opening the house and garden for years for the Queen's Fund, and she felt the royal visit was only her due, and not before time, but was determined not to be awed. She played the knowing Cromwellian to Queen Mary's aristocrat, and afterwards every member of the family received long letters relating the events of the day. Dixter of course had to be appreciated in every detail – every stick of furniture, every bathroom, every pantry and every cake tin – and, as a Puritan Arts and Crafts Queen herself, Daisy was especially keen to show off her embroidery.

The visit was a surprise in that it was expected sometime soon, but finally happened at a few hours' notice. Daisy marshalled her troops ready for the fray, but there was nothing she could do to conjure up Christo from Rugby. Oliver was commanded to forgo a trip to London, and Letitia – 'Titia' – who had just gone to school, was fetched straight back again by Booth. The morning was spent filling the house with flowers, and Daisy and Titia dressed in blue – the Queen's favourite colour. The visit was intended to be private, but according to Daisy somehow 'word had got out'. Crowds of villagers gathered at the gates an hour before the visit and Daisy properly shooed them off, but by the time the royal car arrived at 3 pm the fences were lined with local lads, thick as blackbirds.

Booth had taken the front gate off its hinges to allow unimpeded royal access, and at 3 pm Daisy, Oliver and Letitia walked up the garden path to greet the Queen, who had been well briefed and stood there hatted and coated, towering and glowering. Daisy's report to Pat continues the story:

I knew that however welcoming I felt I must wait for the Queen to make the first move, so I just dropped her a curtsey and called the Puritan Fathers to my aid, and waited for her to come to life.

She hasn't got at all charming manners, this Queen – she is neither gracious nor graceful, which is a terrible pity of the First Lady in the Land – but I think it is awkwardness rather than arrogance, and I don't think she is used to quite such natural and simple people as ourselves. At last she shook hands with me and I introduced the children to her, and there was nothing in the least awkward in their bearing.

I said: 'Now, Ma'am, would you prefer to walk round the garden first, or to see the house?', and she chose the garden as it was so fine. We turned down the steps into the Sunk garden and she said, pointing at the Great Barn, 'You moved that from somewhere, didn't you?' (She has a curiously gruff, abrupt manner of speaking and I have never heard a voice like it before – one would recognise it anywhere). I told her that the garden had been laid out by Lutyens, and that Daddy had designed the Sunk garden after the War, during which we had grown potatoes on the lawn. I also said how much more interesting the tour would have been for her, had Christo been there to guide her! I told her of his early ambition to be Head of Kew Gardens, and she barked emphatically: 'A very interesting appointment!' . . .

The Botticelli Garden [upper moat with flowery 'Primavera' turf] was looking particularly lovely – all starred with purple crocus, and great mats of mauve aubrieta hanging on the wall – it was a brilliantly sunny afternoon, and she was delighted with everything. I was terrified that she might bump her Royal Head going through the Rose Garden Hovel, so I urged her to be careful, and she doubled up! It looked so funny! She was wearing a long coat of 'pastel blue', with a collar of pale fawn fur, and she was very rigorously corseted, and looked as if she had been literally poured into her clothes. She wore very ugly parti-coloured shoes, and her ankles bulged over the top. Titia said: 'Oh Mummy! Did you see her feet! They fairly flapped in the breeze! And her ankles looked simply awful next to yours!' She has a funny, flat-footed way of walking, and stumps along rather like a soldier marching . . . When we reached the Porch, the Queen, who was carrying a very long umbrella with a pink knob, struck the ferule several resounding blows on the brick floor and said: 'Mrs Lloyd, tell me! What made you want to come and live in this house?' I replied gravely: 'Well,

Ma'am, many years ago my husband and I fell in love with it at the same moment, and we have remained in love with it ever since!' She seemed to consider this a sufficient reason, and turned her attention to that framed notice from the War Office about Dixter having been used as a hospital in the Great War. It made a good impression! Directly she got into the Great Hall, she marched straight up to the portraits and wanted to know all about them! I, thinking it would be more tactful not to particularise (as Lutyens once said of 2 of the ROYAL Princesses I met in his house: 'You've got their Head, but they haven't got yours!'), made a comprehensive gesture which included Henry Cromwell at one end and the Virgin Mary at the other, and murmured: 'Ancestors, Ma'am,' in a non-committal manner! . . .

I said to her: 'I'm afraid you must be very tried, Ma'am! I wish you'd allow me to offer you some tea?' 'Well,' said H.M., 'there's nothing I should like better, but the King likes me to pour out for him, and he told me before I went out that he'd got somebody coming this afternoon, and made me promise to be back for tea – and as I'm a good wife, I must go!' Wasn't that nice and human?

Daisy kept her letter to Pat, 'in case she wanted to refer to it', as she put it; and carefully attached to it a letter of 1949, from Wicked Uncle Robin, her hated brother-in-law, who was visited by the Queen at Albany and to whom, rightly or wrongly, he gave tea.

In autumn 1934, Selwyn, Daisy's oldest child and now happily married to Elaine Beck, fell seriously ill with a chest infection, which turned out to be pulmonary tuberculosis. In the 1940s the disease began to be treated surgically. This involved collapsing the affected lung by introducing air or ceramic balls into the thorax, or by disabling a nerve to the diaphragm. Another more permanent, but disfiguring option was to break and turn inwards a number of ribs. But in the 1930s, and more significantly in the days before antibiotics, there was no treatment. Selwyn was sent to Mundesley Hospital in Norwich and was expected to be there, as Daisy explained it to thirteen-year-old Christo, 'for a very long time'. Meanwhile, Elaine, so little loved by Daisy, was pregnant with Daisy's first grandchild, Angus, who was born the following summer.

When Selwyn was confined to Mundesley, Elaine moved with her parents to rented accommodation near the hospital, and this proximity did not please Daisy when she herself was so far away. Every letter Daisy wrote to her own children was full of relentless criticism of Elaine and her mothering skills. She could not abide the idea of Angus being with Elaine and her family the Becks – 'such slovenly people' – and, to lessen her own anguish and anxiety, Daisy actively determined not to become fond of the boy.

In September 1935 Selwyn suffered an attack of vomiting and tore a hole in one lung, so that ever afterwards Daisy was terrified when any one of her children had a cough or a cold, convinced they would also have TB. By October he was losing ground and on 1st November, during a large lunch party at Dixter, there was a phone call to say that he had died unexpectedly that morning. 'Thank God!' said Daisy. 'No one will ever know what I have been through this last year, seeing that boy dying by inches.' Selwyn was twenty-six.

The family rallied round her, of course, and two days later she wrote to the absent Pat: 'My darling, it is so lovely to have a house full of young people again – one can't be sad.' She was filling the void with the healing optimism of young people.* And a void it was: the loss of a child is terrible, and the loss of her firstborn hurt her deeply but she put on a ruthlessly brave face, to herself as much as to other people.

The Becks wanted to know if Daisy would like Selwyn buried near Dixter, a considerable kindness. Daisy countered that Selwyn himself had wanted to be cremated. Perhaps Elaine would like him buried near *her*, returned the Becks. Daisy didn't care: 'I know his spirit will be at Dixter, whatever she does. I should simply *hate* him to be in that horrible cemetery here, and they won't let me have him in the garden – it's not consecrated! Oh, what a humbug it all is! and what *does* it matter!' Finally, Selwyn was buried at Walton-on-the-Hill in the church where he was married. Daisy did not go to the funeral; her father had disapproved of women at funerals on the basis that they encouraged the men to cry.

The Becks put a simple announcement in *The Times*, giving Selwyn's name and Elaine's, but it was not good enough for Daisy Lloyd. She

* As Christo did after Daisy's death.

49

sent her own announcement, published a couple of days later, including the name of Great Dixter and Nathaniel's name and *all* his awards.

For someone as strong-willed as Daisy, relationships with other females would always be competitive, and it was never going to be easy for Letitia to live in the same house as her mother; there was a constant battle of wills. (Ironically, Letitia was Nathaniel's favourite child; when she was born Nathaniel opened champagne – a thing he had never done for any of the boys. Daisy was peeved.)

In this battle with Letitia, Daisy placed the hapless Christo quite unfairly between the two of them. She must *always* have allies. Never a thought of embarrassing the boy, never a thought of putting him in a position where his loyalty would be divided; in Daisy's opinion, what people did – what her children did – was simply a matter of right and wrong, and if it was wrong then it needed correcting. And so all Letitia's misdemeanours were put constantly before the schoolboy Christo in at least one letter a day, while Letitia was at school and during the months she spent at Dixter after leaving school, and when she began to train as a nurse in Cambridge. There Christo lay, on his dormitory bed, reading page after page of Daisy's letters. When he had read them and understood them – quite unable to do anything to help either his mother or Letitia – he folded them back in their bulging envelopes and put them into bundles tied up with string, ready to be returned to Daisy for safe-keeping when he went home during the holidays.

That Daisy passed on her bitter criticisms of Letitia might be understood as Dixter clannishness, in which every member's failings were thrashed out amongst the rest. That Daisy passed on her own troubles to Christo might be explained by the fact that she had for years used him as her conscience, someone on whom to air her private thoughts and from whom to seek approbation. What seems incomprehensible (and unforgivable) is that she did not *prefer* to tell her troubles to close adult friends and spare her young son the burden of partisanship. But Daisy did not have close friends, as other adults did; Dixter and her children *were* her life and she sought no wider intimate company. Her friends were mostly people slightly lower in the social scale than herself, who *owed* her the return of kindnesses; they were not people with whom she would share intimacy, worries or, heaven forbid, problems. For better or worse, Daisy had put herself in a position where she had no one but

Christo and her other children to whom she could tell her troubles. She had built around herself a public image of the perfect mother in her dream house surrounded by her six wonderful children, the product of her legendary happy marriage, and she was trapped in it. Worse, it was a legend that, by its very nature, would not have allowed her to remarry.

When Letitia was at school in nearby Benenden, she was plump, and to Daisy being fat was the result simply of bad discipline. She badgered the girl constantly about her comfort-eating and eventually hired a live-in nurse, for a month during the holidays, to oversee her diet. What exactly was the nature of the diet is unclear, but Titia lost twenty-four pounds. 'I'd be happy if she lost 3–4 stone, never mind 24lb', Daisy wrote, grudgingly, to Christo. Gradually, year by year, Titia began to believe that she would never be good at anything. Yet she bravely put up with the criticism. The Lloyds always forgave Daisy her carping because she had brought them up, right from the start, to believe that if they were criticised, it must be for their own good. It was a fast track to guilt.

In 1937 Daisy placed Letitia with family friends in Vienna, to help her grow up and see the world. The eighteen-year-old was having a tough time of it, not least in managing her finances, and as ever she felt obliged, as her Dixter training demanded, to confess her inadequacies upon Daisy's cold shoulder. 'Poor lamb!' wrote Daisy to Christo, 'fancy being brought to tears because she was in debt, through no fault of her own! Still, it is nice to feel she was so upset, as it shows she has the *right ideas*. Daddy would have been pleased, wouldn't he? Whatever I do, I am always wondering if Daddy would approve – it's awfully difficult.' Daisy wrote off the year in Vienna as a very expensive waste of time.

Perhaps Titia came in for so much criticism because, of all the Lloyd children, she was by far the freest spirit. Much as she loved Dixter, she managed – just – not to be in thrall to its regulations; her ambition, after she finished at Benenden School, was to be an actress *in the movies!* Daisy was having none of it and thought her daughter should be doing something more worthy in politically troubled times. She insisted that Titia become a nurse and arranged for her to be interviewed for training at Addenbrooke's Hospital in Cambridge. Titia acquiesced.

Daisy took her up to the interview and the two of them stayed with

Daisy's old friends Paul and Olga Hirsch, who in 1936 had fled Germany for Cambridge, bringing the Hirsch library of books and manuscripts with them.* To Daisy's fury, Letitia arranged to stay on in Cambridge with the Hirsches after the interview. Daisy wrote to Christo:

> I told the Hirsches that I could not spare [Letitia] but you know how persistent they are, and how selfish. And yet you know how they behave when the positions are reversed. Letitia is glad to be rid of me, as I cramp her style when she is making up her face. Renate, to my disgust, encourages her to use lipstick. I think this is unkind considering how much we all, as a family, dislike it. Letitia's interview with matron on Tuesday morning went off all right – I persuaded her to rub off her lipstick and to tuck her pearl necklace inside her cotton shirt (I can't bear to see jewellery in the morning anyway, and pearls on cotton is real bad taste) but I couldn't do anything about the awful hat cocked over one eye.

The house-trained Christo, the silent schoolboy, listened to every word of Daisy's tirades and agreed with her, for which she praised him. More letters, more bundles tied up with string.

All the brothers were asked to side against Letitia. Quentin, to his credit, was more easy-going and not so concerned. In less-than-perfect health, he had stayed on quietly at Dixter after school, learning to manage the estate and living at home in his childhood bedroom, shared with Christo in the holidays. He enjoyed practical matters, getting mains electricity brought to Dixter, trying to disguise loudspeakers as oak chests in the same way that Lutyens had disguised Dixter's central-heating radiators, and having the water tested to see if its acidity was eating away Dixter's lead water-pipes (it was). More than any of the brothers, Quentin was able to shrug off Daisy's incitements to feuding, and in turn she took him for granted. She did not expect great things of him and anyway he made a convenient manager of Dixter's practical affairs. That did indeed become his occupation.

Nursing may not have been stardom or the movies, but Letitia finally

---

* Their daughter Renate now became the latest surrogate child to Daisy, staying at Dixter for months at a time and becoming Letitia's bosom friend. The two families went to see opera at Glyndebourne together – the Festival had begun in 1934 – and were constantly in contact.

settled for the job. 'Addenbrookes is a fine place,' she wrote, 'and I shall definitely sign on for five years hard labour there, even if it is rather a sacrifice out of one's life at my immature age!' A month later she was installed in Cambridge and found herself with real freedom at last, away from Dixter. There was punting and picnics and May Balls, and she thought Christo would love it if he came to study at the university. Foolishly she wrote home about Cambridge in glowing terms, and Daisy, horrified, had a letter off to Rugby straight away, telling Christo how his sister's life was 'full of dissipation and young men'. When Letitia cut an engagement with a family friend to go punting, Daisy was disgusted. 'I told her so very plainly – especially as the boy was a Jew and very ugly, and, as a race, they must have got a sufficient inferiority complex nowadays without any additional slaps from Letitia Lloyd.' Obviously, ugly was what Letitia deserved.

Daisy relayed all of Letitia's misdemeanours to Pat, including the girl's letters as proof. 'Will she ever settle down seriously to her job?' complained Daisy. The circuitry of Lloyd family correspondence was Machiavellian in its complexity. A's letter would be passed on to B, but not to C; and B could show it to D, but not to E, who would only show it to C; but Daisy would be pleased if D would copy out A's letter for C, omitting the offending passage and forwarding it, together with a letter sent to F from E in Cairo, which had been passed to Daisy by E. This is no exaggeration. How her children remembered who was supposed to know what is a mystery. But it was no mystery to Daisy: not for nothing was she known as The Management.

Faced with her mother parading her inadequacies around the whole family, Letitia pulled back from the spider's web of correspondence with her mother and brothers. Her letters became fewer, to the point where Daisy took to opening and coolly answering mail that came to Dixter for Letitia, as self-appointed go-between: 'Tish thanks you for your letter and returns your love (meaning well!).'

Daisy was totally unable to resist wanting her grandchild near her, and she missed Selwyn terribly, even if he 'had never really belonged to me after Elaine annexed him'. Together with Oliver, now twenty-four, she decided that baby Angus must be wrested from the arms of the slovenly Becks and that the dreadful Elaine must come with her baby to live at Dixter. As a first approach, Daisy wrote to Elaine daily, writing with Selwyn's pen, to 'comfort her', and sending her 'some very nice stockings, just like some of mine that Selwyn admired last summer'. Elaine resisted. She knew Daisy by now. It was not for nothing that Pat would later call Daisy 'a dangerous woman' or that, when Angus himself married many years later, he would keep his parents-in-law well away from Dixter and Daisy, despite Daisy's effusive invitations.

Elaine absolutely refused to have her life prescribed by Daisy. She brought Angus briefly to Dixter in 1936, when he was one, and the boy promptly fell ill. Daisy, terrified of children's illnesses after Selwyn's death, tried to persuade Elaine to hire a trained nurse to care for the boy, but she refused. Daisy at once poured out her heart in a string of self-righteous letters to Christo, saying that she felt helpless in the face of such ignorance and jealousy. Daisy even offered to *pay* for the nurse, but still Elaine refused. Daisy was furious; her faith in her own infallibility as a grandmother was unshakeable, and she was determined that Christo at least should appreciate the fact. She told Christo that Elaine had cried with rage and said that Daisy had never appreciated her, 'but I, as always, returned the soft answer, and putting my arms round her, said: "Darling, you must never get cross with me; you are all I have left of Selwyn, and I *couldn't bear it!*"' How should a fifteen-year-old boy reply to letters like this? In soothing terms of agreement, naturally.

Elaine took the confrontation to heart. When Angus turned two, she informed Daisy that she was a having birthday party for him elsewhere, where there would be children of his own age. Daisy at once confided to Christo: 'I think it would have been kinder not to mention it, since I was not to be invited! What a curious nature [Elaine's]. I sent a telegram to him [toddler Angus] this morning: "We all wish you a happy birthday and would like to be with you."'

When Angus' third birthday loomed, Daisy took the initiative. The first birthday that her precious Selwyn had spent at the newly built Dixter had been his third, and Daisy was determined to have Angus there for this significant anniversary. She demanded that he be brought because he was becoming spoilt. Elaine refused. Oliver, as eldest son now, was sent to visit Elaine at the home of her parents, the Becks, and afterwards wrote to his girlfriend, Patricia Jane Barnett, that he did indeed think the child spoilt and selfish. Patricia replied to Oliver in no uncertain terms:

Judging by your remarks, it sounds as if the boy didn't do anything which does anyone any harm, so why worry about '*breaking* him of bad habits' (horrible nineteenth century expression). And I never know what 'spoilt' means. It is a word so loosely used about children who interfere with the activities of their superiors (in age). And doing things he is not 'supposed' to. As to devilment, well, I like it. It seems to me that this child has one good quality in his environment: the absence of fear of his elders, and so is probably a great deal happier than most, which is the important thing.

Oliver, card-carrying Communist and supposed free-thinker, at once sent Patricia's letter off to Daisy, loyalty to his mother taking precedence over loyalty to his girlfriend, adding the remark that he had heard Patricia's views on childcare before and that she 'generated more heat than light' on the subject.

After Oliver's visit, Elaine replied formally to him in writing, and again Oliver showed the letter to Daisy, who then copied it to the powerless Christo. The problem, Elaine said, in letting Angus come to Dixter for a while, was one of religion. She felt Angus' religion would be at risk in the liberal agnosticism of Dixter and pointed out that, as Oliver well knew, Selwyn had been baptised before his marriage to her against Daisy's wishes, but that *afterwards* it was Selwyn himself who had insisted that Angus be baptised. Elaine continued:

This constitutes the barrier which prevents me from ever allowing Angus to spend any length of time at Dixter where, from my own experience, his religious obligations would not be given any importance, and the influence would in fact be in a different direction, and there *is* a strong influence. You ask me if I do not think it fair that Angus should not be allowed to become as fond of Dixter as Selwyn was? I think I have given the reason why this could not be, apart from the fact that it is not his home, as it was Selwyn's.

Daisy was disgusted and told Oliver:

Of course we have always known that we were up against a fanatically religious person of very narrow views. In spite of all she says,

I am convinced that it is in reality jealousy rather than religion at the bottom of the matter. The influence of Dixter is strong because it is happy and good – I have always striven after the Spirit of the law, rather than the Letter – and that is what Elaine really fears. Poor Elaine! It must hurt to have a mind as narrow as hers – one sees now how people went to the stake for their convictions – though I think she would sooner send other people there.

Daisy continued to set out to Christo her strategy, writing to him in a staggeringly unselfconscious manner:

I think perhaps I ought to tell you what I have written to Elaine – it will prove to you that I, at all events, try to practise the Christian virtue of turning the other cheek: 'Elaine darling, Oliver showed me your letter. Poor child! How sad it must have made you to write it – but, strange as it may sound, it filled me with hope. Here was something definite to go on, and as you are seriously mistaken in one particular, I *feel* you may be persuaded to reconsider your attitude, but before I say anything more to you, I *must* see your father and discuss things with him. But be assured, in the meantime, that I shall always love you as once I believed you loved your poor old *Mother D*. I have been missing my loved ones terribly lately. It was our wedding day on the 20th – as Selwyn once said "the most important day in the year to our family!"'

And so, to thaw the ice in Elaine's heart, Daisy did indeed arrange to see the Becks. At their meeting, she repeated that it had been Elaine who had insisted that Selwyn be christened before his marriage. She said that she, Daisy Lloyd, would not christen her children, but let them choose for themselves when they were old enough. Then, in full dramatic mode, she concluded, 'I have the greatest respect for other people's religious convictions, and have never set myself up as the keeper of my brother's conscience. I *love* God: Elaine *fears* him.' It was Selwyn's dying wish, she said, that his child should be 'at Dixter'. Daisy's high-minded charm won the day, and Elaine was persuaded by her father to relent at least in part. Having got her way, Daisy delivered the *coup de grâce*:

I apologised [to Elaine] very sweetly for any pain or annoyance I might have caused her, but suggested I had been punished long enough. She said 'Well, you must be a very different woman from what you used to be!' I accepted the rebuke meekly, and replied that I hoped and believed that sorrow had softened me. After which I got to wheel the perambulator while I wiped my eyes and blew my nose (I couldn't help crying a little – I was so sorry for her *and* Selwyn) and then she allowed herself to be kissed.

Was there ever a more triumphant kiss!

And so Angus began to spend time at Dixter, though always accompanied by Elaine. Daisy had got her way. But she did not have the last word, since the toddler Angus was unenthusiastic about becoming a Dixter baby. 'Elaine takes the boy to church every week,' Daisy wrote, 'and sees to it that he doesn't really belong here. He's only interested in motor-cars, trains etcetera, and himself. I have done my best in a short time to make him more acquainted with people, animals and flowers . . . he has not been taught to pick with discrimination.' Anyway, Daisy concluded, almost unhinged, she 'hated the shape of Elaine's head'; Angus' too.*

With the battle for Angus effectively won, however, Daisy was in fighting form and Dixter shook with her cleaning and jamming and bottling. Christmas saw the house full to bursting with her dutiful children and their friends, and she insisted that they all dress for dinner every night: 'That is one of the little cleanlinesses that people in our position can afford.'

Her summer trips to Austria continued, right up to the eve of the war, partly to support her Jewish friends and partly to ensure that Quentin got his time in the healthy alpine air. Letitia, in Vienna in 1937, was homesick, but was not allowed to join Daisy in the Austrian alps because of the cost, and being homesick would do her no harm; Christo on the other hand, now sixteen, was to learn freedom by following Daisy out to Austria on his own. 'It will be a very good experience for *him* – and I am letting him "travel hard", as Daddy used to call it – that is, no

---

* It came as no pleasure to Daisy to learn, in due course, that Angus, rather than Daisy's children, was to be Uncle Robin's heir.

sleeping berth, as I don't want the children to be too luxurious.' In advance of his arrival in Salzburg, she took the opportunity to buy him lederhosen, so useful for scrambling around on the hills. And 1938 saw a grand and especially successful family holiday to Skye, organised by Ken, where Daisy fished to her heart's content and Christo identified obscure club mosses and acquired a taste for Scotland.

To her delight, Christo now got his first piece of commissioned writing, when Daisy's 'vice-tochter' Dodo Emsworth, who worked at *Time and Tide* magazine, asked him to contribute some short reviews of children's books. Christo leaped at the chance. Even as a teenager his pieces showed his willingness to criticise. 'I didn't think they were too terribly rude,' remarked Dodo in a note of thanks. Oliver, now working at Mile End Hospital, a Communist and owning shelves full of left-wing literature, brought the family further column inches by making it into the pages of *The Times*. At a violent political demonstration against appeasement of Hitler, he had tried to get through a crowd of police and demonstrators to offer medical assistance. He was hit on the head by a policeman for his efforts. Daisy the Cromwellian found herself delightfully torn between praising his bravery and disapproving of Communism: 'I'm afraid I should have cheered the bobby when I saw him hitting Oliver over the head – he deserves it! Not that I like Fascists, but I *love* policemen!'

Daisy liked to feel that she knew something of politics, and she had strong opinions of politicians' characters. It gave her great pleasure when she was able to find a little political gossip to which the rest of the world was not privy, and her friend Nancy Kinsey was a rich source. Nancy was on the staff of Lord and Lady Londonderry at Mount Stewart House in County Down and was one of very few correspondents who could outdo the Lloyds in the art of writing a good letter. Daisy and Christo revelled in the correspondence. Sometimes it was just tittle-tattle:

July 1938:
The other day there was a great dinner-party (50) here for the Queen of Spain. On the morning of the day I was rung up by an equerry or something who asked me whether Lady Londonderry was wearing a large or a small tiara at the party. She was out, so I tactfully replied that that was for her majesty to decide, and

would he let me know after he had asked her. So after lunch he rang up and said 'Please tell Lady Londonderry that Her Majesty is going to wear a MEDIUM-SIZED tiara'! And then I had to telephone to all the ladies who were coming, to advise them of this momentous fact, and pictured those who did not possess assorted tiaras chipping bits off, or soldering bits on, as the case might be.

At other times Nancy could wax both political and ridiculous, the former making Daisy feel importantly close to events; and Nancy wrote with a vigour that made Daisy's letters look mousy and Christo's pedestrian:

From Lady Londonderry's account, the atmosphere at Londonderry House [London] must have been electric last week, and I am tempted to relate some of her account to you, as I know it will make you laugh and that you will be DISCREET.

Firstly – von Ribbentrop arrives to say Good Bye and 'slobbers all over Lady L.'s hand' (as she puts it) whilst swearing that he knew nothing about Hitler's projected little procession into Austria; and of course WE always believe what Diplomats say.

Secondly – comes Baron Frankenstein (the Austrian Minister) to say that he has been recalled. So a NOTE is dispatched to Hitler telling him that he really cannot take Frankenstein away from all his friends in London, therefore a job must be found for him there.

Thirdly – an Englishman rings up from St Anton to say that Hannes Schneider, the charming and celebrated ski-ing instructor has been arrested. Hot upon that comes a telephone message from Obergurgl to say that Hans Falkner, the young ski-ing instructor there, has also been arrested. So a NOTE is winged to Goering, who, being such a Great Sportsman, will understand that you cannot arrest ski-ing instructors; moreover, he knows that Schneider and Falkner are great friends of OURS and have stayed at Mount Stewart and Wynyard [the Londonderry's country houses in Northern Ireland and on Teesside] – which is tantamount to having a white handkerchief tied round one's sleeve on the Eve of St Bartholomew.

Then Lord L. makes a very courageous speech in the House of Lords, assuring his peers that Hitler never breaks his word and has saved Austria from a welter of Blood. (Courageous indeed: except that probably his peers had all gone to sleep.) No sooner had he got back home after this Display of Chivalry than

Fourthly – Kitty Rothschild rings up from Austria to say that her brother-in-law Baron Louis Rothschild has been arrested. This, naturally, is not quite so shattering as the arrest of the Tyrolese ski-ing instructors, because the Rothschilds are Jews, albeit good friends of ours too. But, really, our dear friends the Gangsters are not behaving to pattern. Hitler with the Soft Eyes and Goering with the jolly laugh and amusing clothes seem to be rather letting us down. These Nazi-methods are all very right and salutary in Germany, where the people *like* them, but to apply them in Austria (and especially in the Tyrol, where WE were shortly going to ski), is monstrous, and has filled us with pained surprise and incredulity.

Then Lady L. came over here and was reminded by Mairi [Lord Londonderry's daughter] that the Londonderry Challenge Cup (a very beautiful old silver one) was in the safe-keeping of Hans Falkner at Obergurgl, and was to have been competed for on April 24th next. Mairi shrewdly suggested that the Nazis will probably melt it down for Reichsmarks. The LIMIT is reached, and

Fifthly – on Saturday morning I was required to type a NOTE (falsely so-called, for it was a very long letter), to von Ribbentrop telling him in round, not to say abusive terms what WE think of German mentality and of Nazi dealings in Austria: demanding that the prison doors at Innsbruck be forthwith thrown wide and the Tyrolese Ski-ing Instructors enlarged – to say nothing of Baron Louis Rothschild, and so on and so forth; and concluding 'But, even if you do nothing else, I hope you will see that your Nazi friends do not IMPOUND MY CUP . . .' A few more invidious remarks about his Nazi friends; instructions for the Cup to be sent to the British Embassy in Berlin: a threat that, if such behaviour continues, WE shall ourselves go to Vienna to see what is really happening – and WE remained von Ribbentrop's very sincerely; – and he will certainly get an earful when the mail reaches Berlin.

With Christo's time at Rugby drawing to an end, a family conference was held. He was keen to be an architect like his father, though concerned that he did not have sufficient aptitude for mathematics.

The final decision, on Oliver's advice, was that he should read modern languages at Cambridge and convert to architecture afterwards, because the good architecture courses were then at Liverpool and at the Architectural Association in London, yet he could hardly turn down Cambridge for them, and Oxford had no architecture degree.

James Mathiesen, one of Christo's friends from Rugby and a member of Ken's musical circle, was already at Cambridge, and he had praised Christo's choice of a career in architecture and told him he would love Cambridge. Daisy had taken to James when he had visited Dixter earlier in the year and had stood up resiliently to the full barrage of Lloyd family teasing meted out to 'new' people. 'To go to the country,' he wrote to Daisy in thanks, from his home in Woodford Green, 'and be able to touch trees and flowers without getting filthy with London soot is marvellous, but when this is coupled with such surroundings as Dixter and the views and walks from it, the situation becomes heaven indeed. I shall always remember every detail of my visit, from family cross-examination to the gift of hair pins . . .'

Such praise was music to Daisy's ears. That James was game to play the piano, and sing, made him even more welcome, not least since Christo was never keen to play his oboe at home for Daisy because she criticised him so much.

So: Cambridge it was to be. But in the meantime the family decided to take Christo away from Rugby and send him for two months to Paris (Daisy said he was anyway too thin at school), where he was to take a summer course in French at the Sorbonne and have a further taste of learning self-preservation. She took pleasure in writing to Christo's housemaster, who had always disapproved of Christo's shyness, saying that he would be leaving at Easter rather than at the end of the summer term. 'It is satisfactory that such an unenterprising creature should *wish* to spread his wings.'

Did Christo 'wish' to go to Paris, or was he packed off? Certainly he had been offered its temptations. John Cobb, now studying art at the Sorbonne, was an extravagant member of Christo's sport-hating circle at Rugby, and very happy eating Ken's grapes and chocolate and making music. John and Christo had kept in touch (school friends were now starting to call him Christo, having been Chris or just Lloyd at school). Christo had written one of his 'three-volume novels' to John, describing the family's 1938 trip to Skye and the wonders of its natural history. John replied with enthusiasm, telling him to come to Paris at once:

Your vocation in life is clearly to become a second H. V. Morton and go round writing books about these places – you'd probably do it pretty well and enjoy it a bag. Anyway, we must return there together some day and you can teach me tapestry work as well, which I long to learn. But if I go north with you, then you must come south with me. I very much fear that you are catching this northern 'stay at home or anyway in the British Isles' complex from [Ken] Stubbs. Be warned by me, it's dangerous and narrow minded! I notice that in your description of your work with him in Warwickshire you underline the words *absolutely English*! And I think it shows sign of stuffiness, also your unwillingness to go to Switzerland – though I think maybe your excuse about snow is justified. Anyway remember this as long as you remember me.

I hope the family meeting about your future was a success anyway, and that they've decided to let you leave before the summer and come over here. It would broaden your mind and French is a help in after life no matter what you are going to do. Anyway if all else fails you and I will take a cottage in the heart of the country and you can garden and play the piano and I shall write books that nobody will publish! I think I'll have just enough money if we eat bread and cheese! We'll invite all the nice people we know down from time to time and put up a notice saying 'All OTC sergeants and other undesirables keep away!' What about it?

Paris! Rugby, Cambridge on the horizon, and now Paris. Here Christo was in a new foreign city and on his own at last, never mind if the bank thought it imprudent for a young man to be travelling in France under the present political climate. It should have been wonderful, and yet Christo's time at the Sorbonne turned out to be no flowering of the self, even if he did learn to travel. He was simply too shy to break free.

'I hope you are having a perfectly grand time and are sowing your wild oats thoroughly,' wrote James Mathieson, now at Cambridge and about to visit Paris himself with the University Madrigal Society. Wild oats were hardly Christo's style. At first he was deeply lonely, and his letters to Daisy were sometimes thirteen pages long. His spelling met with the usual criticism. 'Bight one's food? Tare off a piece of paper? Darling, it looks so uneducated!'

Starting as she meant to go on, Daisy had a box of flowers waiting for him in his room in Paris, and on the day he left England – 12th May 1939 – she began the first of a new volume of numbered letters to him, hungrily asking for information on the family he was staying with, his room, the furniture, how far it was from the bathroom and the lavatory, and did her flowers stand up to the journey? From Ken, there was a box of asparagus waiting at the house on boulevard Berthier where Christo was staying with other English boys, to whom Daisy insisted that he speak nothing but French, to maximise his experience.

She bombarded him with garden news, just as she had when he was nine. How vulgar Suttons' stand had been at the RHS show: '*exactly* what Queen Mary would most like – I need say no more!' How hard she was working for him, putting out literally hundreds of bedding plants, and all before lunch.* She had been showing visitors round the house as usual, at a shilling a time. The Garden Club of America had visited. She had been to a Women's Institute conference in Earls Court, as the Northiam Representative, with '8,000 women there – most of them looking *very* W.I.ish'. And *of course* she would be visiting him in Paris. Meantime, he should buy lots of flowers for himself, cheaply.

Ken missed Christo too, and covered him with Rugby news. He was looking for a new school piano in London and had seen a reconditioned Bechstein on which their beloved Brahms had practised; the keys were left unrestored 'because the scratches showed "the nails of the master"'. And while he was there, he nipped into Heal's to get a comfy chair for the garden, from which he hoped to teach harmony on Sunday afternoons. Ken's eclectic furnishing was not entirely to Daisy's Dixterly puritanical taste, and nor was the glorious disorder in which Ken lived. She visited him, and threw out his flower arrangements, she told Christo proudly, replaced the vases and started again, shut the piano so that no dust would gather under the lid, cleared the smaller ornaments from the mantel (for Ken to put away) and dusted it, made him take piles of small change to the bank and discard heaps of old *Radio Times*. 'And,'

---

* Daisy was not a great gardener of the kind Christo became; she did not have his flair for putting border plants together. She loved them as individuals, and the schoolboy Christo even then did the planning; her specific interest in playing with colours came out instead in her tapestry and embroidery, or in her wild 'Primavera' meadow gardening.

she prided herself, 'it was all done *so* painlessly!' Instead she got him making a pincushion top for her, at 1,652 stitches to the square inch. Intervention of this kind was not new to Daisy; as a surprise, she had rearranged the furniture in Selwyn's house while he was away on honeymoon, which could never have made for a great start with Elaine.

But Christo *did* change in Paris, despite the bombardment of home news. He began, a little, to live a life of his own. At weekends he travelled in and around Paris, often alone, as the whim took him, to see the great tourist sights, going as far afield as Chartres and Bayeux, sending home long, detailed descriptions of the tapestry there and, in his father's footsteps, of the architecture of French cathedrals. He went to Versailles where, in this grandest of grand palaces, he picked wild flowers; he always had to be *handling* flowers, and picking them; it was not enough just to look. Also at the Sorbonne was Rodney Bennet, another of his Rugby musical friends, and they made the most of Paris' musical life, going on the spur of the moment to hear Solomon playing, or Rachmaninov or the young Menuhin. Christo loved taking colour pictures of the city, bought himself a newfangled light meter for the purpose, and sent the exposed films home to Quentin for printing and advice on technique.

But, as relations with Germany worsened, Christo's French sojourn was cut short. On 3rd September 1939 war was declared and the following night bombs fell on England.

Chapter 4

Cambridge, 1939–41

The devil makes work for idle hands.

Christo entered King's College, Cambridge, to read modern languages in October 1939, a month after war had broken out. It promised to be a hospitable place for him. The fine old architecture made him feel comfortable. Letitia was studying to be a nurse at Addenbrooke's Hospital just a stone's throw from his college on King's Parade, Olga and Paul Hirsch were in Cambridge, and Renate Hirsch was also at Addenbrooke's, so Christo had a ready-made circle of family friends before he arrived. Unfortunately, he lived out of college at 14 Harvey Goodwin Avenue, a suburban come-down after Dixter, with a miserable, shabby garden where his horticultural sensibilities were appalled to see his landlady trying to train bindweed clockwise around canes *when in nature it climbs anticlockwise.*

Daisy delivered him in person to Cambridge ready for the start of term, and hardly had she left than he was off for a walk along the leafy Backs, taking photographs and making notes on exposure and light levels. His bicycle arrived a day or two later by train from Dixter, and having got it repaired (it was immediately run over by a post van) he began to make lone Rupert Brooke-ish trips upriver to Grantchester, to take pictures of flowers and the church.

Neither Rugby nor Paris had turned him into a vigorous young man. He had Daisy's wide, firm brow, certainly, and his own crinkled mop of dark, curly hair; but his torso curled back shyly above the hips, as if set there by a strong wind or a punch. With his hands always behind his back, one hand gripping the other's wrist, there was nothing forthcoming about him; it was the image of embarrassment.

He must have seemed a curious character in a college full of loud young men. As much time as ever went into his embroidery and an interest in fabrics. He consulted endlessly with Daisy on which silks might make attractive ties and, rather to his own amusement, which tweed she would use to make him a pair of knickerbockers; scraps of brightly coloured fabrics pinned to letters flew back and forth. Daisy still made all his shirts, as she did for every one of her boys until they married, and meanwhile the knitting needles raced.

To his delight, Cambridge was full of music, and King's College had its own choir of course. Daisy dug into her cupboards and found Oliver's old surplice from his time at King's, starched it and got it in the post as fast as she could. Christo could go to concerts and plays and films as often as he liked and, to keep his own musicianship up to scratch, he hired from Miller's in Sydney Street a piano to keep in his room. At the Hirsches' house he took part in play-readings of the great classics of European theatre – Beaumarchais, Christo's beloved Racine – and they read them in the original language. There was bridge to be played – *intellectual* sport – and he soon found himself treasurer of the Bridge Club. But all his enjoyment came from people and activities he already knew; living in a world-famous university town could not stop him being shy and solitary among his peers, even if his own brand of quiet self-possession never left him. Time passed in studying, writing letters, walking to lectures 'for the exercise' rather than jumping on his bike, and taking days out to Fulbourn fen, where he counted shovellers, widgeon and teal and listened to the snipe drumming. Outside Cambridge, there were a few previously hard-won friendships with boys from Rugby who shared his love of music, and to them he wrote 'three-volume novel' letters about his university life, to which they replied rather stiltedly, unable to compete with Christo's exhaustive power of narrative – and, frankly, embarrassed. Loneliness is not difficult to smell.

To Daisy he wrote only about times with Titia and Renate Hirsch, and if he named new people they were ones he had met through that little family circle and were mentioned more for their shared interests than the promise of real friendship (briefly he took up with a *bedstraw* specialist). He became a weather bore, forever pestering Quentin for rainfall figures and barometer readings.

When he could, Christo got away to see Ken at Rugby. War or no war, musical life at Rugby still thrived under Ken Stubbs. In the first week of November 1940 Letitia went over from Cambridge to hear the pianist Solomon playing the Emperor Concerto with the school orchestra and Ken conducting. In the middle of the concert there was an air raid and the sirens sounded, but neither audience nor orchestra nor Solomon took any notice. It was the greatest night of Ken's life, and he and Solomon shook hands at length on stage, then had dinner together, after which Letitia played ping-pong with the great man himself.

At Dixter, Daisy was far from happy. Her beloved Pat was a soldier away fighting. The economic climate was poor and Nathaniel's estate provided her with an increasingly inadequate income, especially when she began to take in evacuee children from London. Staff were not easy to find, and Daisy was an expert at offending and losing them. She wrote less and less to Christo about the garden, and more about herself, the poor old Mother Sheep left at home. She even played the emotional trump card of promising Christo a future life at Dixter with a wife. It was a game she played with all her sons: she wanted to see them settled and providing her with grandchildren, but no sooner were they actually married than she was complaining because their wives did not conform to her idea of motherhood or were not good enough for her boys. So long as wives could remain imaginary, like Christo's, they were near-perfect.

'Darling,' wrote Daisy to her new undergraduate:

> I have at last found a wife for you! I am afraid she is rather young, but we shall cure her of that in time. Her name is Gillian and she is the adopted daughter of the lady who is now taking care of our boys [nine evacuees staying at Dixter]. She is that rare and delightful thing – a really intelligent and well-behaved child. She always refers to me as 'the lady with the red shoes', so today I am going to try and buy some for her Christmas. [The boys] are all devoted to Gillian and look on her as a very precious toy.

Thus, a wife for Christo: a manageable child.

The evacuee boys themselves were not at all what Daisy was used to: rough, city children, some as young as seven and upset to be away from home in a strange, grand house managed by a strange, grand woman. They ran away and became violent. One continually wet the bed, for which Daisy soundly slippered him until he stopped. She shaved their heads to deal with lice, and, to prove the powerful magic of Dixter, she herself weighed them once a week, to show how they were gaining weight.

But however well she managed these boys, Daisy continued to fail to manage her own daughter. There was no sign of Letitia settling down and marrying; she enjoyed her independence at nursing school far more freely than any daughter of Daisy's should. To curb her excesses, Daisy quietly failed to tell Letitia that, when she reached twenty-one, she was entitled to receive directly her share of the income from her father's estate (she had told the boys, of course) and the money slid into the Dixter coffers for administration by Daisy.

On her nights off-duty Titia used to go 'merry-making' in Cambridge with her roommate Barbara, and she took Christo along sometimes, to try to bring him out of himself, but it was no use; he was as uncomfortable as ever. They took him dancing with some young Czech men, but he sat it all out. 'What on earth do you find to talk about with them,' he demanded, 'they aren't even musical!' But Titia was happy with her easy-going Czechs who, unlike her family, were not perpetually testing and assessing her. They danced well and that was enough.

For all her openness, Letitia had a sharp temper. She fell foul of her demon Sister at Addenbrooke's for not ensuring her blackout curtains were properly in place during an air raid; like her brothers, she had been brought up always to sleep with the windows open and found the closed atmosphere of the nurses' home stifling: 'The blackness of it, – and, apart from its airlessness, all the plaster peeling off the walls. Ugh. Dixter seems an Illyrian dream, an idyll . . .' Daisy, every inch the matriarch, intervened with an imperial letter to Matron, and the Sister was appeased. But then Sister found Letitia sharing a bathroom with Barbara as they got ready to go out dancing, which was deemed improper. Titia was convinced she was being picked on and – furious at the hospital management and knowing she would disappoint her mother – decided to leave Addenbrooke's.

Daisy continued to confide all of this to Christo, in letter after letter after letter; he was her man-on-the-spot, her co-conspirator and confidant, too much in thrall to Daisy to refuse to listen. He made no protest. Even Nathaniel was raised from the dead to criticise his favourite for being weak and obstinate. Even kind Pat was pressed to admit that Letitia had done or achieved nothing useful in life so far.

'Tonight,' Daisy wrote to Christo, 'I have expressed a letter to the Matron, of which I enclose a copy – don't you think I've edited Letitia's letter [of complaint] very skilfully? You may show her the copy, but keep this letter to yourself.' Daisy's letter elicited a warmly, conspiratorial reply from Matron. Regarding the blackout issue, Daisy endorsed Matron's remarks that Letitia was selfish and that, in any other country, people like Letitia would find themselves in jail. So Daisy sent Matron a nice box of Cox's. To Christo she continued:

Letitia has always given more than her share of trouble. *But* she is very fond of you (this always transpires in her letters) and you must make use of this weakness *for her own good!* Don't forget that Wednesday is St Valentine's Day – give her a handkerchief or some pretty trifle – quite *on your own* of course. She is a warm-hearted child in spite of her manifold wickednesses!

When the war came, Letitia decided to specialise in midwifery, which Daisy felt was unpatriotic; the girl should be specialising in nursing the sick and wounded in wartime, just as she herself had allowed Dixter to be used as a Red Cross hospital. 'A plague on her, she is such a nuisance,' Daisy railed.

Letitia had her heart set on studying in Dublin, but Daisy pulled strings through a cousin to get her a place at Edinburgh Royal Infirmary, where her friend Renate Hirsch had also begun midwifery. Letitia called her 'an interfering woman', but once again acquiesced. After one period of leave at Dixter, when to her relief Daisy had gone to visit Oliver (now working at the Radcliffe Hospital in Oxford), she wrote to Christo, the family confessor:

I can't tell you how awful I feel at the disillusionment Mummy and I feel in each other. I know she'd like a nice docile 'yes mama'-ish little daughter, who never wanted to go any place, and who always played 2nd fiddle to her. Well, she can't make a silk purse out of a sow's ear! I know she's perfect in 101 ways, but in so many ways I keep comparing her unfavourably with several other mothers I know. When she was away at Oxford, everything went like magical clockwork here. Everyone was happy. There was an atmosphere of co-operation with *willingness*, and Mabel and Quentin were different people, really they were.

Why can't things be different when she's here? I can never ask my friends in with an easy conscience that Mummy will be nice to them even if she doesn't like them. And what a *waste* of a beautiful place like Dixter if one can't proudly exhibit it to one's friends and make them feel that the world's a better place than they had supposed, because of it.

Poor Christo, caught in all this crossfire. Undoubtedly he could see Daisy's faults, as he could see Letitia's, but he managed to survive all these differing demands on his loyalty. And when Daisy had him there at Dixter, she genuinely *was* kinder; and Christo was *genuinely* sweet to her. Somehow, they were made for each other.

When Christo was home from university, Daisy and he would cement their alliance by gardening together all day long, planting out bedding plants that had been raised in boxes, weeding in the depths of the Long Border, scratching around in the meadow grass to see which crocuses were fertile and had set seed. And all the time they were sharing their thoughts and lives in the quiet way that only working on something physically together can provide. The war was there in the background of their lives, of course, and the thought of Pat away fighting.

When two Spitfires fell down in the valley near Bodiam and a bomb hit the nearby village of Etchingham, the timbers of Dixter shuddered, bringing home the war's reality. Occasionally Spitfires passed over Dixter, loud as giants ripping calico. News came from Letitia, staying with Ken at Rugby in 1940, of there being four or five air-raid warnings every night, and how they could hear the bombs falling on Coventry. A few hit Rugby itself. At Dixter, Mabel the downstairs maid handed in her notice without a new job to go to, but sick of Daisy's criticism, and Flo the cook demanded a pay rise. Sands, the gardener, received the very worst of Daisy's criticisms: if he watered Christo's precious cacti in winter, it was because he was plain stupid; when he forgot to take the regular box of flowers to Northiam church for Harvest Festival, she sent him down to the padre with a propitiatory jar of bramble jelly and a note telling the padre that he too should chastise Sands for forgetting.

The old coal-fired range installed by Lutyens, which had made the kitchen the hottest room in the house, was abandoned for electricity, and overnight it became the coldest room in the house; where once the evening meal had taken place around a big oval table in front of a blazing fire in the Great Hall, it now retreated to the servants' hall, a little oblong room adjoining the kitchen, with small high windows. It was snug enough with a fire lit, but 'Think of Daddy's face!!' lamented Ken.

When Christo went back to King's in term time, Daisy sulked abominably, and after his first long vacation Christo left her in tears at the gate:

I did hate leaving you this morning; you looked so lonely, and will be, I'm afraid, if you don't look out, and gad about as much as you can until my return. After all, two months is quite a short time. For my sake, if not for your own, please *promise* not to sit cooped up in the nursery for hours on end every day, just sewing and listening to the wireless by yourself the whole time, brooding in fact, and hardly pushing your nose out of the door from morning till night. Please, *please* don't do this. Try and be out of doors as much as you can, in the garden or anywhere else, outside Dixter. You may think that's asking rather a lot, but *do*: promise? The last four months have been wonderfully happy, haven't they: it's ten years since we've been so long together. In spirit I am with you the whole time.

It was a love-letter, from Christo the faithful son, and wrapped with a little ribbon of melodrama.

Part of Daisy's problem was that, with Christo away, there was no family there for her to control, apart from Quentin, who was exempt from military service on medical grounds, and, occasionally, Ken, who continued faithfully to visit her. In the bitter winter of 1940, when moorhens and rabbits lay dead in the fields, Daisy and Quentin, held indoors by the weather, got ever more on each other's nerves. Quentin was sick of having evacuees on the farm, and Daisy reprimanded him for his lack of patience: 'I hated going into cottages [as a child], and would always cross the road to avoid anyone at all dirty-looking – you have no idea what willpower and self-control I have had to exercise to force myself to do all these things I (naturally) so much dislike. I'm afraid I am a confirmed aristocrat at heart.' The two of them quarrelled constantly, despite Ken's best efforts as peace-keeper, and then Daisy sulked and shut herself up in the nursery again, listening to the radio for news that might relate to Pat.

Ken wrote to Christo:

It is such a pity that at such a lovely place as Dixter there should be so much unnecessary unhappiness, and, when you and I aren't here, so little else but loneliness and bickering. As soon as you or I come we get Mummy *out* for a start. And then she is very happy of course at having us here. Q. could do exactly the same if he would. I think Mummy does demand a lot from one when one's with her – you know, fetching and carrying – and at times she is unreasonable. But what in the world does that matter seeing how much she gives of herself, how gratefully she accepts little odd kindnesses. But Q. doesn't see this at all and reacts in the wrong way every time. I am so sorry for them both. I think Q. ought to go away for a long time. Mummy would be less lonely without him.

Failing with Quentin, Daisy now tried her hand at organising other people's children – those of Margot Kinsey, one of her lame ducks and sister of her friend Nancy at Mount Stewart. She was pushing Margot to get her children evacuated to the country at once – to somewhere like Dixter – because of the war, and Margot was brooking no interference. 'My Dear Foster Mother,' she wrote:

I sometimes wonder if you credit me or my children with any sense. The way you spoke to me this afternoon about evacuation, as if I had never given it a thought, does it strike you that there might be difficulties that you yourself have never experienced? My children, to me, are every bit as precious as yours are to you, and I don't need to be urged to put them in safety, but it only makes it more worrying when you speak as if you were the only person who gave this a thought. I have always turned the other cheek to many things you have said, because you have been very kind to me. I feel like *you* did *very often* when Olga Hirsch told *you* what to do.

72

Practically every time you see me you try to educate me. I do not mind constructive criticism, but I do mind destructive. I do my best whatever you may think, and you might remember that, surrounded by every necessity and comfort, every sorrow is easier to bear. I hate writing this but you have made it necessary. Yours, Margot.

Daisy found it ludicrous that her maternal guidance should be questioned and she copied out Margot's whole letter and, in outrage, posted it straight to Christo.

There was a feeling among the Lloyds that war was for other people. Proud as they were of brother Patrick, the career soldier, the rest of them felt their energies would be better spent not at the front – not least because, apart from Patrick, none of them was sufficiently tough or focused to be a good officer. Letitia, therefore, was a nurse, and Oliver a doctor, while Quentin worked the land at Dixter. Daisy was just glad to have them safe and could claim that Pat was her patriotic contribution to the fighting. But what would happen to Christo? What could a shy, intellectual, physically inept soul like him have to contribute to the army?

In June 1940 the undergraduate Christo joined the Local Defence Volunteers, as an infantryman. Patrick told Christo to get his name on the gunners' list fast and to volunteer for service in the artillery, to save himself from ending up in the 'awful infantry', when eventually he was called up for army service. Christo obediently applied for a transfer to the Royal Artillery, and Pat weighed in to support his application, but to no avail; there was too long a waiting list. And so Christo was set to do four months' training with Other Ranks, as a private and possibly then lance corporal, with the possibility of then moving to an Officer Cadet Training Unit for five months and thereafter a commission. The Gunners he achieved, but never, to his shame, a commission, unlike his illustrious brother Pat, captain at twenty-five and major at twenty-seven.

Chapter 5

The War Years, 1941–6

What I dread most about Socialism is the thought of being governed by people who have never learned to govern themselves!

Daisy Lloyd, 1938

Christo was the youngest and the shortest of the Lloyd brood. Not surprising then, that when he was finally called up in 1941, the clan called it 'baby-snatching'. Off he went to military camp at Catterick, and his degree at Cambridge was deferred. Nobody suspected what an uneventful war he would have, dreary more than dangerous.

To this sensitive, home-loving, sheltered soul the army was a rude shock, though not, as he later remembered it, so rude a shock as going to prep school or Rugby. But at least in education he was in the hands of excellent teachers, whose purpose was to take care of him and nurture him. In the army, 5829328 Gunner C. Lloyd was entering the school of unsympathetic hard knocks.

For almost two years Christo was at training camps all over England, in Devizes, Bulford, Malton, Haydon Bridge and Catterick, earning the grand sum of fifteen shillings a week, with a further two shillings and sixpence held back for when he left the army, and two weeks leave per year. Like most of the men, he sent his washing home by post – up to fifteen pounds in weight, and in his case frequently a repository for pressed flowers. Daisy did his washing herself, to feel closer to her Lambikins, even his handkerchiefs. 'Bless his blood and bogeys!' she smiled as she scrubbed away.

How he hated army life. The food was bad and he spent his money topping it up with snacks. His quarters were cold and he was obliged to wear a pullover in bed, pressing Daisy to send him warm pyjamas:

74

'there are no eiderdowns here, you know'. He had to live and work with people more foul-mouthed than he knew was possible and who smoked incessantly. Despite the cold, he still pursued the Lloyd obsession with having open windows at night and thus made himself hugely unpopular. Letters were his only refuge, his chance to rise above the life by describing it, and to keep in contact with his family by entertaining them. Wit was his shield against the world. Daisy pounced on his letters the second they arrived, numbered them and annotated them with the date on which they were received:

November 27th 1941
Instead of the usual afternoon work, yesterday afternoon was given over to 'Recreational Training', as the army pleases to call games. When I came here, I did not put my name down for any game, and those who do not play, have to spectate. That is to say it is preferred that one should watch extremely inferior soccer for 1½ hours than that one should take a nice brisk walk, which was what I wanted. The reason for this state of affairs is that most men would rather play a game compulsorily than watch one, and that if they were allowed to do as they pleased if they did not want to play, they would *not* go for a walk, like me, but would just loaf about indoors. So off I marched with half a dozen others, for the purpose of gaping at the dullest game ever invented by John Bull. For the first half of the game I lay reclined upon a heap of greatcoats reading Martin Chuzzlewit, which I'm thoroughly enjoying. After half time, however, I decided that, in order not to become frozen stiff, a walk was definitely *necessary*. I made my way toward the village of Bulford proper, which is quite a bit apart from Bulford camp. I went down a hill and, turning a corner, surprised a thrush eating berries off a privet bush. I *should* say that the thrush surprised me, because actually it, for its part, took no notice of me whatsoever. Close by was growing the first bush of spindle that I've seen since I've been here. The cutting made by the road, had at this point been taken back some distance from the road itself, and ended as a bare, white cliff face. This was chalk, as I expected, but what *did* surprise me was the presence, scattered about in the chalk, of flintstones in all sorts of odd shapes and quite unconnected; also of the cross-section about an inch wide, of a straight

strip of flint running diagonally across the cliff-face. I found there a large type of spurge, which we don't get at home. It was still in bloom.

But the army even managed to spoil walking for him. After Christo's botanical rambles around Rugby with Ken Stubbs, army route marches were a nightmare:

I had no idea that the exercise of walking could be so deadly. A 10 mile walk would be a pleasure to me, but this – ! We marched in 3's, and one is hemmed about by others, always liable to tread on the next person's heels, to have one's own heels trodden on, or to slap the back of one's hand against one's neighbour's. And then there was no question of progressing at the most comfortable pace. The pace was set from in front, and was unluckily continually changing; we were continually having to step out or step short, and nothing is more tiring. And when one is getting rather tired, one involuntarily swerves a bit in marching, and there is no room for that sort of thing. I don't feel inclined for conversation, but the worst thing of all is that in that crowd, for some reason or another, one cannot or rather I could not let my thoughts wander into those pleasant channels which are the best preventatives of boredom and which allow a person to forget almost entirely for a time, his present circumstances. I tried to think of bees and make plans and dream dreams about them, but even this failed. There was no escape.

Yesterday afternoon we all went on what was called 'an assault course'. We all bicycled on army 'cycles to a field right above Richmond [Yorkshire], having walked all the way through and past Richmond up an excruciatingly steep hill. We were then given a bayonet training course, all concentrated into the one afternoon. A bloodthirsty sergeant of Infantry exhorted us to make bayonet attacks with savage cries and filthy language at the right and left breasts, the right and left groins and the stomach of various tiny little stuffed and pendant sacks, representing the ENEMY. But if the enemy really looks as pathetic and forlorn as those poor little sacks, whose tummies were already lacerated from the blows of many former infamous attacks, and whose entrails (in the form of damp straw) were bulging forth in a state of imminent disintegration, I'm afraid I shall never have the heart to combat so impotent a foe.

The actual assault course took place at the end. With bayoneted rifle, we plunged into a maze of trenches, half filled with snow, struggled laboriously through them, 'looking for game meat to be spiked'; then out again past more floating sacks, at which I made feeble little dabs; then a sprawling collapse over a trip wire, put there just to make life more realistic; then a further plunge into another trench and finally out onto a bank and fell onto my gasping stomach, whence I was supposed to go through the motions of firing five shots, which would, however, most certainly have been of more danger to friend than foe, for my weapons had become my own masters. And then, horror of horrors, the whole course had to be immediately repeated, whilst my tin hat shipped in the most sprightly but engaging fashion, all over my head and face, motivated by the weary jogging of two leaden flat feet. I understood how those sacks must be feeling, at the end of it, except that they were spared the heat of it all.

Daisy had trained members of her family always to be right, the only person before whom they might show inadequacy being herself. But in the army Christo's inadequacy was crystal-clear to everybody, and shaming. On his days off he escaped for long walks in the countryside, where he hunted for flowers (his unit threw out hundredweights of maps every time it moved camp, and he salvaged any that might be useful to him). At least he could feel good about identifying plants and relaying his conclusions to Daisy (occasionally plants themselves were relayed too, including great clumps of lesser butterfly orchids from Devizes).

It was of course permissible for any person at all to be more adequate and right than Letitia, as she found out when visiting Christo at camp in Haydon Bridge. He took her on a long walk that involved wading through nettles: he was wearing trousers, her legs were bare. Christo made sympathetic and encouraging noises, pointing out that:

at this time of year, stinging nettles should have no more poison left in them and that there was therefore no need to cry out when brushing past them. I also observed that, had it been spring time, and the nettles young, they would then have been infinitely more unpleasant. Later I pointed out a specimen of the annual nettle, whose sting is far more venomous, but she refused to test the veracity of my assertion.

Christo cannot have been unaware of the Dickensian precision of his prose, and, occasionally, its pomposity. It was a style he was cultivating, after the fashion of his hero-of-the-moment, the naturalist W. H. Hudson, that great observer of detail and painter of word pictures, whose books he collected avidly. He told Daisy:

At present I am reading 'A Naturalist in La Plata'. In a chapter entitled 'Facts and Thoughts about Spiders' he writes:- 'The gossamer spider, most spirited of living things, of which there are numerous species, some extremely beautiful in colouring and markings, is the most numerous of our spiders. Only when the declining sun flings a broad track of shiny silver light on the plain does one get some faint conception of the unnumbered millions of these buoyant little creatures busy weaving their gauzy veil over the earth and floating unseen, like an ethereal vital dust, in the atmosphere.' Don't you think that's very telling descriptive writing?

Christo did his very best to match Hudson in his letters home. Of a walk in the Cheviots, he wrote:

Only five yards from where I stood, and taking not the least notice of me, a little treecreeper was busily engaged in looking for food on the trunk of a sycamore tree. I witnessed a perfect display of all this little creature's prettiest airs and graces. First it ran up the tree, then down and then up again; sometimes it paused a while to investigate deeply into a promising crevice; sometimes it vanished for a little on the far side of the trunk. It appeared at its best as a silhouette; its slim body, warm brown on top, white underneath, motionless for a moment; its long, slightly down-curved beak poised for action and its tail pressed hard against the trunk, woodpecker-like, for support.

So full of plants and Latin names were Christo's letters that it was
suspected by his mess-mates that they might be in code. 'The cherries
are blooming', they said, might mean 'there is a revolution in Paris', or
anything else that had been agreed on. His dreams were far from camp,
full of cacti and bee-keeping, and all he wanted was to be at home.
Frivolously, he suggested to Daisy:

Couldn't you write a letter to the War Office suggesting on my
behalf that the making of string bags is WORK of NATIONAL IMPORT-
ANCE, that suitable receptacles for shopping goods in general and
7lb of potatoes in particular are ESSENTIAL for the WELFARE of the
NATION, that no pains should be spared to brighten the lives of
the English people and that to see me sitting in a large wing chair
before the fire in the Yeoman's Hall, feverishly netting dinky little
string bags, which turn inside out and outside in as easily as may
be, is sufficient to bring a smile to the lips of any intruder, and
THEREFORE will the War Office bring its notice to bear upon the
manifold incontrovertible reasons for my immediate withdrawal
from His Majesty's Forces, where my highly specialised talents are
lamentably displaced and neglected?

There was a kind of ludicrous, Hoffnung-esque absurdity about much
of army life that was pure grist to his mill as a writer:

Since leaving home, I've had two baths – showers rather. Our
quota is one a week, and a special expedition down to the village
is made on Mondays. The first one was the coldest, draughtiest
and most scalding affair I've ever experienced. I can't imagine what
it'll be like in winter. A thin jet of water is operated by a long-
handled and very wobbly tap, depending from above, rather like
the top bolts which work the garage doors. It's almost impossible
to benefit from any water from the jet, without continually banging
one's head against the tap handle. This alters the temperature of
the water, usually to a scalding heat, and at the same time on the
first occasion, a howling gale was blowing all around us from
outside.
    The lats here are up a steep slope behind this hut, and about
30 yards away. They consist of a row of buckets, emptied daily,

covered by a row of loose wooden seats. The ground falls away very sharply in front of them, so that it's very uncomfortable sitting there, and of course if one sits on the edge of the seat, everything collapses. The whole is in a very open, draughty wooden shed. This has the advantage of blowing the smell away, but the roof consists merely of a number of wooden boards side by side, so that when it rains the water drips mercilessly down through the cracks and everything inside is drenched. In winter the whole affair will be choked with snow – a chilly nest indeed.

The huts are built of sheets of concrete, nothing more. They get intensely stuffy when the sun shines, and doubtless correspondingly cold on the other side of the year. It poured with rain this morning, and I found it dripping from several places in the roof onto my blankets. If the officers lived in the same conditions as we do, matters would very soon be improved. As it is, masses of everybody's time is spent in doing fatigues such as trimming the edges of paths and roads, pulling up weeds, scything grass and putting up tarpaulin shelters for the motor cycles and the L/c's car, painting all the doors in the officers' mess with white paint, etc, etc.

In camp life there was always time to kill between the chores, and Christo, never able to be idle, filled his time by applying to his mess-mates the powers of observation and detailed description that he and Daisy would use for botanical matters, and he set about giving her a series of cameos of the men he worked with in camp. Years of listening to Daisy nailing people's faults had trained him to wield the scalpel. And so, while his companions drank and danced, Christo would sit at a table in the corner of a badly lit NAAFI, with a pad of paper, reeling off ten-page letters:

30/8/42

John Bradley is far and away the best of the bunch. He's 31, and certainly no beauty. He's short and a very odd shape. His legs are short, and below the knees very spindly, but above them are a pair of *large* thighs. He has quite a long torso and an enormous head in every direction, quite a lot larger than mine. His hair is brown, stiff and untidy. It refuses to lie down. His face is rough in texture but his eyes are the most important feature as they are so representative of the man. They're a clear blue and very intelligent. When they smile, which is often, they look genially amused. He is a many-sided person and of a complex nature. So much that it is very difficult to make a true analysis of him – especially as I have known him for little more than a fortnight. So I'm not going to try to go into too much detail, lest I should fail to do him justice.

His father is an engine driver; a very honest man; terribly honest in fact; clever in his way but without imagination. Bradley says, he doesn't remember his father ever having kissed his mother, though not because he doesn't like her. He's simply the undemonstrative kind. When his son did frightfully well after his first year at Durham university and the professors of Botany, Zoology and geology had each offered to give him their special attention if he'd specialise in their subject, the father was of course frightfully quilled, and showed it by shaking hands with his son! He was dreadfully religious and Bradley had to go to church every week day and three times on Sunday up to the age of 21. He himself found the church utterly false and corrupt and it says much for the father that through discussing the subject with his son from time to time, he himself became so disgusted with his former idol, that he lost all interest in it and now devotes all his leisure hours to ambulance work and hospitals. Bradley got his BSc in geology and devoted years in the concentrated study of it but I think he underwent many disappointments in the matter of a job, and had to take up schoolmastering. Naturally his family hadn't any money to throw about.

Luck finally shone on Private Lloyd and, at the age of twenty-one, he was transferred as requested to the Royal Artillery, as brother Pat had originally proposed. He was a surveyor, one of a team that, by the use of trigonometry applied to the landscape, could direct the guns where to fire. His training now changed, and already after a month life became less boring. Days were long, but he found himself interested in the mechanics of guns. He learned to drive, on heavy army lorries, although the coordination needed to double-declutch baffled him nearly as much as the making of army porridge. Now he could use his brain, and learn a little about military law and tactics and the workings of the petrol engine.

Christo began to think about getting an officer's commission, although becoming an officer in the Royal Artillery was difficult then, because 'none are getting killed off'. 'There are two essential qualities for an officer,' he wrote home, 'brains and leadership. I dare say you can imagine that when I applied [this idea] to myself, I didn't feel any too confident. Brains I may have in sufficient quantity, but leadership? Well you know me, and I don't think it is at all possible to acquire leadership by experience, but I am certainly not naturally endowed with it.' Of course he failed to get a commission. Not surprisingly, Wicked Uncle Robin had approved of his ambitions to be an officer, and bore a horrifyingly robust – perhaps a tough businessman's attitude – to the war. 'I hope when we get a really decent supply of aeroplanes we shall systematically wipe out town after town in Germany – men, women, children and buildings, and teach them a lesson that war is not a paying proposition when fought on their own land.'

For now, Gunner Lloyd would just have to remain a private and swallow his pride. His friends from Rugby were doing much better. James Mathieson had become an officer in the Engineers and was busy building bridges. John Cobb was working in the consulate at Oporto and had heard about the Solomon concert at Rugby, memories which led to reminiscing about Paris before the war:

I spent a perfect day at Fontainebleau with a darling French boy (who incidentally was killed during the first months of the war). It was a perfect autumn day, sunny and crisp, and the forest was looking its perfect best in the myriad shades of red, yellow and gold. The whole thing was rather like Babes in the Wood, for having walked for miles we sat down, began to discuss religion, and finally fell asleep. When we woke up it was already dusk and, try as we would, we could not find our way back. Finally when the proverbial beads of perspiration were beginning to appear on both our brows we found a road and hitch-hiked our way back to town, blistered and dead to the world but utterly happy.

John was a garden lover, too, and, like Christo, lived at home with his mother. The two of them discussed travelling together after this dreary war had ended, and John suggested where to start:

Dixter, September 1911: workmen on the roof of the kitchen in Lutyens' new wing. The stone paving in the Lavender Garden is in place, ready for the topiary peacocks.

Dixter, February 1956: the Topiary Garden under snow. It was later turned into a meadow garden by Christo. Far left, first floor: the Solar. Far right: the Yeoman's Hall.

The Yeoman's Hall, brought to Dixter as a dismantled timber frame. It became Daisy's cavernous ground-floor bedroom. Note the low oak chest, which was one of Lutyens' disguised central heating radiators, and the bed, £44, which was copied by Nathaniel Lloyd from a Florentine design.

1923: in full Puritan dress, Daisy Lloyd sails from her bedroom into the garden. Not for nothing was she known as The Management.

Daisy and Les Six in 1930: Back row: Oliver and Selwyn; Christo, Quentin and Letitia in the middle; and Pat in front with Bunch the spaniel.

Christo, aged 9, with Daisy in Nathaniel's new Sunk Garden. Never were mother and son
so wrapped up in one another.

Ken Stubbs, family friend and brilliant music master at Rugby.

Christo with his collection of cacti and succulents brought home from European holidays. In his 70s he was to use large cacti as bedding plants. Here in 1933, three months before his father died.

Christo in his typically shy stance, firmly clamped to Daisy who is holding a spaniel puppy.

Christo concentrates on his needlepoint, while Oliver enjoys himself on the diving board with other students singing to a guitar. Daisy captioned this photograph: 'Letitia and Christo in the foreground: Amazon and the Pansy (is that the opposite to an Amazon?)' Weissensee Student Camp, Austria, 1937.

Music in the Parlour at Dixter: James Mathieson viola, Christo oboe, Ken Stubbs piano.

(*Above*) Private C. Lloyd and (*right*) the new, post-War, moustachioed, business-like Mr Christopher Lloyd. Daisy made her own dirndl skirts.

Christo in the potting shed. All his life, he had a passion for sowing seeds on the same day every spring. Note the traditional wooden plank underfoot, to keep one's feet off the cold earth on long winter days.

Selwyn.
A keen business head, he
entered the family firm.

Oliver. Pathologist,
entomologist, speleologist,
communist and composer,
he was the most brilliant
of all the siblings.

Quentin was delicate
and remained at home
at Dixter. He managed
the estate.

Patrick, successful career
soldier and a major at 27.

Letitia, a nurse,
happiest and
most unhappy
of all the
Lloyds.

1970: an open day at Dixter. Daisy, in her nineties, sitting as ever in front of the porch with her dog.

Anna Pavord and Fergus Garrett went with Christo to Turkey to search for tulips in the wild. May 1993.

Pip Morrison, 'looking soulful', as Christo put it

Wild boy Romke van de Kaa.

I read the other day that one could get to Tahiti for £25 (2nd Class) and live there plus house servant and food for £45 a month, so this I think must come first by way of a Rupert-Brookeish relaxation. After that we can return to civilisation and get down to the real hard work of sight-seeing etc. What do you say? I can imagine little more perfect than the colourful Tahiti of Gauguin at the moment, where everything is free and easy, even love.

Shades of Christo's future Exotic Garden perhaps! But what would Daisy have said about Christo going to Tahiti to relax and to love? John regaled Christo with ever more stories of his escapades, of a trip to Lisbon and a Portuguese boy in primrose-yellow pyjamas, of being chased around the hotel by a fast and pneumatic landlady in a golden kimono. His stories must have been music to the ears of shy Christo, sitting there reading letters in the corner of the NAAFI. A bolder life might be lived by proxy. He remained in correspondence, too, with Rodney Bennet, the Rugby boy with whom he had explored Paris. The two of them laced their letters with camp 'Franglais', Rodney – in imitation of Mother D. – addressing Christo as *Mon Agneau* and signing himself *Bien-aimé*. Welcoming Christo to a forthcoming leave to visit him at Merton College, Oxford, in 1940, Rodney wrote, '*Le poule de petit-pois ornamentales est très agité, et ne sait guère supprimer son agitation*' ('The chicken with the ornamental peas is very agitated, and can hardly contain its excitement'). Perhaps, very gradually, life *was* teaching Christo to spread his wings.

The summer of 1942 saw an episode that shook Daisy to the core, whether she would admit it to herself or not, an episode that should have set alarm bells ringing about her Lambikins.

Daisy's elderly cousins in Rye, Horace and May Field, had adopted many years before a girl of six who, when she later married, had two boys. She died while the boys were still very young and, since their wayward and unreliable father Herbert Edwards was living abroad, the aged Horace and May acted *in loco parentis* for the two virtually orphaned children. The boys spent a great deal of time at Dixter under Daisy's welcoming wing and became firm friends of the Lloyd siblings. Their names were John, known at Dixter as Johnny Boy, and Quentin, known as Piglet (as in *Winnie the Pooh*).

The two brothers were at school at Bradfield College in Berkshire. Their financial circumstances being uncertain and troubling to the school, Daisy herself had acted as guarantor of their school fees and had taken the chance to boast to the headmaster of her own family's reliability and of her great sympathy for the boys' predicament: after all, she had lost her husband and eldest son; but her second son Oliver was a brilliant pathologist at Oxford, her third son Patrick a promising soldier, and both were bringing in incomes to the family as a whole.

Piglet was a curious boy: fun certainly – Letitia was hugely fond of him, and the two of them were great gigglers. He was slender, beautiful, a fine dancer in his kilt, and proud of his artistic tendencies, long hair and long fingernails. During the holidays in early 1942, Piglet (still a schoolboy) had begun a close relationship with 'a boy at Oxford', John Mortimer, later to become a celebrated lawyer, playwright and man of letters. Their two-sided correspondence was discovered at Bradfield after the end of the summer term. Sparks flew. Piglet's end-of-year report closed with the words: 'He has allowed himself to be seduced into evil.'

Daisy, being a significant player in Piglet's upbringing, was heavily involved, and the headmaster wrote to her explaining briefly that Piglet would be leaving and needed a job. She, in her own inimitable fashion, managed to get hold of the rather more blunt letter that the headmaster had written to the boy's absent father in Alexandria, and she copied the whole correspondence – 'l'affaire Piglet' – to her son Patrick, soldier and man of the world, keeping a copy of the copy for herself, thus:

Copy of some 'Correspondence for Patrick Lloyd re l'affaire Piglet':

Headmaster's letter to Herbert Edwards [in Alexandria]:
During the holidays Quentin Edwards was introduced by an old Bradfield boy at New College to a group of young undergraduates mostly living in Christ College. From letters which have since been discovered the following facts are clear:

1 The whole group of undergraduates were thoroughly undesirable. Their tastes were degenerate, their morals perverted. One

of them, the writer of the letters, professed a passionate affection for Quentin.

2 This undergraduate visited Bradfield on one occasion. I have no evidence that any serious harm followed from his visit, but I was able to persuade the head of his college to forbid him to come down again.

3 Quentin was certainly attracted by this man, partly through interests in art and the ballet and literature to which he introduced him, partly because the attentions of this older man appealed to his vanity and made him feel less 'lonely'.

4 Much of the 'art' concerned has been decadent and unhealthy. One or two of the boy's own works with pen and pencil have shown the same tendency.

5 It is probably true that Quentin, while encouraging the interest of the older man, refused to have anything to do with his perverted affections. Quentin absolutely denies that he has given way on this point, though he has gone far enough to shock most old-fashioned people.

6 These letters and Quentin's own work and the whole atmosphere that he has created for himself, make it undesirable, for his own and for Bradfield's sake, that he should remain any longer in the school.

In view of this I should have been justified in expelling the boy. That I have not done so is because I feel he has been more sinned against than sinning, and that some allowance must be made for a boy whose father is far away and whose mother is dead. But I do not wish him to think that he is not responsible for his actions. The attack on his virtue may have been insidious; it may have been made through what were originally perfectly healthy interests; but he ought to have realised from the start the essential unhealthiness of the men whom he chose to make his friends. He has had warnings from me and from his housemaster; for both of us, though we knew nothing of this evil till after term was over, suspected he was too much engrossed in the more decadent form of art.

Rightly or wrongly, I have decided therefore not to expel him but to let him leave to take up work of national importance until he is old enough to join the services. To this lenient treatment I must add his acceptance of certain conditions.

1 The work must be of national importance, and he must not seek employment on the stage or in the films.
2 He must break away absolutely from his former associates and have no further dealings with them by word or through the Post Office ...

The man has given an undertaking to my solicitor that he will have no further dealings with Quentin in any way ... And that he will return all Quentin's letters to be destroyed. No more can be done without an action in the courts which would be harmful to all concerned, and against which I consider it my duty to protect Quentin and the school ...

I have impressed on Quentin that he is normal, that he can perfectly well be like others. And I strongly advise him, as soon as the harvesting is finished, to get work in a factory where large numbers of very ordinary young men and women are at work. He professes an interest in the working classes; this should give him an admirable opportunity of meeting them as equals.

Then he will look back with a shudder on this period of his past as an unaccountable and evil dream.

In spite of the difficulty he has been, with his waywardness, his unwillingness to accept the ordinary run of school life, his failure as a prefect, his defeatism; in spite of the harm that he has himself done this last term, both directly and indirectly, through his perverted interests; I still cannot help rather liking the boy. And I must add that he has very real literary talent which will someday, I hope, be put to worthy use. I will do everything that I can to help him ... on one condition. He must 'play straight' by me. If he says 'yes' he must mean it. And he must ...

All this Daisy sent to Patrick. But why? Was it for advice on what to do, or to enquire from whom she herself should take advice (did Daisy ever take advice)? Did she copy all this to Christo as she did everything else?

Surely even Daisy cannot have failed to see the innumerable parallels between *l'affaire Piglet* and Ken's relationship with Christo – the shared artistic interests, the passionate affection. The only differences were that Ken was a sweet middle-aged soul and virtually part of the family (Christo called Ken and Daisy 'his two mothers'); and Christo, for all that he was not a leader of men, had a toughness and a Lloydian self-assurance that were absent from Piglet, and which would preserve him from manipulation by most others, if not by Daisy. *L'affaire* and the resulting insinuations certainly prove that Daisy knew perfectly well what homosexuality was.

If Christo was indeed burdened directly by his mother with *l'affaire Piglet*, what must he have thought? Did Patrick perhaps tell Christo the story? They were close enough. Was it Letitia? She was as close to Piglet as she was to Christo. Or did none of them feel it was quite nice to tell their little brother anything they considered so sordid?

Certainly Christo did know about *l'affaire* because he discussed it with Ken. He must then have understood very clearly the shame that could fall on a young man who was suspected to be actively homosexual. He must also have seen Daisy's reaction to the crisis. If Christo already knew that he himself had homosexual tendencies, and if Daisy suspected this, then *l'affaire Piglet* must have lain between them as an unspoken warning against something that, if indulged, would destroy Dixter's reputation and therefore undo their affection for each other. How much easier for them both simply to play loving mother and devoted son, and to flirt occasionally with the prospect of a wife. How easy, too, to let this moment be the start of a gradual casting-off of Ken Stubbs by them both.

It is tempting to think *l'affaire* was forgotten at Dixter and that everyone got on with their busy lives. But no. The letters from the school and Daisy's longhand copies remained at Dixter, torn into small pieces and saved, like silent jigsaws. Who felt strongly enough to keep those fragments? Daisy? Christo? Pat? It was alongside letters to Christo from the period that they survived.*

Daisy, to her great credit, set to work to help the unfortunate Piglet

---

* I found these documents in a cupboard at the top of the Dixter stairs. They were in a mouldering leather suitcase with rusted catches. The material about *l'affaire* was torn into small pieces, which I laboriously jigsawed together.

emerge well from *l'affaire* and he was duly found a place in Rugby where Ken, of all people, could keep an eye on him. He worked in the British Thomson-Houston heavy electrical works, and spent his evenings at Horton Crescent with Ken, who fed him well and allowed Piglet some peace and quiet. He slept in a hostel for boys at the works. Ken wrote to Christo of his progress, presumably without his tongue in his cheek:

> Piglet is here a lot. I am sure it was the best thing for him to get some sort of job and he certainly loves coming in here almost every evening. I am trying to stop him smoking cigarettes. This I have managed to some extent by giving him a pipe on condition that I give him one hard smack on his bare behind for every cigarette he smokes. So far it only comes to eight in over eight weeks, so I think I am winning. He can't at any rate feel very grand if he has to take his trousers down for every fag he smokes. I feel sure he will soon be entirely cured. At one moment he took to wearing a horrid cheap silver ring on his little finger but I and the other boys laughed him out of this. He is a delightful boy, but too much inclined to talk when he should be listening, but Bradfield is a rotten school and he has had a bad start in life. He is far less socialistic than he was since going to the BTH Works and seeing what really happens in that sort of world. I only wish he could be here for a longer time. His trouble is that he is so naturally attractive that he gets all the wrong sort of attentions. I am glad to say that he quite realises this and resents it very much, but he can't help taking advantage of it. I am not at all sure that the Navy will be the best place for him.

So concluded *l'affaire Piglet*, with Ken doing the tidying up for the Lloyds. Within weeks, Ken was again telling Daisy how words failed him when talking about that 'divine creature Christo!', and to Christo himself, 'You don't know how often I think of you. And *how* I want you when the birds sing.'

And of Piglet and his amour? Both John Mortimer and Quentin Edwards became QCs, to meet in later life across a crowded court room. Edwards, now a retired judge, has since referred to the affair as nothing more than a crush; a romantic but not homosexual relationship of the kind that was common in single sex public schools at the time.

In 1942 Oliver, now Daisy's oldest surviving son, became engaged to his girlfriend Patricia Jane Barnett, a coolly spoken young woman with a penchant for dressing entirely in black. What a mixed blessing this must have been for the atmosphere at Dixter. Titia told Christo after the engagement that their mother was 'so overcome at being a mother in law again that she has almost taken to her bed'. Daisy now had to share the affections of her eldest son with a woman with whom she had already crossed swords over Angus, but at the same time she was gaining the promise of grandchildren to whom, this time, she might devote her total attention.

Oliver was to bring his fiancée to Dixter in February, and even before the girl arrived Daisy was busy appropriating the wedding for herself and establishing the correct alliances. Pen flew to paper. 'I have written her a nice little welcoming letter,' she scribbled to Christo, 'and pray I may have better luck with her than with poor Selwyn's wife. I have written to Oliver, and have asked, if she is horribly religious, if he will have to be christened, and if she will allow the wedding to take place in the Great Hall.' Daisy envisioned vast armfuls of flowers coming in from the garden, and she and Christo arranging them on every surface.

Her letter must have been one of genuine welcome because Patricia Jane, in her reply, said, 'I shall keep your letter all my life.' Daisy found this gratifying and copied out the whole of Patricia Jane's letter for Christo. As for the letter itself, 'The writing is individual and full of character, and if she can learn to dot her 'i's, and refrain from mixing her founts, it may well become really beautiful.' But, still, Daisy was impressed and hoped the girl might be a steadying influence on the mercurial Oliver.

Naturally, rich and childless Uncle Robin was given the news straight away and he countered by asking who Patricia Jane's father was. Did she have connections, any money? Daisy claimed not to know: 'I once heard Tan say "My wife's pedigree is long enough for us both!" Perhaps Patricia Jane may say the same of her husband's! I certainly had no money to speak of when Tan married me, and I know he would have loved me just as dearly without my family tree.'

The rest of the family – even Letitia – was made to form ranks to welcome Patricia Jane, and Daisy decreed that she should be called Jane, so as to avoid confusion with Patrick. Oliver steered a middle course and called her PJ.

It was to be a civilian wedding and, bizarrely, Daisy now tried to persuade Oliver against this. Not that she disapproved herself, but because it might harm his career if others assumed that he was less than reliable for not having had a church wedding. But then *her* parents had had a civil wedding and it had never harmed them, so she acquiesced. Oliver had expressed his intention to honeymoon under his mother's roof at Dixter and, said Daisy, 'he has chosen the North Bedroom, so now I must make a proper black-out for the bridal chamber'. But PJ and Oliver decided that their wedding should be held in Oxford where they both worked, and her family was nearby. Daisy threw her toys out of the pram. Once again she was losing the upper hand to a daughter-in-law. In a flash of armour-plated self-righteousness and self-pity, she wrote airily to Christo:

I did tell you, I think, that I'm not going to Oxford. It is not of national importance [in this time of fuel rationing], and I am the only one who will be missing anything, and I think it will be a good example in these difficult times when we are begged not to travel unless absolutely necessary. Jane and Oliver are quite reasonable about it, and don't feel hurt or offended, as some less intelligent people might.

Pat was best man at the wedding, where he took warmly to the Barnett family and, to represent the Lloyds further, Wicked Uncle Robin turned up in a new seven-seater coupé driven by his chauffeur. Of the ceremony itself, said soldier Pat, 'the business only lasted about five minutes'. Daisy smouldered alone, at Dixter. Mrs Barnett posted her some of the wedding cake, which Daisy decreed must have looked 'like the Tower of Babel'. 'This wedding cake has just come,' she wrote to Christo, 'so I am sending you my share *and yours*.'

A month later Daisy completed a dirndl for PJ, so that she might feel obliged to look like Daisy, even if they did not see eye-to-eye, and off it went in the post to Oxford. In a gesture worthy of the Brothers Grimm, Daisy then told Christo that she had made an embroidered *belt* for it and, with no sense of irony, that she was already embroidering one 'for future Mrs Christopher', but that if need be it could be turned into straps for lederhosen.

Despite everything, Daisy wanted Oliver and PJ at Dixter. She also wanted Christo to be there, to make a family occasion. Only four months after the wedding, she was using, as a lever, the dates of Christo's army leave, when he would be able to come home to his beloved garden. But PJ had to work and would not ask for extra time off. More to the point, she was newly married and wanted to be in her own home. Oliver supported PJ and precipitated a second family tiff. The couple offered Christo a day in Oxford with them instead, but no, Christo had to resist as that would leave poor Mother D alone at Dixter . . .

Oliver and PJ did not have the most usual of marriages; it was more a meeting of intellects. He was certainly the most talented of the brothers, an eminent pathologist, expert botanist, entomologist and accomplished composer, but he was curiously independent of anyone. Letters from Oliver never had any preamble, they were always straight to the point, however complex. As a boy he had doubts about whether, when he grew up, he wanted to be the Archbishop of Canterbury or an actor. He was also, when it came to marriage, not especially interested in 'the bed business'. PJ's independence intrigued Oliver. 'She is a charming girl' wrote Renate Hirsch, 'but she and O. give the impression that there was no absolute need of their being together, and that each of them could fight their own way in life, selfishly and independently. But I may be wrong.'

Certainly they were no Tan and Daisy settling down to golf, babies and houses. Oliver got a new job at Epsom Hospital in Surrey, and PJ took up a course at Liverpool that would qualify her to be a welfare officer in factories and munitions works. She hoped then to find a job near Oliver. It must all have seemed very odd to Daisy and not the sort of settled conditions from which to expect grandchildren. In any case, as she pointed out to Christo away in army camp, the girl had irregular periods.

Christo's real army life began just before the war ended. April 1945 saw Lance Bombardier Lloyd away from training camps at last and on a troopship bound for Mombasa in East Africa; it proved to be neither more polite nor much more dangerous than training camp. Lunches of greasy stew and potatoes; official laundry days on deck (cold water, no soap), with every bar and rail festooned with drying clothes. Punctilious Christo always included his pyjamas in the wash until the day he dropped them, sopping wet, on his *Complete Shakespeare*, which stained them so red that he never dare hang them out again. And he was seasick. 'The sea,' he opined, 'is most to be admired when seen from the shore.'

He wrote his letters at night under the moon, and watched the flying fish. On still days, dolphins followed the ship and there were fine sunsets. In ports, he bought oranges and studied the street trees, sat reading Conrad and Shakespeare in his much-envied sun specs. One day fifty kites hovered over the moored ship. 'I can't think where they've come from,' he wrote to his mother, 'unless they migrate, in which case I would willingly be one of them and fly away home.'

Lonely, he once again began to write entertaining portraits of his shipmates:

Opposite (bunk) is a chap by the name of Murphy (a Londoner) and another whom I refer to (in private) as Halitosis. The latter, while pencilling a short, laborious note shortly before we left, called out to Murphy 'How do you spell beauty; B_A_U_T_Y?' Answer: 'Yes.' Murphy's a good-natured fellow. His girl friend types her love letters to him, a proceeding of which he tells her now and again that he does not approve. Love should be scrawled, apparently. I should be good at it.

On arrival in East Africa the troops camped by the sea in an un-expectedly green landscape; not at all the parched terrain Christo had expected. The great succulent trunks of baobabs delighted him, as did the lizards and snakes and the millions of flying ants out mating in a rainstorm. Lime juice tasted like nectar after the days at sea, even better than his first banana for five years.

His survey unit was installed at the Athi River Depot, at an altitude of 5,000 feet, outside Nairobi in a landscape reminiscent of Salisbury Plain, except that you could see Mount Kilimanjaro and Mount Kenya 100 miles away. The days passed rather as they had in training camp, in physical training and assault courses, and half-hour queues for food that was sometimes cold or ran out altogether. One day the troops were sent to Nairobi to see a film of the German concentration-camp atrocities, which filled Christo with horror; learning Swahili was more to his taste – how amazing that the word for tank was the same as the word for rhinoceros, and the word for river the same as for pillow.

As he got to know the area, he found seeds and corms of plants that he fancied and sent them home every week, some of them proudly passed on to the Royal Horticultural Society by Daisy. On his days off, he went into Nairobi and scoured the shops to find a snakeskin handbag and cottons and silks for Daisy, or taught his mess-mates in camp to play the game 'Slippery Anne', for which he was popular. 'I have been thinking,' he wrote to Daisy, 'what an imposing sight roast neck of giraffe would be for a Thursday lunchtime in the Yeoman's Hall.' To keep him amused, brother Pat, home on sick leave, began to type out and post to Christo the last volume of Gibbon's *Decline and Fall of the Roman Empire*, the reading of which Christo had never managed to complete at home.

There was full lighting only in the NAAFI, so he would sit there on the concrete floor to write, with his back to the wall, scribbling and missing the long, light evenings at home. At night there were thefts from the camp, by 'skilled' natives, of clothes and kitbags. Once a tent was stolen from over its sleeping occupants. And then there were the hyenas that prowled the camp at night, kept off only by the unit's Alsatian dogs. In one camp, Christo heard, a man had slept with his foot out and it was bitten off. To Daisy he wrote:

I awoke around midnight to the familiar sound of every dog in the camp (a good 30, I daresay) barking furiously, even hysterically, the nearest being some 20 yards away and ranging up to nearly a mile distant. This excitement is usually roused by the wailing of our even more distant hyena. As I lay listening and yet trying not to listen, I was suddenly startled into rigidity by an animal bumping heavily against my bed and then gliding into the tent. There it remained, motionless and silent; I could only hear its breathing. All sorts of horrid visions raced through my mind. I didn't dare, somehow, to reach with my hand beyond the protection of my mosquito net for a touch. After all, you never know. So I said 'Shoo; go away,' not very bravely. At least nobody can accuse me of being incapable of saying 'Shoo' to a hyena. I didn't say it *was* a hyena now; but it positively *seemed* like one to me, then and there, so that's as good as saying 'Shoo' to an indisputably *visible* hyena. In any case the brute took no notice; perhaps it didn't understand English. It just went on breathing, quietly and ominously. So then – it's a relief to get to this part of the story even in relating it – I resorted to the *successful* expedient of clapping my hands. IT barged out of the tent by the other exit. I was safe again. But I still don't know what IT was; just a dog, you will say, but, well, you never can tell.

It might be said that in wartime hyenas are likely to be the least of one's worries, but Christo was lucky; a month later came VE Day and it was over. The army presence was gradually wound down and he was demobbed in 1946. In the meantime he took the chance to visit Renate Hirsch, also now in East Africa, newly married to Walther Schuster and farming there (they had honeymooned at Dixter). Christo became godfather to their son Michael three years later.

It was a curious time for him there on the farm – the war over, Dixter and Daisy waiting for him – and yet as free as he would ever be. Here was another moment to begin a new life, if he chose to, to try for Tahiti. But everything began to point home. For Renate he made his first flower arrangement for fifteen months, of hot-coloured lilies, dahlias and snapdragons; he climbed through cedar forests and found pink twayblades; he saw coffee growing, exotic birds and, on the way back to Nairobi, half an acre of orange and yellow kniphofias and thought how 'very much' he would like to grow them by the horse pond at Dixter. Inevitably, home he went (via Italy and a walk up Vesuvius), back to square one.

Chapter 6

Wye College and a New Start, 1946–57

*Either we shall want our garden to be an alfresco room in which we may
sit, meditate, write, eat and doze; or we shall want it to satisfy our craving
to grow, enjoy and make happy, beautiful, interesting and exciting plants.*
Christopher Lloyd, *Country Life*, 1973

October 1946: what a relief to be home! The garden was shabbier, the
pruning imperfectly managed, perennials in need of division. These
could be fixed. Daisy, too, was there to greet him, almost speechless
with joy at having her baby safe and home again. But things were not
the same – the kitchen was cold, the live-in staff driven away, Daisy's
grand ground-floor bedroom now a sitting room, and Nathaniel's
Florentine bed stored away in the cellar. Pat was overseas, Oliver with
PJ in India researching malaria, Letitia a staff sister in a Cairo hospital
and likely to stay there. Christo himself had seen too much of the globe
to ignore it now. Much as he loved Dixter, he would have to accom-
modate the world outside, find himself a real place in it, earn himself
more self-respect than he had ever earned as an incompetent in the
army. Cambridge again? No: it had been somewhere he was pushed by
family and circumstance, and it had been a lonely time, a time when
he had not yet possessed the resilience that he learned in the army. He
needed now to do something in which he actually had some skill, and
that meant something to do with plants, horticulture, gardens. He would
take his gardening seriously, study it, qualify, show what he could do;
and in the meantime he had Dixter, the best playground and laboratory in the world. London University's Wye College was down the road
at Wye, in Kent, so he applied to take a BSc in decorative horticulture. He was off.

Studying nearby enabled him to be at home every weekend and occa-sionally even during the week, which kept both Daisy and Christo happy. She let him take charge of more and more of the garden (she would soon be seventy) and he slipped into the role happily, leaving her instruc-tions about what should be done during the week while he was absent.

Sometimes his studies took him away for longer, as on an exchange visit with students from the École Nationale de Horticulture at Versailles, where he was fascinated to see the technical side of gardening – the management of fruit trees, propagation, pests and diseases and the use of chemicals. These were subjects that he was glad to have under his belt, professionally speaking, but they were only an important means to an end, not of interest in themselves; his writing never dwelt on such issues, although he made no bones about mentioning chemical controls if they were effective. He was never tempted to garden organically.

On his way to France he stopped at Wisley, in Surrey, to see the daffodil trials and there, on his knees, was old man Bowles, E. A. Bowles, the famous bulb specialist and garden writer. In Paris, Christo took time off alone, walking the streets as he had done in 1939, visiting his old landlady, looking in on high mass at Notre-Dame and under-standing nothing, but loving the dressing up and processing, walking through the Luxembourg and the Tuileries, trying for tickets for the Comédie-Française, and watching a gypsy wash her hair in the Seine. A nightingale sang in the Bois de Boulogne and Christo was glad to be chatting away in French again.

Very gradually sociability was at last creeping upon him at the grand old age of twenty-six, now that he was with people who shared his passion for plants. Daytimes in Paris he spent with the group, looking at vegetable breeding, azalea, canna and orchid production, and flowers bred for the military cemeteries. 'I can't praise the visit enough,' he pronounced, 'such an exchange deserves to be encouraged and spon-sored by all nations of the world.' The last night in France involved a party and dancing, but that was one step too far for him; he sat it out in a long conversation with a bearded Lebanese monk studying horticulture.

At home, his notebooks filled with lists of things to do and ways to improve the Long Border: scrap A, more of B, put C next to D, twelve new annuals to try, ten to discard, twenty-five to grow again; seven types of cannas to put out. There were plants new to him in the grounds at Wye and he brought them home to add to the Dixter melange, especially bearded irises, which he later professed, by and large, to despise. 'Finished the Long Border,' he wrote in his diary, 'in 5 weekends in perfect weather.' How exciting it was, to be busy and focused at last.

Not everything ran so sweetly. Ken Stubbs was hungry for Dixter, but Daisy was tiring of him since his usefulness at Rugby had declined. And now he was ill. 'Sorry there is no name for my complaint,' he wrote, with almost a sense of shame. 'Judging by my own feelings it is some obstruction between the upper and lower bowel. I am lying on a couch in my study this afternoon. I probably won't write again for a bit unless something happens.' He did get to Dixter for Christmas 1948 and managed the great feast in the Great Hall, but it was his last Christmas there. He endured the 'dread operation', but was horrified when advised that he might have to go through it a second time. Within the year he was dead of bowel cancer.

Christo was heartbroken. The man who had been his mentor, and his personal and family friend for so many years, was gone. And yet at the same time it was evident that, long before Ken's death, Christo had begun to move on; Ken was no longer the friend he had been, they wrote little, and Ken was seen less and less at Dixter. Christo's relationship with Ken belonged to his youth, a time when he had been so insecure; now he had grown up. If Ken's platonic passion for Christo was still alight, any reciprocal passion in Christo was curtailed to admiration.

Ken was not one to talk of illness or chase after sympathy. Rather it shamed him and disrupted his busy life of nurturing schoolchildren. For the Lloyds' part, they never dwelled on illness: to do so was a sign of weakness to be treated with impatience. They had all risen above Selwyn's death following Daisy's example, and now they would do the same over Ken's. Anyway, Lloyd hearts soon healed. 'I sometimes thought him a little silly about *you*,' concluded Daisy to Christo, 'but I never thought you silly about *him!*'

More generous sentiments came to Christo from Letitia, in Cairo:

I have been thinking of no-one but you for the last two days, ever since I had the sad news of Ken. Beloved as he was by the rest of us, I know how even more devoted you were to each other . . .

97

How thankful I am that he didn't suffer long and not at all towards the end. He lived a full and generous life, never sparing himself to serve others, and it should be written of him that he died not only without a single enemy, but with treble the number of friends of anyone usual. But then he was not usual.

What fun we had at an early age, when he'd read aloud to us the Pooh books and Jack Pumpkinhead of Oz, and how jealous we were of whose turn it was to sit on his knee *this* time! And how thrilled I was when he allowed me, whenever I stayed at Rugby, to sit beside him at chapel in the organ loft. And I'd love the way he'd twinkle at me when I'd chatter with the boys who came to see him, and gradually, make them lose their shyness. He always achieved what he wanted far better than anyone else, but somehow never scolded.

I called him 'Heffalump' when I first knew him, why I don't know, but he answered just the same. I had a cold, or something, about the first time he came to stay, and had to stay in bed in daddy's dressing room. I remember shrieking frustratedly after him when he left, as I couldn't go and see him off at the gate or station. Then the old cry at holiday time – 'Who's going to meet Ken?' 'I am!' 'No, I am!'

And what fun you and I had, waking him up in the early morning. How he could remain so good-tempered with us, subjected as he was to the severest treatment at that early hour, goodness only knows. People tickling his toes and jumping on his tummy, *poor* Ken! But he really loved it all. Which is why we all doted on him.

So when we think of him, we must only be happy. For that's what he always radiated, happiness and an intense interest in everybody and everything they were keen on.

Never did a Lloyd write a kinder word. No other Lloyd but Letitia would dare to spend time in such nostalgia.

And for Letitia herself, things had looked up. She had gone out to Cairo to work as a staff sister and there she had met Nils Lind, Middle Eastern representative of the Gulf Exploration Company. They fell in love and married and, for the first time in her life, she felt valued and happy.

No matter that he was twenty-five years her senior; perhaps a stable father figure was what she needed. Daisy was charm itself to Nils, even flirting with him and telling Letitia that he was nearer her own age than Titia's. That Nils was so much older than Letitia was one aspect of the marriage of which Daisy could approve, since Nathaniel had been fourteen years older than her. To Daisy's great delight, Letitia became pregnant and a daughter Olivia was born in Cairo in 1951.

Nils had been born in Sweden in 1894, but, aged three, his family had taken him along with the entire village to live near Jerusalem in anticipation of the Second Coming (they were wrong). Much of Nils' immediate family died of malaria, but he stayed on. In 1922 he left for the USA, made money and then came back to the Middle East, fluent in Arabic and a useful man for international business. His life had not been easy. His first marriage was an arranged one, producing two children, but ending in divorce. He remarried, but his second wife turned out to be a resolute lesbian and he divorced again. Letitia, who had faced her own demons in her personal life, was his last chance, and they married in Cairo with a full Arab ceremony – dancing horses, belly dancers and a feast. Daisy did not attend. Pat once again represented the family.

After graduating from Wye in 1949, Christo looked for more experience of commercial horticulture, which included work for Wallace and Co. at Tunbridge Wells. But 1950 saw him back at Wye for two years, as an assistant lecturer. The toothbrush moustache appeared, never to disappear; and the shabby army uniform, the gawky young man with one hand behind his back, gave way to a new serious Christo, buttoned up, suited and tied. He had found his métier, as a teacher, in which he was successful, something that gave him real self-respect at last, and he was respected in his turn because he knew his subject so well. For his students he would organise the most extraordinarily difficult plant-identification tests – thirty plants at a time – using armfuls of plants brought back from Dixter, and he took the young people on regular trips to Wisley, Kew and Hampton Court, all the time making sure that he made notes for his own use. He even examined students on the characteristics of their flower arranging – which came out as rather sweet character studies of the students themselves. He set about helping to manage the college gardens with unprecedented flair and got them properly labelled for the first time. Rather like Ken at Rugby, he would hold parties in his rooms with music and cider for the students, and he took colleagues home to tea to see Dixter and to meet Daisy. Of course he cut an odd figure in college, this rather posh young man with his grand house and his own shabby, second-hand car, but he was *liked* at last and he made lifelong friends. There was live music at Wye too, a choir, an orchestra, and a quartet in which Christo played his oboe.

After two years of teaching, Christo was asked to sign on for two more years, by the college principal, a friend of Nils Lind. Christo agreed: 'It makes a lot of difference to me, and gives me something to live for, from week to week.' It seemed as if Christo had found the perfect life, gardening and teaching gardening – until, that is, he blew it up in his own face. Patience was never his strong point and, like Daisy, he always had to be right in an argument. He fell out spectacularly with the principal and, calling the college management 'incompetent', resigned from the job that had given him such self-respect and went back to Dixter.

Now it really was just Christo and Daisy.

There he was, sharing again his spartan childhood nursery bedroom with Quentin, with Daisy in her little rickety bedroom over the porch. What to do now? Christo decided he would make a living out of Dixter alone, open the garden more, teach by example. At the bottom of the garden, by the staff cottages, he would open a nursery to sell the plants he most admired, and which people could see growing at Dixter.

Proudly he built some long cold frames, double-skinned for insulation, and set about propagating from the garden, taking a part of the vegetable garden for lining out his stock plants. He began to revitalise the garden itself too, making good use of the plants he had brought from Wye and installing in the Rose Garden varieties that he had raised from cuttings. Neither he nor Daisy found the increased opening of the garden to the public 'quite nice'; it had an unwelcome whiff of commerce, which did little to glamorise the legend of the Lloyds. But they did it, including a day every year for the National Gardens Scheme. 'The public', as Christo disparagingly called them, meant petty thefts of plants, which outraged him. *Daphne tangutica* disappeared, 'the rarest thing in the garden', claimed Christo. 'Skunks!' spat Daisy. Still, numbers had to be made to rise, and to supplement their income they sold cut daffodils too. 'Market gardening!' Uncle Robin disparagingly called it, and grudgingly printed 250 leaflets for her: *Great Dixter. 2–6 pm daily, April 1st to October 30th. Tickets 2/-*.

Christo reasoned that there ought to be money in writing about gardens. He knew he could write, and his photography was of a standard to be published. So he travelled to see gardens, making trips to Italy, the Lebanon and Sweden. He and Rodney Bennet took ten days in Paris, Christo making sketches of the great architectural gardens and considering the possibility of a book on French gardens. Stealing plants from Dixter might be forbidden, but when it came to the countryside different rules applied, and wherever he went Christo seemed to find orchids longing to be dug up and taken home. He could make them happy and multiply at Dixter; besides, the countryside then was so much more full of wild flowers. Daisy thoroughly approved of Rodney, as an only child a potential lame duck and with the kind of prodigious memory that both she and Christo thought so important in life.

Christo began to travel more within England, to see gardens and to meet other people who were making gardens in the post-war years. He was impressed by the new 'island beds' being promoted by the great Norfolk nurseryman Alan Bloom, who said that perennials planted not in borders against a wall, but in beds out in the open lawn, would grow more stockily and would support themselves better. The gardener and writer Margery Fish – how he loved to refer to her as '*Mrs Fish*' in his later writing – became a friend, and he would lend a hand weeding her garden at East Lambrook Manor, which he found run-down, but full of good plants. Her writing was, and still is, admired by lovers of cottage gardening, and is direct and comfortable, but Christo's wit and incisiveness were something she never possessed.

Christo and Daisy would go to Sissinghurst to visit Vita Sackville-West; 'Mrs Nicolson', as Daisy insisted on calling her. Vita called college-trained Christo 'The Expert', and the two of them would tour Sissinghurst, shooting off Latin names at each other, while Harold Nicolson kept Daisy occupied. Christo usually came away with cuttings, 'but they were left for me to put in,' complained Daisy. When Vita came to Dixter, Daisy – for once meeting her match in this forceful woman – allowed her to smoke inside the house; it was one of the few actions for which she lost Christo's respect. Vita was writing pieces on gardening in *The Observer*, and her collection of them was published in 1961, under the title *In Your Garden*. Christo himself began to write a little, placing a first attempt in *Gardening Illustrated* and the odd piece, illustrated with Quentin's photographs, in *The Home Gardener* and the Rose Society of America's journal.

It was with a dreadful sense of resignation that Christo now had to watch Daisy's latest battle for custody of a grandchild: Letitia's daughter Olivia. Sparks had flown even when she was born, Daisy being furious that Letitia had waited until three days after the birth to write to her with the news. Letitia, she proclaimed, was a selfish pig.

Nils' job meant living in Beirut. But, at Daisy's insistence, Olivia was placed with her at Dixter from time to time while Nils and Letitia travelled, including trips to America where Nils' two boys from his previous marriage were based. Daisy had hopes that Olivia might be the first of an army of grandchildren flooding into Dixter. Her problem was letting the child go at the end of her visits. If she was not there *full-time*, under Daisy's educating eye, how would she grow up to be a Dixter baby? Three months with her parents again and Olivia's morals had gone to pot, a shame since 'she was such a lovely, sunny, well-behaved little thing when Dixter had finished with her'. To make the child feel secure and to save Daisy work, Letitia sent Olivia with her Greek nanny, but Christo and Daisy disapproved noisily; they wanted to employ instead a handy Dane, who had also proved herself excellent at weeding in the garden.

It looked as if Letitia was going to be Daisy's only source of grandchildren, for the time being at least, since Oliver's wife PJ was admitted to Holloway sanatorium in 1951, suffering from a mental breakdown. There she remained for a year, apathetic, not even opening Oliver's letters and convinced that her food was being poisoned. Two years later she came out briefly, outwardly restored to normality, but not understanding at all why she had been confined. To Daisy, mental stability was a matter simply of will power, and PJ obviously had none. 'The Barnetts are all pretty unstable,' she announced, and became convinced that, even though PJ was always a selfish and inconsiderate guest, getting her down to Dixter would help promote the discipline that PJ needed to recover. Daisy put both PJ and Oliver in the North Bedroom, but kept the porch room spare, in case Oliver 'needed a bolt-hole'.

Christo's greatest friend at this time was John Treasure, whom he had met at Wye. They had everything in common: both, for what it was worth (a great deal to Daisy), were descendants of Oliver Cromwell;

both lived in substantial country houses – John at Burford House at Tenbury Wells, Herefordshire; both were keen on clematis and were developing nurseries specialising in them, sharing their experience and even running a joint catalogue for some years; and neither was really a man of business. Both were gay too, John discreetly but bravely living with a partner, at a time when homosexuality was still illegal.

And so Burford became the first of Christo's home-from-homes, a home free of Daisy and Dixter strictures. He and John loved to see gardens together, even managed a trip to the opera at Bayreuth, and enjoyed hunting down old varieties of clematis. In particular, they discovered what they were convinced must be the 'lost' *Clematis* 'Madame Julia Correvon' growing at Hidcote Manor, Lawrence Johnston's garden in Gloucestershire and now a property of the National Trust. Seeing only one specimen of the plant lingering feebly on a wall, they wrote to Graham Stuart Thomas, then the chief gardens adviser to the Trust, asking if they might propagate from it. Thomas was as precise a man about plants as Christo, and he too had been gardening since he was a child; but he was a much drier stick, and there was no love lost between them ('a *very* dull man,' according to Christo). Thomas replied that, thank you no, the Trust would do the propagation in-house. John and Christo, fearing that the clematis would receive a less skilful treatment than their joint expertise could offer, decided to take the law into their own hands. John kept guard and Christo did the deed, and 'Madame Julia Correvon' is now safely and universally available throughout the nursery trade.

When Christo quoted the episode in *Country Life* twenty years later, there was a public outcry, but he felt this particular thievery – like his liberating of orchids from the meadows of Europe – was in a good cause. Productive and efficient. He loved to quote the technique of the light-fingered Lionel Fortescue (of the Garden House, Buckland Monachorum in Devon), who, when visiting a garden, would leave his umbrella at the bottom of the garden, then 'forget it' and have to go back just as he was leaving, to retrieve it. Into its folds he could conceal who-knew-what plants. Christo himself had other means: at Sezincote in Gloucestershire he took a fancy to a deutzia bush and, managing only to break off a long stem, hid it by passing it down his young companion's trouser leg, from where it had to be extracted, in a downward direction to avoid damage to the twigs, when they reached the car park.

Within four walls, John was openly gay; and later, as the legal position on homosexuality softened, more publicly so. Staying with John suited Christo well: it was like being in the right gentlemen's club – he need not be an active member, he had no partner, but he was comfortable just to be there, with no obligation to pretend to be straight or anything else; he could be himself, alone but not lonely, bearably withdrawn from the physical needs of sexuality. With John there were no tense, wearying, unspoken layers of awareness to every relationship as there were at Dixter; it was just a warm, fun-loving, close and long-needed friendship. Yet thirty years later when Christo's friend Tom Bennett drove John and his partner to Dixter for the last time, when both were obviously starting to fail, Christo was in the middle of a busy weekend and made no effort whatsoever to spend time with John. The Lloyds simply did not have time for illness – they had to move on.

John, the raconteur, claimed that his only heterosexual experience was being chased and conquered by Stanley Baldwin's daughter. He did not think much of it. His farewell to the world was a complimentary remark, paid enthusiastically to a male nurse's behind, as he was being rushed to hospital in an ambulance with a burst aorta.

With the war long over and times more settled, there was still no sign of marriage for Quentin, who jogged along, running the estate and managing an amicable relationship with his mother and her ally Christo.

Pat ought to have been the most marriageable brother: tall, aquiline features, physically active, charming. Yet he remained a committed career soldier in a world very different from Dixter. He was not suited to the settled life: he needed excitement and, since 1954, had commanded a light anti-aircraft regiment of the Arab Legion for 'Glubb Pasha'.

January 1956 found him at El Zerka in Jordan, keeping the peace in the turmoil leading up to the Suez crisis. On 8th January he was temporarily separated from his troops in Zerka Street and became trapped between two Arab mobs, who pulled him from his Land Rover, stoned him and then shot him, probably with his own revolver. The incident was kept quiet at the time by strict censorship, to prevent hostile Arab radio stations relaying news as an incitement to further incidents. He was forty-two.

In Pat, Dixter lost its professional; and its personal peace-keeper.

He was the sensible one, the one who took command, the kind one, the one who mediated when the rest of the family was quarrelling. Now Letitia must fight her own fight; Quentin must have no ally in camp against Daisy and Christo; Oliver no conscience to make him return to Dixter occasionally; and Christo no hero. Pat was the brother Christo had loved most tenderly – brave, valiant, strong, his own man, everything that Christo envied.

Daisy was two sons down now, and she clutched Christo ever closer. No more little jokes about Mrs Christo.

Chapter 7

A Writer Emerges, 1957–72

'Your fingers are brown, go live in a sea-view flat in Bournemouth.'
Christopher Lloyd, *The Observer, c.* 1970

In 1957 Christo published through Collingridge, with his own black-and-white photographs, what was to be the first of his significant books: *The Mixed Border in the Modern Garden*. The same year saw the publication of Alan Bloom's *Hardy Perennials*, and Christo would write his own book under the same title ten years later. Bloom was a Norfolk nurseryman, an excellent plantsman within his field, but a rough diamond, sporting long, flowing hair and a gold earring. His passion was steam trains, not Glyndebourne. His son Adrian went on to become a pioneer of the fashion for gardens of heather and conifers, a style that Christo loathed. 'Heather is for grouse,' he concluded, although, open-minded as ever about plants, he later admired the bulging, formal borders of heather and evergreens at Belsay Hall, Northumberland, where he and I spent happy times discussing what evergreens I might plant to spice up the mix.

Alan Bloom wrote in a less easy style than Christo, and his market was the amateur gardener with a small garden; he referred to 'midget borders' of 5 x 16 feet. In *The Mixed Border* Christo was still thinking big, Jekyll-style, and took it for granted that his readers would want to learn about his own 100-yard-long, one-sided showpiece border. A border to be seen from *two* sides he suggested should be eighteen feet deep.

The object of *The Mixed Border* was to put aside the public's admiration for purely herbaceous borders and add woody plants. Gertrude Jekyll and William Robinson had brought perennials to the fore fifty years before, when Victorian bedding fell out of fashion, since which time shrubs had become more popular, often used on their own in shrub-beries. A mixed border would bring them together. It would not be labour-saving, but then Christo loved *work* in the garden. Didn't everybody? 'The most telling effects usually are the result of considerable painstaking and many of us will not begrudge the effort involved,' he suggested. Shrubs were necessary, after all, to give firmness and solidarity to an otherwise all-herbaceous border, and the addition of bulbs and half-hardy plants would extend the season further again. It was his breadth of experience at work here, his dislike of compartmentalising plants.

The book was moderately academic in tone (most gardening books then were), and moved through planning on paper, planting and seasonal maintenance, followed by a listing of shrubs, hardy perennials, half-hardies, annuals and biennials. It did not have space to list cultivars to the same extent that Bloom did, or as Christo himself did later in *Hardy Perennials,* and the subject of colour – later a whole book for him – was given a mere two paragraphs, but it set out Christo's stall as a gardener. It showed what he and Dixter were about. There he stands on the book jacket, tied and collared, earnestly fondling 'Nelly Moser', and no doubt looking just as Daisy thought he should look: a man proud of his cold frames, a man not afraid to use DDT and certainly a man who knew his plants. You could tell that from his writing. 'To get the best out of plants one must know them personally,' he wrote. 'This is one of the main satisfactions of gardening.'

Writing would help to keep Dixter financially afloat, and both Christo and Daisy felt the book could be the start of great things. But there was no huge addition to the coffers when, in 1958, Uncle Robin died, aged ninety, in great pain from gout and gout-related surgery, and walking with two sticks. Quentin and Oliver flew up to Glasgow for the funeral, and when the will was read – it was Angus, Selwyn and Elaine's son, who was his principal heir; the boy whose mother Daisy had so despised and antagonised. Selwyn's line ceased to have a financial share in the Dixter estate. Angus went on to become a successful art dealer in London with two children, one a writer by the name of Christopher Lloyd and an earnest Christian, like his grandmother Elaine.*

Selwyn, in his short career working for Robin, had shown a drive

---

* In the years after Daisy's death, Elaine and Christo became friends and the young Chris Lloyd became a regular visitor at Dixter.

and business sense that Robin had admired, even if Selwyn himself was intimidated by Robin the tycoon. Robin was fond of Selwyn, and had become only too aware of Daisy's treatment of Elaine before and after Selwyn's early death. In making Angus his heir, Robin was leaving Daisy and the Dixter Lloyds to sink or swim, without the injection of capital that would so have helped them.

Nevertheless there was confidence at Dixter now. However tight funds might be, Christo was buying and laying down some really very good wine. Dixter lived a little more. Nils retired and in 1961, to Daisy's great satisfaction, he and Letitia – and of course ten-year-old Olivia – came to live in the Garden Cottage down by the nursery. Nils took up in a small way the selling of antique furniture from the barn adjoining the Sunk Garden, and made Dixteresque oak tables himself.

Quentin, handsome and broad-featured, now in his forties, was still running the estate, but had discovered a most un-Dixterlike pastime – dancing; and, through dancing, Quentin found a wife. He left the narrow little bedroom that he had shared with Christo for all those years and moved with his new wife Pamela into Little Dixter, a cottage a few fields away. He had made the break from Dixter, even if he was still within sight of it. There was work to do of the kind he liked, improving the house and making it a normal family home.

Daisy, as ever, thoroughly disapproved of the match: Pam was just 'one of his dancing girls'. Daisy's family, the Fields, had loved dancing, but not *this* kind of dancing. And as for those two fat children who came along later, she would rather have her dogs. It was a dilemma for her; the children were close enough not to need actually to *live* at Dixter, and Pam certainly wanted it that way, but they were also *close enough* to be easily made into Dixter babies, and yet Daisy *so* disapproved of their mother . . . At least she *had* grandchildren from Quentin. There would in all likelihood be none from Oliver: his disturbed wife Patricia Jane had never become stable again and died in the asylum in 1963.

Dixter now was divided into three camps: in the big house, an alliance of Daisy and Christo; at Garden Cottage, Nils, Letitia and Olivia; and at Little Dixter, Quentin and Pam. There was a constant tension in what might have been a fine family ménage, everyone silently or not so silently troubled by the emotional demands of Daisy Lloyd. And all around them the beautiful garden, wintersweet and pink goblets of magnolias in spring, red-hot pokers and peppery phlox in high summer, and the promise of apples to be picked in autumn.

In 1963 Christo, the up-and-coming forty-two-year-old writer, was summoned to the offices of *Country Life* magazine, in which Dixter itself had been featured so long ago. The editor, John Adams, was looking for someone to write a new gardening column and Christo seemed a likely candidate – he had the right background, a sound training and apparently he could write well. In his office, Adams produced a recent article by Roy Hay, from *The Times*, and asked Christo if he could produce something similar. It was all about lawns, lawn care and mowing machinery. 'With embarrassment to us both,' admitted Christo, 'I had to confess this was not my line. I did not emphasise that there was no side of gardening that I found more boring, but that was the fact.'

On the floor above worked the editor of *Amateur Gardening*, Arthur Hellyer; Adams summoned him as mediator and an accommodation was arrived at. For £12 a week, Christo was given half a page in very small print and with no illustration, but, as a result of the simplicity, he could write his copy just eleven days before publication, making it relatively close to events. He was off. A card index was set up, noting what plants he had referred to when, and week by week the words poured from him.

There was no brief (there never was), so he could take his prompt from what was happening at Dixter, confident that his readership at *Country Life* had an appetite for the kind of subject he could offer. Any small nugget of interest would provide a stimulus and he would handle it in full, practical detail; but there were always plenty of tangents too, references to places and people, flower shows and literature. There was no need to start everything from basics, because he knew his readers well enough to take some knowledge for granted and to use his words more productively, elegantly, wittily and concisely, to take the subject forward. (How he slated many years later the writer and broadcaster Monty Don, for using the word herbaceous twenty-eight times in one article when he could have 'done so much more' with twenty-eight words.)

Year in, year out, his typescripts arrived at *Country Life*, the editor's dream, always on time, always the right length and with no signifi-cant editing required. He covered everything as the mood drove him:

propagation, pruning, meadow gardening, vegetables, plants he saw on holiday, other people's gardens, new plants, old plants, what flowered when and with which other plant. Over the years editors came and went, but Christo had become an institution and one for which many people bought the magazine. Readers felt they knew him.

The same year that he began working for *Country Life*, Christo made his first visit to Dundonnell House, near Ullapool in Wester Ross, a place that would become a second home-from-home, and where he stayed almost every year for decades. The owner, Alan Roger, was ten years older than Christo (they had met through Royal Horticultural Society connections) and was to become a regular visitor to Dixter, often in order to attend Glyndebourne. Alan was the son of the late Lord and Lady Roger, the youngest of three brothers, all gay and with no one to whom to leave their family fortune. The oldest, Bunny, was a fashion designer famous for his lavish and outrageous parties in London; Bunny loved the lacquered and faux-bamboo interiors of Dundonnell. Alan was more the gentleman, classily dressed but a touch louche with it, and sometime High Sheriff of the county. He had spent the war in Persia, in intelligence, and was now settled at Dundonnell, where he lived rather beyond his means with staff and a Rolls-Royce. He shared Christo's interest in plants and gardens. Dundonnell was not one of the great gardens of Scotland, but it was wonderfully, delightfully, mossily romantic and, like the severe eighteenth-century house itself, perfectly suited its highland location. There was statuary, some nineteenth-century box hedging, a large laburnum arch, a walled garden, Alan's bonsai collection in valuable Ming bowls, and a fine conservatory. Beside the house was a tumbling Scottish river, and within minutes of Dundonnell you could be walking the hills of Wester Ross.

When Christo was there he was wined and dined in the company of all the interesting figures of county society, and was taken to visit their gardens or to lunch. Many of them became his friends, and he spent time with them when Alan was in Edinburgh on business. The wine and food were always excellent (where else would one be offered bamboo shoots culled from one's favourite, rare, non-culinary species, *Chusquea culeou*) and all in all, life was very much as it might have been lived at Dixter, had the Lloyds had capital. Some days were 'social', and lunches or dinners predominated; on others days guests did what they fancied

– walking, reading, fishing – then reassembled for supper. Christo loved the place: he was in good company, frequently gay company, company in which he was given automatic respect for his wit and expertise. Dundonnell was a complete break from Daisy and Dixter, a chance to recharge his batteries, breathe some different air and perhaps see some different, *simpler* plants up on the hills.

It was now that Christo began seriously to keep notebooks. Usually he had two on the go: one for plants, in which he took notes at shows, conferences and gardens; the other was his personal notebook, not a diary in the traditional sense, because he only wrote when he was away from home, but an aide-memoire of the places he visited, the friends he met, places he stayed, what he ate and drank, and his opinions on people and gardens. They were not confessionals or even particularly introspective, but they were very personal and a record of his life independent of Dixter. He valued these notebooks so much that he always put his name and address inside the front covers, with a plea to anyone finding the books to return them to him. 'Reward' moved over the years to 'Considerable Reward!' and latterly 'Reward and Goodboy Biscuit!' Dawn was his regular time to write, sitting up in bed with the light on; no fun for other people when they shared a room with him. It accounts for the looping scrawl that could be almost indecipherable to anyone but himself.

The success of his column in *Country Life* meant that the magazine was happy to publish his next book, *Clematis*, in 1965.* What an excellent book it is. Never again did Christo produce a monograph like this, which is a pity; it was such a good mixture of botanical review combined with readable instruction and opinion for the gardener, springing as it did from having shared his enthusiasm for the genus with John Treasure for many years, and from personally growing and selling clematis. There was a gap in the market for such a book, he knew, and it became the standard reference for gardeners, the first place to look when choosing a variety for a particular use or position. Sound sense on pests and diseases and on pruning. Good on species and cultivars. Rigorous but readable. Written for a reader who was assumed to be the author's equal in intelligence and enthusiasm, if not knowledge. What more could anyone want?

* When it later went out of print, it was revised and published by Collins in 1977.

Trees and Shrubs for Small Gardens came out in 1965, and was a different kettle of fish. It was the first in a new series of slim paper-backs, the Pan Piper 'Small Garden' Series, aimed at the kind of 'ordinary people' for whom Vita Sackville-West had written her *Observer* columns with her special brand of benign superiority. This was the time when gardening books were starting to be written for the suburban gardener working on a genuinely small back garden. There had been writing aimed at suburban gardeners in the nineteenth century but their so-called suburban gardens were in reality pretty big and often had staff. These were one-man, domestic gardens in streets of houses, and hardly Christo's home ground.

The editor of the series, C. E. Lucas Phillips, presented his prize writer to the world in glowing terms: 'Christopher Lloyd, M.A., B.Sc.(Hort), is not only a highly trained horticulturist, but as his twin degrees testify combines the humanities with science. He lives in a marvellous XV-century Manor House, Great Dixter, near Rye in Sussex, and has turned part of the superb gardens into a nursery.' It was far from what Christo himself might have written – the 'marvellous' manor, the reference to Dixter as a 'gardens' – but he was glad of the respect and was tickled to be a contributor to the series.

Lucas Phillips added that the reader would find Christo writing about all sizes of small garden, from the 'pocket handkerchief plots of cities' to the 'average suburban garden of half an acre'. Christo was willing to downsize his ideas – in *The Mixed Border* eight years previously he had been referring to Dixter itself as too small – but he was not set to deal with pocket-handkerchief plots. 'Even within the compass of a garden of no more than an acre,' he opened, 'and very probably a great deal less . . .' He assumed that he was writing for gardeners who lived in the countryside, however small their plots, telling them to soak pot-grown plants 'in a pond' before planting them, and to tie up trees with 'hay-baler' twine.

He had been told to address 'the little people', who were not begin-ners, but were by his standards spectacularly ignorant. Consequently he wrote in an earnest, almost condescending, teachery fashion. There were a few of his usual black-and-white photographs, and a number of line drawings in case things got too technical. He made forays into garden design, explaining how to make a decent shrubbery, 'not a series of small circles surrounded by turf'. Used to employing Latin names since prep school, he was not going to fall into the imprecise world of common names, and he justified at great length his use of Latin names by saying that 'he would give all the *useful* common names too'. If they were not what *he* called useful, they were not used.

It was in effect a reference book, starting with the basics of planting, pruning and propagation and moving on to an A–Z of popular trees and shrubs. Each entry was brief and the language was clipped. Why use a sentence for 'the little people', when a phrase would do? Christo must have polished off his copy in no time at all.

1967 saw the publication of *Hardy Perennials*, from publishers Studio Vista. It was another of his neat little books of that decade and perhaps the first to cement his reputation for being a 'perennials' man, a label that would last throughout his life. For Christo there was nothing new in the book; it was just a tidy listing of 200 good perennials and grasses (no ferns or bulbs here, as there would be in his *Christopher Lloyd's Garden Flowers* of 2000); it was just *Lloyd's* take on perennials, in contrast to *Hardy Perennials* (1957) from Alan Bloom. There were just a few photographs, some in colour, some in monochrome, and all by Christo.

After a four-year gap, Christo's second book in the Pan Piper 'Small Garden' Series, *Gardening on Chalk and Lime*, appeared in 1969. Again there were a couple of dozen of Christo's black-and-white photographs, mostly plant portraits and many of them conspicuously and proudly taken at Dixter. He was getting into the swing of being an author (it was written in thirty-eight days, at 1,000 words per day), and Lucas Phillips, the series editor, gave Christo similar glowing scientific and humanitarian references on the jacket. In the chapter on 'Hardy Perennials', Christo the man of words, writing for a living and with no shame at self-publicity, stated 'I have lately written a book under this title (published in 1967 by Studio Vista at £1 5s), and can clearly not do the subject justice here.'

If *Trees and Shrubs for Small Gardens* had set out to be a revolt from old-fashioned, segregated shrubberies and herbaceous borders, *Gardening on Chalk and Lime* was a swipe at the supremacy of the acid-soil garden, the kind filled with rhododendrons by nineteenth-century aristocrats and by nouveaux-riches, would-be aristocrats. 'The wonder is,' joked Christo, in some exasperation, 'that no one has yet selected the title of Lord Rhododendron when included in an Honours list.' Such remarks led to Christo being labelled a rhododendron-hater, whereas in fact, when planted in an appropriate place, he loved them; in Scottish gardens they were a constant fascination to him. He even planted a few species at Dixter, under the trees above the horse pond.

Gardening on Chalk and Lime was a far more sophisticated book than *Trees and Shrubs for Small Gardens*, even if still addressed to the little people. It set out to demonstrate how to make a garden, dealing first with trees and structural shrubs, and moving on to 'flimsies' that provide the decoration, stopping along the way to focus on particular groups of lime-loving plants such as viburnums, junipers and roses. There was an excellent chapter at the beginning of the book, which sets out brilliantly – the Wye lecturer coming out here – the distribution of limey soil in the UK and is useful to any gardener even today.

Christo was getting into character as a writer now. The book opened with an imaginary scene worthy of Karel Čapek (a Czech playwright and author of *The Gardener's Year*, a naïve comic masterpiece much loved by Christo, and adored by his friend and nurserywoman Beth Chatto when he introduced her to it twenty years later):

> There is a tendency to commiserate with the keen gardener who is working on a limey soil. 'You really should grow Rhododendron yakusimanum,' we begin by telling him, and then, with a sudden hushing of the voice, while he turns aside with flushed face and moist eyes: 'Oh but of course, you poor thing, you're on lime.' Actually we knew perfectly well from the outset that he couldn't grow rhododendrons, and our remark was just a bit of one-upmanship, to stress the fact that we could.

Whether they liked it or not, this time the little people were getting treated to some serious garden talk. There was a chapter on grey-leaved plants – 'the great mixers' – giving them the respect they deserved for once: they had been till now, he suggested, a woman's thing, especially all this loving or hating of them. 'The men are all too busy cultivating prize Jap chrysanthemums or Giant Decorative dahlias, to have a mind on such a matter.' (The only Giant Decorative Christo ever grew was one named after Daisy.)

Christo could not resist taking a swipe at 'the flower-arranging set' when one of their favourite plants such as hostas, bergenias or butcher's broom gave him the opportunity, despite the fact that he was such an eager participant himself. His mother had trained him to pick flowers almost as if it were a science, and Dixter was always filled with great vases of flowers and foliage. His great friend Beth Chatto began to take an interest in foliage plants directly as a result of her interest in flower arranging, and he greatly respected her for that. The odd thing is that he never got round to writing a book about flower arranging himself. It may well have been that he saw it as something which, at its best and most unaffected, was really very simple, only requiring to be generously done. For him, a great vase of celastrus branches in full berry, on a polished table in the Great Hall, said quite as much as the most artfully arranged competition vase. He preferred armfuls to vases full.

Like much of Christo's writing, *Gardening on Chalk and Lime* just stops. No conclusion, no rounding off, just a completion of the information on the plant in hand. It was the Lloydian 'what's done is done' manner, and no going back. What followed was merely a glossary of horticultural terms and a useful list of specialist nurseries, information that, in those day of greater economic stability, did not date so quickly.

Information was fast becoming Christo's commodity for sale, as much as the garden; and partly because of his books, he found himself being asked to give talks all over the south-east of England to amateur groups and societies; his range of subjects was huge and brave. Here was an expert indeed:

Planting for Small Gardens
Bulbs the Year Round
Making the Most of Garden Plants
Borders with a Difference
Plant Propagation
Plants with Personality for the Ordinary Gardener
Fruit
Wall Shrubs and Climbers
Choosing the Right Plants for Your Garden
Wildlife in the Garden
Placing your Plants
What Makes a Garden

Of course Christo was far more at home thinking about large gardens with greater scope and it was this that, in the 1960s, made him offer to act as a consultant on the garden at Glyndebourne. Christo and Daisy had attended the operas at Glyndebourne ever since they began in 1934. They would take along rugs and a picnic basket – the same ones Christo continued to take for nearly sixty years, he in his evening suit and black tie and The Management in her smartest dirndl or occasionally her formal, full-length Quaker dress – a Cromwellian for all to see (or ask). Christo knew George and Mary Christie, who then ran the festival, and he offered to help Mary polish up the garden, his musical home-from-home.

He and Mary Christie began a three-monthly check-up that lasted almost to the end of Christo's life. He would pick up the phone one day and announce his intention to visit and there would be a grand circuit of the garden by Christo, Mary and the head gardener. They progressed slowly down the long, double borders on the terrace in front of the house and the more informal beds around the lawns, making note of what could be improved, what might grow in such a warm position, what would look good with what, and what to get rid of. All his life, when scrutinising a border, Christo had a characteristic, Poirot-like pose, hands behind his back with one hand gripping the opposite wrist, chin on chest, and glaring at the plant in question as he decided on its use or abuse. If the person beside him had something to say about it, he would respond by turning towards them from the waist only, his eyes moving to their feet and his ear to their opinion, but never letting the poor plant out of his 'basilisk eye'.

Mary would organise a good lunch for him, in the company of such directors and singers as happened to be rehearsing or performing there at the time. He loved the musical gossip and the chance to meet people who actually made music themselves, as he and his family had always done, people for whom music was something you *did*, as well as listened to. In later years his head gardener Fergus Garrett would drive Christo over and lead the team.

The publication of *The Well-Tempered Garden* in 1970 was a landmark, not just in Christo's writing, but in garden writing generally. It was the first of the classic Lloyd books – for some people, still his best – and it marked a new, freer, more entertaining, more *personal* style in gardening

116

books. It was the writing as much as the subject that made it good. Christo was there talking to you, in your living room or in your garden, and certainly in his garden. It made you want to go and visit Dixter and meet this intriguing man. How different it was from Marjorie Fish's books of solid domestic meanderings in the 1960s and Vita Sackville-West's *Observer* journalism, in which she had spoken to the reader like an enthusiastic but rather patronising, aristocratic flower arranger. What set Christo apart was that he was *conspiratorial*; it was just *you* he was addressing, and it was obviously going to be fun.

The title was a reference to Bach's collection of keyboard pieces, *The Well-Tempered Clavier*, that great showpiece of technical and emotional display, and it set his book apart from the good, solid gardening titles of the day. It did not aim to cover a specific subject – clematis or alpines or rhododendrons – but took a broad look at plants and gardening generally, from the basic to the most sophisticated issues, from muck to magic, because, like music, gardening was 'a humanising occupation'. The result is a timeless book into which one can dip even today, to discover what a gardener needs to know about a plant, to find nuggets of closely observed experience, not just the generalised facts you would expect to find in an encyclopaedia. To make it easier to return to a subject later, he put into bold type the names of the plants under discussion so that the subject would jump off the page at you; and at the page top (running heads) he put little captions as aides-memoires (a trick he continued through several more books) – *Categorising scents*, perhaps, or *Campanulas as indoor pot plants*.

Not surprisingly, it was also a book about gardening at Dixter; Dixter *was* his experience. That gardening there was ambitious and sophisticated did not matter to him; he was writing now for *keen* gardeners at last, or at least gardeners whom he hoped would become as keen as himself. With these readers he could chuckle at the follies of inexperienced gardeners, striking a parallel again with Karel Čapek, the Czech playwright:

One could trace the steps of his [the total amateur's] education by his answer to questions on the much disputed subject of rose pruning. 'When do you prune your roses?' 'In the first week of April,' the novice will answer. 'Why then?' 'Because it says so in my book.' Ask him why he doesn't prune them at mid-winter and he will just look blank. But put him this same question a little later in his education and he will wax indignant: 'Prune them at mid-winter? Do you think I want to kill my bushes? Have them lured into fresh growth in the first mild spell only to be hit by frost immediately afterwards?' He has been reading the correspondence in a gardening journal and feels the ground is safe.

Christo was letting his personality shine at last. He was as happy quoting from *The Lancet* and the *National Farmers' Union Journal* as he was from Keats' remarks to his sister or a character in Wagner's *Ring* cycle. Sometimes he was a little schoolmasterly, but then he was not so many years away from lecturing to students, and besides his humour outshone his earnestness, especially when the humour was at his own expense. 'There is room,' he wrote, 'for more than one opinion on this matter (mine being right, yours, if different, wrong).' He was developing one-liners so much to his liking – 'I am a confirmed fig pig' – that, knowingly or not, he used them again and again for the rest of his life.

As the years went by he came to be loved by his readers for being opinionated – a word generally used in a pejorative sense. In Christo's case, it was used in admiration by those who knew his writing, for daring to say things which were anti-establishment or flew in the face of received wisdom, for being pleasurably wicked and provocative, but at the same time (and this made it acceptable) sincere. People new to gardening, who had not read him, understood that this man Lloyd was given to airing his opinions wittily, and they labelled him opinionated in a friv- olous way. There was an expectation that he was always ready to produce a clever, cruel jibe that was ultimately at somebody else's expense. In fact Christo was never frivolous, although on occasion his sense of humour could venture into the surreal. To be deemed frivolous was, to him and to Daisy, the ultimate condemnation.

What strikes a gardener reading *The Well-Tempered Garden* today is that Christo was already dealing with the interests and fashions that would comprise his entire career, that at Dixter he had *always* been doing the things that he later became famous for: extolling the virtues of grey-foliage plants, and meadows, and succession planting, and annuals, grasses, and exotic planting with cannas and dahlias. But *The Well-Tempered Gardon* was no attempt to be a fashion forecast, and since he was working on a garden established fifty years previously, he also wrote about the stalwart, slightly old-fashioned plants of early twentieth-century gardening – lilacs, forsythia, snapdragons and, of course and at great length, roses, the plants which, when he removed them from his own Rose Garden in 1993, the popular imagination assumed he had always hated.*

More than any other of his books, *The Well-Tempered Garden* is the one that stands the test of time, because it is so appealing and, to an English gardener, so very, very useful. It stands at a tipping point, summing up the plants and preoccupations of early twentieth-century gardening, and looking forward to the great surge in the popularity of gardening that followed. Back then, in 1970, it was welcome simply as a breath of fresh air, and people loved it. What better spur could he have to get on with his next book: *Foliage Plants*. But in the meantime he had a holiday in mind.

Christo's friend, the gardener John Codrington, had been on an organised holiday to Kashmir in 1969, and persuaded Christo to come with him on a second trip, to see the wild flowers and high alpines. Christo was used to twenty-mile Scottish walks and had ample stamina, even if the idea of a packaged holiday made him nervous. During the winter of 1969 he began work on *Foliage Plants*, while looking forward to summer in Kashmir. John, a tough ex-soldier and spy, was well-known in the world of large private gardens, in many of which he helped with design and planting. His own 'mad jungle' of a garden on Rutland Water was familiar to serious plantspeople. If it did not entirely meet with Christo's approval, it was a treasure-house of interesting plants, and the two of them got on well.

Off they went in June 1970, part of a guided, English-speaking party of thirty, none of them young and all well-to-do. The Indian decor of the Indian Airlines jumbo jet kept Christo highly amused as they flew to Bombay, Delhi and finally to Srinagar, where they spent a couple of days on a houseboat on the lake, Christo delighted by the water-lilies, willows, poplars, luscious apricots and handsome Kashmiris with ready smiles. The few days spent as a tourist intrigued him: the 'masses of

---

* So it was with rhododendrons and heathers and even dwarf conifers; one good, witty put-down of a plant badly used, and the public chose to think he hated everything to do with that plant.

bedding out in just the taste one would expect', the delightful old town. 'Everything that was old was beautiful; everything modern, hideous. Picturesque but rather squalid, of course, though everyone seems happy. Tiny shops in which the goods are manufactured before your eyes. All mosque roofs now seem to be of corrugated iron and flattened kerosene tins have been much used.'

They ate hugely filling meals in local restaurants, entertained one evening by local bands, though Christo of course managed to avoid joining in the dancing. Then, disaster struck: he went down with diar-rhoea, making the piles that already troubled him suddenly a serious problem. 'All very demoralising and painful, not to say lowering,' he quipped.

In this embarrassing state, the upcountry expedition began. He and John shared a two-man tent, the first night camping at 7,500 feet by the side of a noisy river pale with melt-water. In this camp at least there were servants aplenty, but they could not make up for Christo's dis-comfort, which was in part alleviated by one of the party who was a surgeon.

While the group went off seriously botanising, the frustrated Christo took short walks from the camp, and managed with typical lack of care to wander into the middle of a military exercise, 'just like a field day at school'. There were flower meadows to be explored, and he found a potentilla to try in his meadows at home. But finding flowers barely made up for nights ruined by pain.

Journeys from camp to camp were made by bus rattling along rough roads, but the leg to the Sindh Valley (at 9,000 feet) was to be 100 miles; Christo could not bear the thought and so, intending to claim on his medical insurance, he and John took a taxi. Now he was happy, never mind the state of the vehicle. The friendly driver agreed to Christo's shouts of 'Stop!' whenever something caught his eye, be it to identify a jasmine or take pictures of a vulture.

But the new camp, too, was a problem: beside a beautiful ruin, yes, but perched above a river and plagued by flies. While the others made their day-long expeditions, Christo stayed on his camp-bed or pottered out from the camp, finding catmints, lilies, epimediums and a sheet of the day-lily *Hemerocallis fulva* spectacularly covering an overhanging rock. These things just about made the trip worth bearing.

Climbing again, they camped at 9,500 feet under the path of a glacier where rocky moraines lay side by side with promising smooth meadows. Many a day it poured and poured with rain, on other days they ate out beside a bonfire in woods of white-stemmed birches, while shepherds with sheep, goats and ponies filed past. But the very meadows that had been the point of the holiday turned out to have been entirely grazed off by goats; the entire trip was a waste of time.

Christo took off alone with John, into a landscape of bare boulders, John on a pony and Christo (still unable to bear a saddle) behind on foot, like Sancho Panza, and in woods they found orchids, arisaemas and skimmias, but these too all grazed down (Christo liberated a few fritillary bulbs to save them from the hungry mouths of cattle). Stopping to picnic one day, John decided to stay and sketch while Christo determinedly pushed on, finding himself shortly on an open hillside of yellow *Rhododendron campanulatum.* 'An Indian came down the hill, swinging a paper bag. Eaten up with curiosity, I couldn't resist asking him what was in it – thinking wild fruits, perhaps. He said a word I couldn't understand and eventually pulled out a handful of snow!'

In luxury at last at the Sun and Sand Hotel, Bombay, Christo complained about the 'over amplified "music"'. What would a Lloyd holiday be if it didn't end with a row with the hotel management?

It was so very, very good to be home.

Just as well, for, at Dixter, pen in hand, there was much to do. *Foliage Plants,* of course, but he was also busy writing for the excellent *Amateur Gardening* (thoroughly professional, by today's standards) and again, as he had in *The Well-Tempered Garden,* he was starting to push ideas for which he became famous later in his life: gardening in grass with bulbs and perennials; succession planting; even pushing particular plants like the dahlia 'Bishop of Llandaff', which only became truly, commercially popular as late as 2006. The list of *Amateur Gardening's* writers is a galaxy of stars from the world of serious gardening. The following represents just a selection: Arthur Hellyer, Frances Perry, Margery Fish, Graham Stuart Thomas, Sheila McQueen, Miles Hadfield, Sylvia Crowe, Roy Hay, John Street, Will Ingwersen, Percy Thrower, Tony Venison, Allen Paterson, Brian Mathew, Christine Kelway, Reginald Kaye, Alan Bloom, Christopher Brickell, C. E. Lucas Phillips, Mrs Desmond Underwood, John Brookes, Lanning Roper and more.

Christo became especially enchanted with Lanning Roper, whom he had met through the Royal Horticultural Society. Lanning was an American, blond and preposterously good-looking, and a character of such gentlemanly charm that he was loved by everybody. He was heavily involved in the garden at Scotney Castle not far from Dixter, making a herb garden there in the 1970s for the owner Betty Hussey, a Lloyd family friend and a fine gossip. Christo often met Lanning socially there, taking plants for him from the Dixter nursery. Enchantment led to infatuation and a relationship that was probably ended by Lanning. Even in his eighties and in his cups, Christo could be reduced to tears by the thought of Lanning, and it may well be that he was Christo's one physical sexual partner, but on this the fossil record is silent. All that remains at Dixter of the handsome, lively American is Lord Snowdon's black-and-white photograph of him sitting on a stool, spade in hand, smiling that winning film-star smile; the photograph is tucked into the leaves of the book in which Christo kept portraits and memorabilia of his few great loves – Ken, Lanning, Romke van de Kaa, Fergus Garrett, Pip Morrison.

By the late 1970s Christo was writing monthly for *The Observer* magazine, in the footsteps of Vita Sackville-West ('ghastly magazine – if readers like its vulgarity that doesn't say much for the readership', wrote Christo) and was penning the leader to its pull-out *Good Gardening Guide*, later put on ice for reasons of competition between newspapers. But at least there was no talking down in his journalism; he wanted readers to follow him into interesting gardening: 'Your fingers are brown,' he wrote, 'go live in a sea-view flat in Bournemouth.'

Why shouldn't his work be good? By 1971 Christo was fifty, yet he had almost fifty years' gardening experience, whereas most of his rivals quite naturally had experience only through their adulthoods, their childhoods being normal and plant-free. And Christo's terms of reference were admirably huge: anything from the Horticultural Trades Association, government or university research, vegetables, holidays abroad, flower shows, nineteenth-century garden practice, literature, readers' letters, chemicals, pests and diseases . . .

Times, then, were very good for Christo. His beloved garden was strong; each border set thickly with bold plants, some standing at the back, others ready to run mid-border, and still others forming solid ranks at ground level. The place was full. Christo was becoming recognised as an author and journalist and nurseryman; he was managing to travel; he gave lectures, with The Management sitting at the back and regularly chipping in.

Inevitably his relationship with Daisy had begun to change. To outsiders, she still appeared to rule the Dixter roost, but she was slowly winding down physically and mentally, a heavy, forgetful little old woman, and she knew it. On open days she sat outside in the sun, by the front porch, under her bedroom window, headscarf drawn tight to keep herself warm and to keep her powerful glasses firmly on her nose so that she could see her embroidery. The *doyenne of Dixter*, taking questions and passing the time of day with her public. But in reality, Christo was now the management.

In June 1972 the inevitable happened; Daisy suffered a stroke. Christo nursed her at Dixter for ten awful days until she died in his arms in her little bedroom over the porch. She was ninety-two. Dixter was sixty-two. Christo was fifty-one.

It was always in times of stress – school, the army – that he turned to story-telling and now, oddly inserted in his work notebook following his jottings about the Chelsea Flower Show, Christo recorded Daisy's last days and moments. For whom? For himself, to refer back to, as he referred back to his notes on plants? To prove that death was something unremarkable, to be ignored? As Daisy had said when Tan died, 'There are two things in this world people make too much fuss about – money and death.' She had asked for no funeral, and Christo left the next day for the Scottish holiday that he already had planned. The day after that, he was in Edinburgh lecturing on 'Hardy Perennials in the Garden'.

Thursday 1st June
M. 'You and I are very much alike.'
Xr. [Christopher] 'We are?'
M. 'I can't say I mind.'

When I kissed her hand several times in succession, 'lovely sound.'

Xr. I'm going away for a few hours and shall be back this evening so be good.
M. I will be, dear old thing.

Sunday 4th June
M. How have we done today? [garden visitors]
Xr. Only 33 people. The weather has discouraged them.
M. (with flushing eyes) *I'm* not discouraged.

Tuesday 6th June
Very flushed but still holding on. Sweetie Pie [a dachshund] a
great comfort. 'I think she wants to bite someone.'

Wednesday 7th June
After taking her egg in milk at breakfast, 'Well now, the thing is
to get rid of ourselves as quickly as we can.' Still very responsive
to love and affection.
Later: 'I'm just waiting.'

M. rallies a bit. 'What can I do (pause) to show you that I love you?'
She is delighted with the plant of Begonia 'Cleopatra' I brought up.
'I'm afraid there'll be trouble,' indicating Sweetie Pie and Crocus
[another dachshund] who were both demanding to be loved equally.
Xr. 'The trouble is they both want to be loved, we all want to be
loved.' M. 'Yes, and some of us want to wash our hands' (indicating my grubby, garden-stained paws).

Thursday 8th June
She's still quite bright. Begonia 'Cleopatra' still her darling. Holds
up her hands in delight as I bring it for her and 'let me touch it',
stroking its leaves. I tell her I'm going to Scotland the next day
and she takes it perfectly clearly, showing interest in the different
places and people I intend visiting. When I come to Alan Roger,
she brightens 'Ah, I love him.' Asks why he [the doctor] can't get
rid of her. 'All this fuss over an old woman.'
Awake and delighted to see me return from Glyndebourne in the
evening.

Friday 9th June
She's asleep at 4.50. I stroked her arm to wake her but she still
sleeps so I go back to bed till 6. Now she's ready for me. 'I've been
waiting for you.' 'I was here an hour ago.' 'I've been here much

longer than that.' Help her to the commode but first tell her I'm getting some hot water to wipe her tail. 'That will be nice' (a touch of sarcasm!) Does wee wees. Back to bed but very breathless. 'I'll get you a hot-water-bottle'. M., trying to hold on 'That's through that way' pointing at the door. She's roaring like a boiler when I get back and in a sweat. 'Don't let them kill her' are her last words, apropos of Crocus who is on heat and who she's sure will be run over by a vehicle. Looks very peaceful at the last.

Saturday 10th June
To Scotland. Dixter to King's Cross in 1hr 35 mins.

Sunday 11th June
Had forgotten what splendid views there are over Edinburgh. The rocks below the castle are pink with campion. Much Swedish white-beam flowering in Prince's gardens. Pathetic bedding and gardening standards here, but the floral clock is not quite as repulsive as some of this genre . . .

PART TWO
Life after Daisy

Darling X r: Chris, - to - , pher, Lambikin,
do you recognise this terrible drawing?
I'll give you
full marks if
you do! The sheep
(for sheep they are
indeed) look, I am sorry to say, more like a
mixture between Sand's pigs. & a couple
of angry buffalos. The nice little boy was you!
And. in short, feeling I had to draw something
sheepish with which to greet you, I took a

Part of a letter from Letitia to Christo. Her drawing
captures exactly the shy posture Christo still had when
picnicking at Glyndebourne at eighty.

Chapter 8

The New Dixter, 1972–81

Christo (disapprovingly, as he discusses with Ruth, Lady Crawford,
her garden at Balcarres Castle): '*Have you got a notebook?*'
Lady Crawford: '*No, darling, I've got you.*'

1974

How does a man move on after fifty years with his mother? Daisy's and
Christo's relationship had been a marriage of minds, a marriage that had
brought together their skills as botanists, plantspeople and gardeners and
had given birth to a wonderful garden; they had put flesh on the bones of
Lutyens' design to a degree that happened in none of Lutyens' other gardens.
But it was also a marriage in which Daisy had given Christo the garden to
develop largely as he wished, in exchange for loyalty to herself. Other young
men would have craved their freedom; but, for the shy Christo, creating
a garden with Daisy had saved him the embarrassment of having to cope
with freedom in the wider world. He had been willingly in thrall to her.

Now he was older and more his own man; her death therefore came
as a huge relief as well as a great loss. But loss was something he had
been taught to put behind him; it was an indulgence. He might be
alone and middle-aged, but he remembered Daisy's prescription about
money and death: 'This house has always been a particularly happy
one, and I am determined that it shall continue so.' Filled with similar
determination, Christo took a deep breath, turned his back on the past
and heeded her words. He would make a new life at Dixter, but in a
fresher, easier way. No more Edwardian rules and regulations, no more
dinner bells, no more management. He was scarily, *unavoidably* free now,
whether he liked it or not. And he still had his other lifelong loves, the
garden, and the wonderful house.

But first, his trip to Scotland. At Dundonnell he was thrown into the usual routine of walks and meals with the local land-owning and garden-owning gentry, followed by bridge. 'Lunched at Lady (Sophie) Slade's hideous new house just outside Ullapool. Read and slept this afternoon – E. M. Forster "The Longest Journey". Flashes of insight alternating with flashes of pseudo-insight that don't ring true.' Reminders of his loss seemed not to touch him: 'It was nice to see Alice Maconochie. Apropos of her late mother, who died in spring, she says she misses having someone to look after. Her mother was buried, at her request, according to the local custom, being carried on a bier to the graveyard with no coffin.'

To escape from any inclination to look back, he spent his days in botanising, bird-watching and long, lonely mountain walks, pushing himself to the top of An Teallach in two and a half hours and marching on to Sgurr Fiona in a snowstorm; or, on kinder, sunnier days, walking into the corrie below An Teallach to look down through a clearance towards Loch Toll, where the ripples were catching the sunlight; or sitting on the heather at Loch na Sealga, listening to the wavelets lapping the shore. In the small hours of the morning, sitting up in bed, he wrote his diary – not just notes any more, but now his confessional, somewhere to talk as previously he might have talked to Daisy, of the history of the gardens he saw, his reactions to them and the characters he met. It confirmed his new existence.

And with no other social plans after Dundonnell, still he kept Dixter at arm's length for two more days, staying alone at a hotel in Tongue, determinedly hunting down a wild population of *Ajuga pyramidalis* on the hills. There he met a pleasant enough insurance salesman who always holidayed alone in the hotel, and the two of them drove out to Strathy Point, to watch the sea from the car, in silence. Wasn't that kind of lonely life a trap, no good, a waste of time? He must get a new life. *Now* it was time to go home. He packed his bags, checked out and drove south, taking stops with his friends – Bob Seeley in Northumberland and John Codrington in Rutland – before getting back, for the first time, to a Daisy-less Dixter.

Letters of condolence waited for him, all in praise of her: *she had ruled over Dixter for so many years . . . difficult, but she could also be very kind . . . always most entertaining . . . one of the last great eccentrics.* The finality of their remarks put the onus even more on Christo to move forward and take charge of Dixter. Quentin had his own young family and ran the mechanics of the estate, and had no desire to move into the big house; it was accepted amongst the Lloyds that Dixter and the garden must continue under Christo. He toyed with the idea of giving it to the National Trust, but nothing came of this and he realised that for his lifetime the responsibility – the opportunity – to keep Dixter going was his.

He pursued earnestly all the precepts of Dixter life: he threw himself into the garden, read novels by the dozen, worked furiously at his needle-point. Significantly, he was planning for the garden alone now. His staff were servants, not colleagues, and he had no longer a soulmate with whom to take the garden forward. The garden itself was now a lonely business. So now, most of all, Christo threw himself into writing. That was a lonely process too, except in so far as he was talking intimately to his readers, but one he was able to do well. In 1973 *Foliage Plants* was published by William Collins, and it was good.

In the hand, *Foliage Plants* feels much the same as *The Well-Tempered Garden*: novel-sized, something you can read in bed. Once again there are glossy inserts of colour or black-and-white photographs, bold type for the key plants, and page headings to steer by. Alphabetically the book runs through the plants, from woody plants to annuals, and Christo throws in a few suggested planting designs.

'A book which is too good not to recommend to you at once,' wrote Robin Lane Fox in the *Financial Times*. 'Readers of his *Well-Tempered Garden* will need no reminders that Mr Lloyd is the most articulate gardener now practising regularly in England. No other gardening writer can give such sophisticated advice.'

In *The Times*, Roy Hay agreed: 'It is a pleasure to read the work of a discerning and infinitely knowledgeable plantsman who is offering the distillation of half a lifetime's study of plants. This is a book in the best Christopher Lloyd tradition.'

A tradition already! Christo was mightily pleased. It seemed that writing about gardening *as he experienced it* was a successful recipe. No matter that his garden was big; no matter that he imagined everyone else's border could have a three-foot-wide service path at the back and every garden wall could be nine feet tall. The gardens that Christo visited were mostly big gardens, that was what he knew about, and he always wrote from experience. Enthusiasm was there aplenty and all of it was genuine; none of the forced enthusiasm that editors and television producers later required. There was a great physical sense of the writer too, there in the parlour with some huge flower arrangement beside him, in conversation with the reader.

As Christo became recognised for his witty and personal style, he began to play up to it. Why shouldn't he slate things as well as praise them? His admiration for Alan Bloom's island beds of perennials, so clearly expressed in his own *Hardy Perennials* six years before, had now withered: 'There is a fashion, nowadays, for borders of informal outline. In an informal setting, these will generally be appropriate. But fidgety outlines, sudden kinks and wiggles and meaningless bulges are distracting. You keep looking at the border's shape instead of its contents.' There speaks the man who would never find much pleasure in a garden where the beauty is in the line and space rather than a *richesse* of planting. Oddly, too, there speaks the man who was fond of Beth Chatto's Essex garden, which was confessedly designed by laying out hosepipes in great curves.

Ahead of the game, Christo wrote of the tide of hosta varieties that would sweep through gardens in the next thirty years, and was already joking about them:

And so we arrive at the fashionable genus Hosta, erstwhile Funkia. What can Lloyd say about it that has not already been said many times over? I suppose it might help to try and keep its members in perspective. For hostas have lately achieved apotheosis of a sacred-cow-like nature. They are so easy to grow, so ground-covering, so weed-suppressing, so indispensable to flower arrangers, so many things to so many people, that the fact of their having faults also and of not being the be-all and end-all of herbaceous plants in a garden, is apt to be forgotten.

But those few hostas that Christo chose to write about were the best and most distinct, described with extraordinary clarity and attention to seasonal detail.

That a garden should change and develop was always on his agenda, then as much as in his old age. '[Experienced gardeners] should always,' he said, 'be living on the frontiers of their experience; always be experimenting and trying out something new. It's only those who are afraid of having to admit to mistakes who are frightened of making them.' He himself was already trying out the kinds of planting that came to fruition so spectacularly in his Exotic Garden, later: stooling ailanthus, pollarding box elder, bedding out house plants. But even he was prepared to concede that he had his timid or sentimental moments, as he did over two clumps of Gertrude Jekyll's favourite *Bergenia cordifolia*. 'I loathe them,' he groaned; but they remained there to the end of his life, as did odd little clumps of heather on the edge of lawns; and he positively refused ever to consider changing the soil and planting what was once the coal-heap – a prime piece of garden right under the walls of the house. It wasn't sentimentality so much as a refusal to be *pushed* to do anything; resolution was something to be proud of, like dirt under the fingernails or his wrecked old gardening shoes.

Foliage Plants was not a book principally about the architectural foliage we so admire today, but about all plants with good foliage, of any kind, from gunnera to parsley. All foliage plants needed help and recommendation in those days of simple flower power (curiously, today, the grasses-and-perennials fashion is returning us to structureless flower power, if in a more scattered, washy, pointillist way). With *Foliage Plants*, once again Christo was ahead of the game, pointing up a trend just as it began to happen. Sadly, *Foliage Plants* was not a financial success, perhaps because it had so many similarities, not least visually, to *The Well-Tempered Garden*.

In summer 1973 he made his annual summer trip to Dundonnell once more, taking the notes made by the naturalist John Raven as his field guide. On the way to King's Cross in London, where he was to put his car on the motorail, Christo took his eye off the road and ran into the back of the car in front, which then repeated the process on the next car. Blame was admitted and the RAC came to tow Christo to a garage. By the time they had found one and he had got a cab to King's Cross, it was 1 a.m. and the train had gone. All the local hotels were full, except one very small one run by 'a fat sleazy Jew with a thick accent (like a music hall imitation of a Jew)'. It stank of cigar smoke and he was offered a room for £4. There being only six hours of the night left in which to sleep, Christo found this outrageous and proceeded to spend the night dozing on the platform at King's Cross (the waiting room was now closed). He woke in the morning, as he stewed in his indignation, surrounded by 'Peace!'-chanting hippies in white robes, and felt rather small.

It was this kind of un-Dixterly experience that made his Scottish trips such a valuable change. Different places, different responsibilities, new horizons. Of a lone trip to the island of Harris the next year, he wrote:

> It gives you the feeling of unchanged tradition and a belief in its unchanged way of life, whether anachronistic or not. The country is unspoilt by caravan camps etc. The sandy beaches are still as they always were – empty. Wild life prospers. The roads are good but empty. The debris of all kinds left lying around, including a large number of derelict motor vehicles, is astonishing.
>
> Above all I liked the hotel I stayed at and its being a family concern likely to continue unless – OIL! Ah me! Anything could happen as a result of this being discovered off shore. Let us hope . . .

If he could stay on these trips with friends rather than in hotels he would, and every year for decades he lined people up in advance, like coaching inns. The Seeleys or myself in Northumberland, David Scott and Valerie Finnis, or John Codrington in Northamptonshire, the plant-collector and nurseryman Michael Wickenden in Dumfriesshire. One pit stop he almost invented, for his own convenience. Christo wrote to Francis Hepburne Scott, who had studied modern languages with him (they had been completely out of contact since), to ask if he would be coming to a reunion dinner at King's College. Francis could not join him at the dinner, but said: Come to see us one day. Christo rang two weeks later to ask himself to lunch and was rather pleased, on the day, to be pressed to stay overnight. Thereafter the Hepburne Scotts were on his list and, truth to tell, glad to be so, as his company was always stimulating.

Garden Cottage, where Nils and Letitia had made their home, stands literally under the eye of Dixter and therefore had been under the eye of Daisy; and Daisy had been forever in and out leaving the little family with hardly any privacy. Technically, of course, Daisy owned Garden Cottage. Letitia felt invaded and angry and, frequently, desperate.

134

In the autumn of 1971 Olivia left home to read art history and languages at Warwick University. Daisy's death followed in June 1972. Then, early in 1974, Nils died of emphysema.

Letitia had lost her mother, her daughter had flown the nest, and now her husband was gone, too. Nils had been Titia's rock, as well as her link to more cosmopolitan worlds beyond Dixter. Now she was completely at a loss. She had considered starting up a bed-and-breakfast business at the cottage, but Pam and Quentin at Little Dixter blocked this. What should Letitia do except be depressed? She felt guiltier than ever for being such a disappointment to her mother. Christo had thought Nils rather a lazy man around Dixter and, kind to her though he was about Nils' death, was in no mood to help her snap out of depression. He was starting life again himself, so why couldn't she? Quentin's attitude was much the same. Death! said the Lloyds. Get over it! The family did not give her the help she deserved. And then Olivia told her that she was going to get married in December and live abroad.

In October 1974, in despair, Letitia took her own life, there in Garden Cottage, Letitia, the most naturally carefree and yet the guiltiest of the Lloyds.

Christo took a deep breath and put his only sister behind him. There was too much of Daisy in him. He had no time to spare for sorrow or guilt. He bought a book on suicide to see if he could work out how someone could want to do it.

Olivia came back to empty Garden Cottage of its contents, to make room for a head gardener. Three months later she was married. She went to live in Germany, and has never again lived in England, although she continued always to visit Dixter and Christo twice a year until he died.

Olivia admired Christo. She owned – after Letitia's death – a considerable stake in Dixter, but was content, for the next thirty-two years until Christo died, neither to charge a rent for her share nor to realise its worth by demanding that the estate be sold (Christo had not the capital to buy her out). The same patience was true of Oliver and Quentin: Dixter was the family creation, with their little brother Christo at the centre of it running the garden; Dixter was somewhere to come back to; Dixter was something one would naturally hang on to. Christo was very lucky.

*   *   *

People found that having Christo to visit them – the return match – was almost as exciting as going to Dixter, because of the generosity of his attention to their interests. Sir David Scott was a retired diplomat, married to the photographer Valerie Finnis. After Christo had visited them in 1974 at their house in Northamptonshire, Sir David wrote: 'It's a joy to be able to show an expert round our patch. So many people, even those who call themselves gardeners, are pretty heavy going and leave one exhausted rather than, as with somebody like you, (how rare, how rare such people are) exhilarated.'

Word got about that Christo, for better or blunter, could be a superb (and free) garden adviser. Friends of friends with gardens would ask him to stay on his journey north, curious to see if this legendary gardener could be as sharp and difficult as some people said he was. Sometimes he certainly was and even conceded the point: 'Bob [Seeley] says I was a bit merciless to [a lady gardener in Orkney] at times and as we parted she invited me to come and be rude again whenever I was back, but I was never unkinder than good-tempered teasing and she could take it, pointing out how easy gardening is for us in the south, which it is.' If the garden was large and interesting enough, the Lloyd inspection could last up to five hours, offering brilliant insights. At Belsay I was recipient of a few of his five-hour marathons, divided by a break for tea, and we both enjoyed them. When I went through his diaries, I read, to my shame, that he had found these visits exhausting. But it was he who set the pace.

One day in 1976, the year of the great drought in England, a gardener from the Royal Horticultural Society's garden at Wisley, Romke van de Kaa, was spending the day with friends in Northiam in search of Real Ale pubs. It was a sunny day and lunch was a boozy one, and since in those days the pubs had to close between lunch and evening, Romke and friends decided to visit a garden. There was a garden in the village, apparently, called Great Dixter. Romke had never heard of it or of Christopher Lloyd, but they walked in, slightly the worse for wear, and got chatting to the rather stuffy owner.

Tom Moffat, head gardener at the time, had decided to move on and Christo was going to need a new one very soon, so taking a shine to this rather rough, scruffy blond with an accent from foreign lands (Dutch), he offered him the job then and there. Daisy was gone, why not live dangerously? Christo wrote to confirm the offer and, shortly afterwards, the hard-smoking Romke arrived in Garden Cottage, fresh from Wisley, where he had worked not on herbaceous plants, but in the Rock Garden. Coming from an institutional garden he found the running of Dixter antiquated and the nursery amateurish; there was not even a tap and a hose, only cans with which to water the pots that endless hot summer.

But what a change Romke brought socially to Dixter! Garden Cottage was never without visitors day and night – young gardeners from Wisley and Holland, way-out friends from the pop-music business – and reggae belted out across the garden. 'The Zulus are at it again,' the other gardeners joked; but Christo tolerated it, or rather he was intrigued by it. Perhaps this was how *he* should be living, with people coming and going, having fun; *his* house was a darned sight bigger, and pop music was not so terrible if you took the trouble to listen. Entering the nursery in the first week, he called out 'van de Kaa?' His new member of staff was offended. 'My name's Romke,' he replied, 'why use my surname?' 'But that's what we *call* gardeners in this country,' maintained Christo. But he gave in to the Dutchman's request. Six months later Christo announced quietly that Romke could call him 'Mr Christopher', and after a year 'Christo', so long as it wasn't in front of the other gardeners.

Some of the hopefulness of Romke's time spilled over into the garden. On the way to the High Garden is a small paved area looking back to the roofscape of Dixter and surrounded by Nathaniel's topiary peacocks. The peacocks were linked along the edge of the stone paving by hedges of lavender planted by Daisy. Hence its name, the Lavender Garden. And now, with an inordinate sense of pride on Christo's part, he and Romke pulled out Daisy's tired lavender hedges and replaced them with 'hedges' of *Aster lateriflorus* var. *horizontalis* growing from pink mats of *Persicaria vacciniifolia* – a combination to remain a mere forty years, compared to the lavender's sixty-eight. In the orchard, most of the towering old Bramley apples were felled and replaced with Christo's new loves, ornamental rowans and pears. It has made the orchard look relatively thin and scattery, more so than a house of Dixter's bulk is flattered by, but Christo was happy.

As Christo and Romke got to know each other, Christo began to ask Romke to lunch occasionally and, becoming devoted to his wild boy, took him to Scotland and Dundonnell. One night Romke, rather well oiled by alcohol, fell asleep in Garden Cottage with the television on;

it caught light and burned itself out (but not the cottage) and Romke was dragged out the next morning, lungs blackened like the inside of the cottage, and unable to speak for weeks. While the cottage was refitted he lived at Dixter, where Christo became ever fonder of him to the point, finally, of professing his love. For the worldly-wise Romke, the confession was more embarrassing than surprising; but it made life at Dixter uncomfortable. Shortly afterwards he moved to a garden in Ireland and from there back to Holland, where he married and set up a nursery. It was only after he left that he and Christo were able to become true friends, and Romke explained to him how difficult it had been to be both employee and friend. 'I didn't find it difficult,' maintained Christo sincerely.

Years later, in 1984, Romke asked Christo to visit him in the Netherlands, where he was now in partnership with the nurseryman Piet Oudolf* at the Hummelo. Christo had made Romke a gift of several thousand pounds to help set up the business and was keen to see how he was getting on. It was Piet who met Christo at the airport; he had been to Dixter on a cycling tour in 1976 and Christo had briefly shown him round then. Christo found Piet sympathetic and interesting and was glad Romke had found a worthy partner. There was an open weekend – effectively an advertising stunt – and Christo was there to advise visitors and sign books, but fate was against them: rain slewed down all weekend and, to save his shoes, Christo found himself paddling around in the mud unsuccessfully in clogs; but the real bugbear was that he spoke no Dutch and he always hated being out of the conversation, however kind people were to him. With no words, he could not do what he did best; it was no better than being deaf. At the end of the first day there was to be a party, and as usual Romke the Lad had too much to drink. The next day Piet took Christo around nurseries and research stations before delivering him back to the airport. 'Piet is kind, thoughtful and generally understanding. I expect he and Anja and the boys will come to Dixter.' They did, visiting for eight days a few weeks later, and Christo enjoyed their company.

* Piet has gone on to be an internationally renowned nurseryman and designer, notably working at New York's 9/11 Garden of Remembrance, and more famous in the English-speaking world than in his home country. His style centres on the use of grasses and perennials, marshalled by volumes of shrubs, sometimes clipped into organic shapes.

As time went by, Romke began to write in the national papers and get some television work and his widening reputation brought attention to himself and to the nursery. It was the cause of jealousy and friction that led to fisticuffs with Piet, and Romke being bought out. The two went their separate ways most successfully, Piet as nurseryman and designer, Romke as writer and broadcaster. Christo's loyalty to bad-boy Romke remained absolute, as did his anger with Oudolf.*

Christo's influence was beginning to broaden. By the late 1970s he was now giving advice professionally, at Hole Park in Kent, and sitting on the RHS's Woody Plant Committee. The International Plant Propagators' Society held regular weekend conferences at different locations throughout Britain every year, and Christo took careful notes at them all, especially on propagation, which would be useful in the nursery. In recognition of his writing and gardening, the Royal Horticultural Society awarded him its coveted Victoria Medal of Honour in 1979, a privilege and recognition shared by only a small and select group of people at any one time.

Dixter, however, was not yet the open house it became in Christo's later years. Alan Roger would stay occasionally, and John Treasure perhaps once a year, but mostly visitors still came only for lunch or to play bridge. Christo's old housekeeper knew how to cook just as he liked it, sticking to all Daisy's old Frankfurt recipes, but when she died her replacement was not so obliging. They quarrelled, and she left in 1978, after which Christo decided he must learn to do without a cook and provide for himself. It was easier.

In loco parentis, Christo was now at loggerheads with Pam next door and found Quentin a lazy estate manager. Eventually, they were not on speaking terms, communicating either by notes or via Romke. Quentin and Pam came to Dixter only for that obligatory Dixter institution, Christmas lunch in the Great Hall, where the atmosphere was like ice.

The garden began to coast along rather understaffed and under-polished, Christo himself being effectively the head gardener and Romke there as his second. Visitors complained about the lack of a tea-room and that the grass had not even been cut. This remark came of being

---

* Mention of Piet Oudolf was one of the few things that could reduce Christo to the use of bad language (never very bad, by anyone else's standards).

met, right at the front gate, by Christo's flower meadows, which had not yet become an item of popular fashion, even if they appeared in larger, 'more gentlewomanly' gardens. Certainly meadow grass then had no association with ecology and biodiversity; it was an aesthetic issue for Christo, and remained so all his life.

The year of 1977 saw the revision of *Clematis*, which had been published by *Country Life* in 1965. Now, instead of photographs, it came with watercolours by Marjorie Blamey, and was a thorough revamp of the 1965 book, but every bit as enjoyable and quirky as its predecessor. Although Christo admitted to using the same framework and some of his original text, it *was* a more comprehensive work, drawing on his new experiences of old favourites and latest introductions, and reflecting carefully on the progress that had been made in propagation and disease. It remained the freshest and most definitive book on clematis for many years, and was way ahead of its contemporaries (he later revised it once more, in 1989, this time in collaboration with Tom Bennett). Never again did he write a monograph: his interest was much more in putting plants *together*.

His hunger to see more plants never abated. With brother Oliver, Christo visited south-west Ireland to see the gardens at Fota and Garinish, and to look at the rare flora of the Burren. His annual Scottish forays provided him with new subject matter for *Country Life*, and at Dundonnell he met rare-book dealers Colin Hamilton and his friend Kulgin Duval, and was invited to see them next year at their house, Frenich, near Pitlochry. He loved the place at once, its rushing spate river surrounded by blue poppies and martagon lilies, its golden meadow garden running down to the loch, and after the blaze of Dixter Christo was jealous of its stylish simplicity and cool, northern ambience.

The three men – Colin Hamilton, Kulgin Duval and Christo – had much in common – gardening, a love of Glyndebourne, ceramics. Colin and Kulgin owned pieces by Lucy Rie, whose work had entranced Christo in the early 1960s, and Dixter contained many pieces of valuable majolica, collected by his parents. He himself collected some modern, heavily glazed ceramics in later years. Gradually, like Dundonnell, Frenich became another home-from-home. 'They have a great range of clothes!' quipped Christo, the man whose outfit so rarely changed. Not for him the pale, elegant linen suits that looked so well on tall, quietly spoken Colin.

Colin and Kulgin were also liberally commissioning new furniture from the designer Rupert Williamson, near Salisbury, and Christo fell in love with its pale curves and immaculate surfaces, so unlike Dixter's ancient stiff-legged pieces fixed under generations of wax polish. It was not just Rupert's designs that appealed to Christo, but the idea of putting new high-quality work into an old house. It gave him confidence to do this inside Dixter, just as – outside – he added fresh ideas to the garden.

As Christo started to have friends to stay regularly, his miserable cooking skills at last began to develop – there was more to an evening than two whiskies and a banana – and he took great pleasure in it. Daisy's recipes were there in the drawer, familiar all his life; and they formed the backbone of his future cuisine. Cooking was yet another field in which to study and make detailed observation, nowhere clearer than in a series of highly acclaimed tasting notes on apples for the RHS, of delightful accuracy. Of the variety 'Jester':

Apple 'Jester' (A116/28)
Worcester x Starkspur Golden Delicious
Good globe shape. V. waxy finish. Soft red on sunny side. Green undertone though I've kept it over 3 weeks. Flesh soft but crisp. Unusually white. Slight aroma with little personality. Sweet. An easily eaten apple that leaves you without a thought in your head.

His words came to the attention of the gardener and wine-writer Hugh Johnson, who discussed applying Christo's nose and words to wine, but it never came off, although wine entered his life in other ways. Since his visit to Kenya in 1946, Christo had lost touch with Renate and Walter Schuster, to whose son Michael he was godfather. Walter had died in 1962, and Renate and Michael moved back home to Cambridge. When a friend of Renate visited Dixter in 1979 and praised the garden, Renate wrote to Christo to renew contact, and he – rather ashamedly – wrote to his godson, now an adult, asking him to come for the weekend, 'to see if they liked each other'. They did, and became firm friends for life. For Michael's birthday in 1980 Christo wrote 'Many happy returns of the day! Paul [Hirsch] gave me your details on a post card 32 years ago and this is the first time I have used them. Better late than never.'

Michael adored Dixter, and he was just as interested as Christo in music and in wine, which was his profession. When he and Oliver were both at Dixter there would be live music-making, Oliver on piano, Michael on his horn, and it thrilled Christo to see the place ringing with music again. He had largely given up playing himself, and the only means of making music at Dixter was, at this point, the ancient 78s that the family had collected before the war and which lay closeted like Babylonian tablets in a cupboard. Michael persuaded Christo to buy a brand-new, upmarket hi-fi, the greatest piece of hi-tech Dixter saw for many years, and it struck a curious but lively note among Nathaniel's old English furniture; it was this kind of everyday domestic parapher-nalia that visitors to the house loved to see – the sense of the house being lived in.

Michael and his wife Monika became regular visitors at Dixter. By way of return, their house became Christo's base in London, and Michael would book four or five operas a year for Christo at Covent Garden or the Coliseum. Christo insisted on paying, because he always wanted seats right at the front on account of his increasing deafness. He came up to town on the train, and Monica took him off for oysters before seeing a film, usually something foreign, often sexy and with subtitles. He might squeeze in a visit to his dentist. And then in the evening, after the opera (always half a bottle of champagne first, the rest at the interval), Michael would drive him back to Dixter and stay the night. (Only eighteen months before he died did Christo give up his London nights, realising that he was too doddery for his own good and his minders.) In Michael, Christo had found someone he could write to as he most enjoyed, and his letters covered anything from a recent produc-tion of The Oresteia or the complete works of Emily Dickinson, to a particular interpretation of Parsifal or a request for a couple of cases of a specific claret. Letters provided him with companionship during those quiet evenings at Dixter when live company was absent.

It comes as a surprise to people familiar with Christo in his later years, the King of Perennials, to discover that he was just as interested in woody plants and especially in conifers. He loved to go to the arboretum at Bedgebury and see the pines and spruces and hone his skills in identifi-cation. Such was his breadth of expertise. There one day he got chatting to a young man up a tree, who it turned out was an impecunious

Hungarian researching for a book on conifers. As he so often did, Christo generously threw out the hand of friendship in the dark and asked him to Dixter, and they became friends, Christo even lending money in due course towards the publishing of the book. They talked and talked, and the result was a trip to Hungary in 1979 as a guest of his new friend, Zsolt Debreczy, international specialist in cacti and conifers, but who also had a wide knowledge of the European flora that Christo wanted to know better.

Hungary was a different world for Christo and the roughest he had encountered since the army, but now he was in entirely sympathetic company. Budapest, when he stepped off the plane, was an oven, and Zsolt met him in a little two-stroke car and whisked him off to his sister's flat on the edge of the city, Christo staring out of the window at poplars, walnuts and apricots and mounds of fragrant oleaster, as they passed through streets mauled during the German occupation in 1944–5 and still under repair, their good baroque fronts remaining where the Russian army had got in sooner. Everywhere balconies sagged, propped up with wooden scaffolding.

Zsolt and his wife lived in an unenviable tenement on £40 a month, but were happy and endlessly hospitable, and glad to take Christo to local beauty spots, an open-air museum, concerts, the opera, and a restaurant where gypsies were playing Brahms' *Hungarian Dances* around the tables. As an honoured English guest, Christo was serenaded with a foot-stamping rendition of 'Daisy, Daisy, give me your answer, do!'

There were horticultural visits: to the Botanical Institute of Hungary ('*awful* clematis collection') and, more productively, to the countryside around Lake Balaton, where there were large suckering colonies of dwarf almond and smoke bush, and self-sown petunias reverted to the wild form and fabulously perfumed. In the plains to the south-east of Budapest they visited sand dunes and wetlands, and everywhere there were birds – golden orioles and great crested grebes.

Christo was touched because his generation was respected by young Hungarians; everybody he met was poor, but nevertheless they honoured and protected him. They found him generous, fascinating, but perplexingly, physically buttoned-up and unadventurous. *Why* would he not try the thermal baths – they were not just for the young. At least Zsolt managed to make him take his first swim for thirty years, an enterprise so exhausting that he fell asleep for an hour afterwards. The swim, unexpected as it was, required Christo to lash out on a pair of trunks, which did not even have elastic at the waist, just a string cord with a large bead at each end to stop it slipping. 'One bead immediately came off and disappeared. A safety-pin was brought to the rescue . . .' It seemed as if, for Christo, physical pleasures were just not meant to be. Would he dance now, would he try? Would his new life set him free physically? *Certainly not.*

He coped better and more happily with physical *endurance* – he was a Lloyd, after all – and that is what he got on his next three-week trip to Hungary in 1981 (Christo was now sixty), when Zsolt drove him to see alpine meadows in the Carpathian Mountains, in Czechoslovakia near the Polish border. Five of them clattered round in one car, sleeping with friends and family, three to a room on bed-settees or cots, in places where fuel was scarce and the bath was only ever used as a hand basin. The police were suspicious of Christo since he was a lone visitor, not on a package holiday, and in one town he and their hostess were required to report to the police for a full half-hour's interrogation. Since Christo was an important visitor, she was allowed to sit in the police's presence during the interview. As ever he was cross, but not fazed by petty authority.

They drove into Romania too, through rice fields where storks stood on chimneys and electricity poles, past churches that were filled with madonna lilies. The police searched the car this time, and fined Christo 200 florints for not reporting at once to the authorities. He might have got away with it if he had been more cooperative, ready to negotiate and wave a note or two; but what he lacked in physical bravery he made up for in stubbornness and in resistance to unreasonable authority, even if it meant suffering for it. But how he now hated so much of Romania – the queues for food, the vile, cheap (to him) state-run hotels, the dreadful roads, the meanness of it all (even his Dundee cake ran out!), and then in Transylvania the military camps and the towns smelling of stale piss; the camp sites full and Romanian citizens not allowed to put up foreigners for the night, especially Hungarians, as it deprived the hotels of income (for putting up a Westerner such as Christo, ordinary people could be punished). To his astonishment, the pretty churches were the only places where Hungarians living in Romania were officially allowed to meet and speak Hungarian. Romania offended Christo's civilised, liberal values, and yet he was having a wonderful time in the company of Zsolt's family and friends, seeing flowers, trees, fascinating pines and spruces, and listening to Zsolt play his guitar, which he did at the drop of a hat. It was like looking through a window at another, easier life. Like Romke's. Christo could have it on loan, for the holiday.

Chapter 9

The New World, 1981–90

Gardeners cannot rest on their spotted laurels.
Robin Lane Fox to Christo, 2001

Parts of the Long Border at Dixter could be lush to the point of wanton-ness. To make a good day out, garden lovers often combined Dixter with Sissinghurst, now in the hands of the National Trust and so well kept that Vita herself would not have recognised it. Weed-free, every-thing superbly labelled, good facilities for the public . . . By comparison Dixter was shabby, weedy in parts, and of course unlabelled (the best one could do was look to see if the same plant was in evidence in the nursery). Sissinghurst, then, was at a peak of technical brilliance and complexity, but Dixter had soul; also, one thing Dixter had over Sissinghurst was a potential sighting of the old man Lloyd himself, weeding, and reputedly as snappy as his dogs.

Dixter was perhaps an unfocused experience, but it had wonderful highlights: the Long Border, rich in shrubs for foliage effect and with muscular perennials in a mixed range of often very strong colours; Nathaniel's Sunk Garden centred on its pool, where Christo could play with areas of bedding out; and the meadows, which had been steadily developing in richness since the 1920s. It was overall a more peaceful garden then, there were more contrasts of atmosphere, more relaxation, a steadier if less ambitious agenda. Some visitors found the garden's shabbiness unacceptable, while others found it charming. Technically, the whole garden was certainly at a low ebb, the soil weary and hungry, and all of it ready for a big kick in the pants. It was, in effect, as much as one man's drive, with plenty of hands-on help, could manage. Especially a man whose eye was looking beyond

Daisy Lloyd, happy with motherhood, c 1913. (*Inset*) Daisy with her husband Nathaniel.
Proud of her descent from Oliver Cromwell, she enjoyed wearing Puritan dress.

Dixter: stencil work on plaster, in Lutyens' new wing. Every year the window ledges were laden with drying gourds and seedheads saved from the garden for next year's displays.

Christo's simple arrangement of oriental poppies in the Great Hall. He loved huge arrangements; but guests always found a perfect posy in their bedrooms.

Lutyens' staircase, with banister details by Nathaniel Lloyd. In the bedroom beyond, over the single four-poster bed, a pendant light bulb dangles hazardously from the canopy. So with all the beds. Water on the bedside tables was known to freeze.

Dining room table and suede-upholstered chairs by Rupert Williamson, used for many a fine dinner when set with silver and white linen and candles, in the little servants' hall, with barely room to get in and out of one's place. Christo loved to mix the old with the new.

Olivia, Christo's niece, at work in the kitchen, Christmas 1986. Note the Lutyens' dresser still containing Daisy's recipe books; the servants' bells in the corridor beyond; and the fridge dating from the 1950s.

Holders of the Royal Horticultural Society's Victoria Medal of Honour, 1997. Christo (second from right) sits alongside luminaries of the British gardening establishment. On his right: Valerie Finnis; next to her with button-hole: Graham Stuart Thomas (Full list on page viii)

The Meadow Garden with camassias. The small room above the porch became Daisy's bedroom after the Second World War, and then Christo's bedroom after Daisy's death in 1972.

The porch in 2003, with displays of potted plants. Christo, photographed with his friend, the American designer Anne Wambach, is sporting a T-shirt, for sale in the shop, with his own face lurking among various other pieces of printed Dixteriana.

The enclosed
Rose Garden in
the early 1980s,
its hedges and
paths designed
by Lutyens, and
planted with roses
by Christo and
his mother.

Christo and Fergus,
partners in crime,
uprooters of English
rose gardens.

In 1993, Christo and his head gardener, Fergus Garrett, removed the roses and replaced them with exotic perennials. After the storm of controversy had died down, the Exotic Garden became a fashion icon.

Coffee after lunch, by the Horse Pond, with friends from the north, 1985. From left to right: Colin Hamilton and Kulgin Duval from Frenich, Christo, Alan Roger from Dundonnell, Rosemary and Bob Seeley from the Tyne Valley. Tulip, 'the dachs', loved to lick the coffee grounds from the cups.

In the Yeoman's Hall, 1991. On the sofa: Beth Chatto, the 'incandescent' Ed Flint, Christo. Behind: Beth's nursery manager David Ward, Otto Fauser, Michael McCoy who acted as guide to Christo on his Australian tour.

Still gardening in his 80s. Christo at work with Fergus in the Long Border, which was designed by Lutyens to be equal in length to Gertrude Jekyll's border – 200 feet – and extended by Daisy and Christo to 300 feet

Dixter for stimulation. The renowned horticultural fireworks that appeared in the Exotic Garden, in 1993, could never have been made in the 1980s.

The nursery had begun to develop a reputation for much more than just clematis, in that time when specialist nurseries were developing fast. Every year in mid-April Christo would shut himself in the potting shed and sow seed, scores of packets, until it was all done; not a job for *staff*, that. There was a huge range of uncommon (but not necessarily new) perennials, unusual and occasionally tender shrubs, and some of the perennial plants he was using for bedding in the garden. Visitors came looking for the unusual, browsing through seas of pots or through rows of young clematis, kept upright by fastening them to lines of wire, like raspberry canes. But it was hardly hi-tech, and Christo stuck resolutely to many of the techniques he had set up in the 1950s, selling his plants out of little clay pots. The plants themselves were small too, not just because they took up less space in the nursery like that, packed side by side in the cold frames, but because he felt it was important to plant things out small, for the sake of their better development. The plants were not individually priced or labelled, but by going round the nursery with a wire supermarket basket and a copy of his famous little catalogue, you could see what you were spending; then the basket was taken into the gloomiest of potting sheds, for a sum to be done on a bit of paper and money taken into a cash box. Unless you had a catalogue with your purchases marked upon it, you could get home and find, if the plants looked similar, that you had not a clue which plant was which. The expectation was that you knew what you were buying; making you take note was rather like telling gardener friends to keep a notebook – they must pay attention to detail. The Dixter sales technique has never significantly changed to this day.

At the end of every day Christo would appear in the nursery, conspicuously checking his watch to see that no one had left early. The day's takings would be delivered into his hands and the wad of notes stashed in a pocket, where it might turn up weeks later, occasionally having been through the washing machine.

Oliver came home regularly to join Christo for the Glyndebourne summer opera festivals, and every year Christo would lay on his annual summer party at Dixter for twenty to thirty Glyndebourne staff and artists. Oliver was now a skin-cancer specialist at Bristol University and was more conspicuously eccentric than Christo: hugely tall, long-faced and moustachioed, a Terry-Thomas of a man. His home in Bristol was Withey House, a well-known Modernist house once immaculately kept, but since the death of PJ he had ceased to do any cleaning. The house, with its spinet, piano and bottles of diver's oxygen all grossly shrouded with cobwebs, won second place in a competition for the worst-kept home. His garden was chaos, a wildlife refuge. Not that he cared; he would rather indulge his considerable expertise in caving, produce plays, and write music for the University Dramatic Society. (At Cambridge he had had his politically incorrect pantomime scripts censored by the Vice Chancellor's office.) For the 600th anniversary of Bodiam Castle, down in the valley below Dixter, Oliver composed a score for a celebration with fireworks and champagne. At Bristol he was known as 'the man who wears no socks' (he liked to keep his feet hard for walking) and his sixtieth and seventieth birthdays were both celebrated with sherry and cake in a cave. In 1985 Oliver – nine years Christo's senior – died, suddenly, aged seventy-three. Of Daisy's six children, only Quentin and Christo now remained alive.

There were the warmest of obituaries for this remarkable, multi-talented man. If his sister had been the kindest but most guilt-ridden sibling, Oliver was the least touched by the emotional demands of Dixter and Daisy; he had not so much escaped Dixter as never been pinned down by it. Christo and Daisy had deliberately resolved not to look back, but it never even occurred to Oliver to look back. He was a free spirit. Christo knew that, and was lonely without him and the link that Oliver had provided with a wider world.

Christo continued to visit Scotland in June or September, often adding in Orkney or Skye. Sometimes he would take the motorail to Inverness, then perhaps stay with garden-owning, castle-dwelling friends, or nurserymen friends, but always ending up at Dundonnell. Here he walked, come rain or shine, kept up his embroidery (stitching away through aperitifs before a meal) and wrote his long letters to drop into Dundonnell's own letter box close to collection time; too early a drop incurred predation by its population of ravenous slugs.

Dundonnell had become a clearing house for the horticulturally minded and it was here, by chance, that Christo first met a dapper young American, Tom Cooper, who was looking at gardens that might be featured in *Horticulture* magazine in the USA (he was its editor) and who, coincidentally, had already written to Christo asking if he would contribute. It was a connection that would lead to a great many trips abroad.

Staying with his friends Colin Hamilton and Kulgin Duval at Pitlochry, Christo became ever more thrilled by their Rupert Williamson furniture and began to commission pieces of his own. It was the pale woods he loved – the maples and the hollies – which looked good in the simple, low interiors of Frenich, but which would always seem a little ingénue at Dixter among the spindled, old English furniture bought by his parents, and which seemed so at home in Lutyens' stark, dark oak interiors; the problem was not that Williamson's furniture was modern, but that it was not chosen to complement what was already there. Colin Hamilton said that Christo missed a trick by not letting Williamson furnish a whole room at Dixter in a vein sympathetic to the building, instead of commissioning one-offs for different rooms about the house: a table here, an armchair there, a standard lamp, a waste-paper bin, a door . . . Williamson's dining table and chairs for the servants' hall at Dixter are in themselves superb, but hardly seen to advantage there, for all the happy times they witnessed. But for Christo, commissioning new work was keeping himself young. He enjoyed changing things and adding to things, just as he did in the garden. Williamson was asked down to Dixter, to discuss his commissions at length; it was enjoyable and fascinating to see his furniture in its slightly disconcerting habitat, but the time taken up wiped out a considerable amount of his profit.

At Pitlochry, Christo would help with a little light gardening and enjoy the chance to read uninterrupted his beloved Chekhov stories, which were always placed at the bedside. The lonely poetry of Philip Larkin one might have expected to strike a sympathetic chord in Christo, but no. Of 'High Windows' he wrote, 'Not for me! How much Larkin missed of the warmth, kindness and loving of human relationships.' Daisy would have been proud.

Some years he would take a friend to Scotland, perhaps Michael Schuster, with whom he made distillery tours to try single malts. Once or twice he took his friend Beth Chatto, whose garden in the badlands of Essex was becoming a pilgrimage site for gardeners who loved good foliage. Christo admired Beth and adored her company, although he could also reduce her to tears with a kind of rudeness that he only ever used against people he knew extremely well, people he expected to be as tough as himself. Theirs was a strange relationship. 'Too much of a slave to what she calls ecology,' said Christo of her desire to put together the kinds of plants that, wherever their origin, shared similar conditions in the wild. It was a principle learned from her beloved and scholarly husband Andrew, latterly an invalid, and who, Christo insisted self-righteously, held her back from having a fuller life. Still, Beth and Christo got on like a house on fire, happily, chattily – he liked sparky women – and the evenings during their trips would always end with a conspiratorial nip of whisky, brought by him in a bottle for cheapness, and a slice of home-made Dundee cake. Wherever in the world he went, the cake and the single malt went with him.

Return journeys always included a pit stop. His diaries were as blunt as ever. Of Robin Spencer at York Gate, 'I can't believe his appalling teeth'; of Jim Russell, the famous nurseryman and woodland gardener at Castle Howard, 'Indefatigable, generous, civilised, humorous, a snob'; and of the famously camp, double-breasted flower arranger George Smith near York, 'lots of *good taste* – the hotter colours confined to *one* bed . . .'

In the summer of 1981 he drove down to Devon to stay with Dr Jimmy Smart, whose garden at Marwood Hill was well known. Christo, by his own admission, had two near-misses when overtaking, and the whole trip could be described as a third. Jimmy he found a chilly mortal, while the garden was 'just a rash of plants, none of which (or very few) have personality in the landscape. No vision for the *scene!*'

It was the day of the wedding of Prince Charles to Diana Spencer, and Jimmy recorded it on video so that they could watch it in the evening, in the course of which Jimmy fell asleep. The next day they went to Braunton Burrows, that great area of fixed sand dunes with its extraordinary flora, which Christo had last visited with Oliver in the 1930s. They wandered edgily round the site before setting off for Anne Palmer's garden at Rosemoor. This too was not to Christo's liking: 'Excellently kept but she is even less good than Jimmy at interrelating her plantings. As in public gardens, every plant is disassociated from the next by bare earth.' (The garden now belongs to the Royal Horticultural Society, of whose gardens Christo was apt to say the same.)

The following day Christo was due to speak at the Garden House near Tavistock, a garden under imaginative development by Keith Wiley, but created by ex-schoolmaster Lionel Fortescue. At the lecture there was a grand audience of thirty and Jimmy managed to stay awake, but the occasion felt very much like small beer, however much Christo wanted to please Wiley. Crying off a visit to Knightshayes, he scuttled back to Dixter with some new plants, some good photographs and a few ideas for his *Country Life* column.

But Christo's tours of Britain, and especially his beloved Scotland, were about to be eclipsed. 1983 saw the first of his international lecture tours, on this occasion to the USA and Canada. He was uncertain at first about how he would take to the Americans and expected to find them appallingly brash, not least in comparison to his generous but poverty-stricken Eastern European friends. Should he accept the invitation? Would it be worth it? It was, and very quickly Christo came to love the Americans for their enthusiasm and spontaneity, qualities which he knew he had lacked himself for so much of his life. After Hungary, Western creature comforts were not unwelcome, either. American trips began to form a contrasting part of Christo's life: there were the steady, cold-climate trips to Scotland for the company of old friends and acquaintances; home life at Dixter; his rough and intriguing tours to eastern Europe, which made him feel rather brave and adventurous; and then America, his bit of glamour, where rather to his surprise he was not just a writer, but a celebrity writer, and was treated like one. Who would not love it? He could even *flirt*, in his oblique sort of way, with young men he took a shine to, and, in his diary, he could be as rude as he liked about the apparent failings of American horticulture.*

In Vancouver, he spoke on 'Hardy Perennials and Foliage' at the VanDusen Botanical Garden. It went well beyond his greatest

* He was once no more than usually rude in his diary about the husband of the couple with whom he was staying; leaving the diary on the dresser in his bedroom, he came back from a day looking at wild flowers, to find his diary read and his suitcases sitting on the doorstep, which he was never, ever to darken again.

expectations, and his smallest joke was greeted with gales of laughter. Naturally he was flattered, but it made him realise how desperate the American audiences were to be entertained. It was difficult not to play up to it.

His host was Ken Hadley a gardener at the Vancouver Botanical Garden. He looked ten years younger than his thirty-four, and bubbled over with energy. 'Typical plantsman,' harrumphed Christo, 'down on his knees to minutiae. As one expects, it's the welfare of the plants that concerns him, not their arrangement.' That soon changed; Christo was caught up by Hadley's irresistible gift for cheerfulness and was pleased to be driven by him to Seattle for his next engagement, a Hardy Plant Society study weekend. 'We see things in very much the same light,' Christo was soon saying, 'the difference in upbringing seems to make no difference here.' The journey involved stopping at nurseries along the way (Ken loved his alpines) and they were late for the lecture. Fortunately for Christo, Brian Halliwell, famous for his ambitious bedding schemes at Kew, had been talking on propagation in his inimitable, harsh, northern drawl for fully two and a half hours and the audience was intact, but exhausted. This was something to be got used to in America: audiences wanted value for money, *lots* of slides, and *long* lectures. People had come from as far afield as San Francisco to hear Christo and there were 'endless' books to be signed.

The trip included a visit to the Olympic Mountains to see the temperate rainforests, and it was no picnic: 300 miles in logging traffic and a night in a logging town whose sole attraction was a bed of junipers top-dressed with a bright-red mulch, which turned out to be cranberry skins. But the trees and the mosses that hung upon the mountains were entrancing, and on Hurricane Ridge there were erythroniums, creeping dogwood and lupins. Flying to Portland in a sixteen-seater, Christo looked down on the smoking Mount St Helens volcano and on logs tossed aside like skittles by the eruption of 1980, then gave a lecture at the Berry Botanic Garden. 'I don't think [the curator] really has a clue about making a really good garden,' he wrote, 'but then neither does anyone else out here.' After a last couple of days with Ken and his wife Sonya, he flew home, puzzled, delighted and appalled by the New World.

* * *

The year of 1983 saw the publication of Christo's *The Adventurous Gardener*, under the imprint of Allen Lane. Along with *The Well-Tempered Garden* and *Foliage Plants*, it established his reputation. It is even the same size and weight as the previous books, and Christo imagined these three titles as a natural progression for his readers. All were words books, with very few pictures. He had established his audience for this kind of book, having received good reviews for the first two, and now he felt free to paint himself large in the picture, to drop in the names of other gardeners and writers without explanation – Beth Chatto, Roy Lancaster, John Street – and to refer to his previous books as if they were already part of gardening literature (they were). He credited his readers with plenty of background knowledge, so that no time needed to be wasted, and just assumed they would be comfortable with references to plants and gardens in Scotland and Hungary, and know about the International Plant Propagators' Society and the Rose Society's garden at St Albans.

He never wrote better than when he was rolling a subject around, talking plants and practicalities and principles all in the same breath, and *The Adventurous Gardener* let him do just that. It was a free-ranging collection of chapters lumped into four sections; but they could just as effectively have been arranged at random. One minute he was talking cuttings, the next discussing plants in dry walls or garden visitors, and it all flowed like a dream.

Nowhere else does Christo write quite so freely about other garden writers, and this sets his own style in context. Reginald Farrer, for instance, the author of *The English Rock Garden*, was praised for his ability to eulogise lyrically as well as to debunk accepted wisdom, but mostly for practising the attention to detail equalled only by the powers of observation and annotation that Daisy had instilled in Christo. Farrer wanted his readers to take a notebook to any garden they visited: 'If you force yourself to describe [a plant] in a note you force yourself to look at it properly, analytically. Thereafter you must re-read your notes within twenty-four hours and then again, within the next few days, do a bit of looking up.' It was what Christo himself did and the thing that, he felt, enabled him to do as Farrer did – to write something that was 'a joy to dip into because you keep discovering gems of description and comment that you had missed hitherto'. When Christo saw people in the garden at Dixter with notebooks, he went up to them and spoke straight away.

Daisy and Christo were both admirers of Gertrude Jekyll and the soundness of her writing, her 'masterpieces', because she knew how to grow plants superbly well and also how to use them artistically. She recognised that the best kinds of gardening are not easy, and respected the value of using sufficiently large blocks of plants; no spottiness for her. At her home, Munstead Wood, there was a border 200 feet long by 14 feet wide, and Christo constantly compared it to his own Long Border which was originally the same length, but a foot wider (Daisy and Christo were responsible for lengthening the Dixter Long Border, as designed by Lutyens. Did they do this to gain more growing space *or* to compete with The Great Gertrude's border? In truth, the Dixter border was livelier than Jekyll's, precisely because it changed so much more over its lifetime and was an experiment over and over again.)

In Jekyll's writing the idea that there is such a thing as 'good taste' was totally accepted, especially when it came to the use of colour. Christo was also keen to pronounce on individual preferences. He denounced those 'dreadful brash juxtapositions' of plants (mostly rhododendrons) in April and May at the Savill Garden, the Hillier Arboretum, Inverewe and Exbury. 'I just don't happen to believe that "it's all a matter of taste" excuses or justifies every indiscriminate use of colour in gardening. I believe there are absolute standards of what goes and what doesn't in matters of taste.' But in Christo's last years he notoriously took to using bright, loud colours in combinations that the 'good-taste brigade' found quite inexplicable and truly awful. Yet he would justify his juxtapositions with absolute confidence. Certainly, some pinks might look grim next to some yellows, but the *right* pinks and the *right* yellows could be wonderful. He was thrilled to see a great field full of pink ragged robin and yellow buttercups, when he and I went to look at meadows on the German-Austrian border – the right pink with the right yellow. And some plants he admitted he was almost blind to, despite their appeal to others: 'How can Persicaria "Donald Lowndes" be so handsome and effective and yet, basically, such a horrid plant? Well, there are people like that too.'

All the way through *The Adventurous Gardener* you can *hear* how Christo had his finger on the pulse of gardening. Though he was known as a shrubs and perennials man, he still loved his conifers and cacti and alpines. He was already starting to knock the popular obsession with dreary ground-cover plants ('ground un-cover plants', as he once called the vicious prostrate rose, 'Nozomi'), which had been fostered in part by *Plants for Ground Cover*, written in 1970 by his sparring partner Graham Stuart Thomas. Christo's catholic enjoyment of ambitious gardens was clear; he liked cool Scottish gardens just as much as dry Essex gardens and, in his book, he speculated on a gravel garden, of the kind that Beth Chatto would make a few years later: 'I should want an oleaster, shimmering with the heat and imparting gusts of sweet fragrance . . . nothing taller than a 4ft cistus or phlomis would gain entrance. The garden would undulate and billow between this height and nothing at all, with flat, pale flagstones or expanses of shingle emphasising the glorious, life-giving heat and glare.'

Hard on the heels of *The Adventurous Gardener* came his next book, *The Well-Chosen Garden*, Christo's first large-format picture book, illustrated throughout in order to explain the text and pinpoint the relationships of one plant to another. He was modernising.

It would be easy to dismiss this book as an also-ran, and certainly it did not have the writerly craftsmanship Christo had shown in his trio of major books to date; no great verbal dexterity or wit. But it did now stray beyond the bounds of his 'workshop' Great Dixter, allowing him to cover subjects that he had enjoyed in gardens elsewhere: little roadside gardens, raised beds, planting on tiled roofs, reflective foliage, and (exploring positively two of his bêtes noires) misused dwarf conifers and heathers. Its free-ranging scope was because the book sprang from a lecture that he liked to give, 'Placing Your Plants', but to complete its educational slant the book included a brief A–Z of good perennials, and geographic hardiness zones so that it might sell in the USA. Like all his books, it is admirably useful. But if one has become addicted to the Lloyd wit and provocation, then it seems tame.

September 1985 saw Christo off to the States once more, lecturing to audiences of 500 and 600, and this time on the east coast. The thrill of America had not diminished. How he admired the white clapboard villages and pale maple furniture. When dinners were hosted for him, everybody seemed to know Dixter already and many had visited. In New York he enjoyed Wave Hill and the New York Botanical Garden, but when his hosts took him to see Madison Avenue, Wall Street, Chinatown and the Statue of Liberty he found them all grubby and less impressive than he had expected, although Verdi's *Falstaff* at the Met soon cheered him up.

Then it was off to Boston and the Arnold Arboretum (in poor shape after a hurricane) for a symposium organised by Tom Cooper's *Horticulture* magazine. Christo was starting to get the measure of Americans now; they might seem self-important at first (how he struggled to like the great garden designer Jim van Sweden), but once he was through the professional façade he warmed to people soon enough; he and the 'dreadful' van Sweden parted good enough friends to share a trip to Glyndebourne. He was told one evening that Americans are all nice to each other because they may be *useful* to each other. 'But there must be times when they have to get it all out of their system,' protested Christo. 'They shoot each other,' he was told, 'in England you don't.'

Ohio was next, to see sassafras and tulip trees, magnolias and many different oaks. He was taken to see an Amish community and took a shine to their quilting and leatherware, and visited the Holden Arboretum. Good-looking young men with beards were everywhere.

Cleveland next (he was starting to feel his age – sixty-four – from burning the candle at both ends, but still he was on a high), tucking in a trip to hear Erich Leinsdorf conduct the Cleveland Symphony Orchestra. Now Washington, DC, and the US Botanical Garden, and Dumbarton Oaks, making his audiences laugh, but giving them plenty of information too, feeling he was giving his money's worth, spotting plants for his own garden and collecting people for Dixter – women who *organised* and men who appealed. A trip to see the swamp cypresses (he had always wanted to do that), then Baltimore, and Washington high into the hills to look for autumn colour (too late). There were nurseries to see and always more people to meet and gardens to visit. Of Baltimore House, the Vanderbilt house: 'The gardens are awful and everyone thinks they're wonderful. Not a single feature that couldn't or shouldn't be done 100% better.' And finally, Heathrow again. He was having the time of his life. So what if his head gardener Tom Shepherd was leaving: he would do without one, he was really head gardener himself anyway, and there was more to life than Dixter.

Six months later he was off to the States again, this time to the west coast, and starting at the University of California Botanical Garden in Berkeley, which met with the disapproval he meted out to so many institutional gardens. 'As is fashionable nowadays,' he sniffed, 'the garden is laid out in Continents, or smaller areas. We only did Mexico and California and that took 1¼ hours. Well, it's better to be thorough about a bit than to strain over the whole thing.' The lecture went well and he was given an ovation. Interested young men were keen to talk and ask questions of the Master. 'You can get into terms of intimacy with people like this, in a few minutes, which is enormously stimulating.' He was too roused to sleep.

It would be easy to conclude that Christo was out to find fault with American gardens; but it was not so. Rather, it was that everything he ever saw he judged by Dixter standards, against his own garden, which had no agenda except to be ambitiously beautiful. No educational agenda, nothing ecological or social, just one big, earnest, painstaking, outgoing, aesthetic indulgence, which he carried off superbly well. Few gardens measured up, and those that got most marks received them for trying to do what he did, not for fulfilling their own aims. That was the way he was. Right and wrong by the Dixter rules. It gave him great confidence.

Now he was taken on a tour to see the Sierra Nevada, covering 200–300 miles a day, camping at night, and stopping the car all the time to look at plants. Carson City to Reno to Sacramento, and back again. He saw Ruth Bancroft's garden, which made a big impact – he loved it, and it cannot but have contributed to the genesis of his own Exotic Garden. 'She's a tiny little thing,' he put in his diary:

> 70 or so, green eyes, very bright and sweet. She has gradually turned her garden into one for cacti and succulents, agaves, aloes, etc. It's very well done with large island beds. One has beautifully constructed shade/winter protection, open sided, over it, a kind of conservatory. Her plants create beautiful living sculptures which make fascinating groups from a great many viewpoints. Much of her garden has to be swaddled in protective devices in the winter. She doesn't go into it a lot then.

It could almost be a picture of his Exotic Garden in winter, put to bed in November until the next summer, some plants wrapped in straw and fleece, others under their individual tents of plastic, and the whole thing out of sight and mind within Lutyens high hedges.

Next day he was up before 5 am and was driven 900 miles in two days to Seattle, to speak at a Hardy Plant Society's weekend symposium. The first speaker showed, 'uncritically', fully 200 slides, followed by another 200 from gentlemanly English bulb expert Brian Mathew. Now, exhausted, they were shown four members' snaps of Great Dixter, and all this as an introduction to Christo's own lecture, 'Plants I Enjoy'. Christo knew the Americans like value for money, but this was ridiculous. He despaired at such long-winded enthusiasm and having to speak after it. 'Incidentally,' he added, 'they've a video of the whole conference. Heaven help anyone who has to sit through it again – only a reporter needing evidence, I imagine.'

In Vancouver he went camping again, this time with Ken Hadley, to see more native flowers. Once again they got on well and it was agreed that they should go to Japan together, when Ken had scraped together enough money.

With *The Well-Tempered Garden*, *Foliage Plants* and *The Adventurous Gardener* under his belt, Christo rightly felt that he had a strong position in the world of gardening books, so it was with pleasure that he accepted an invitation from Viking (a Penguin imprint) to write unashamedly about Dixter itself, under the title *The Year at Great Dixter*. It was a move forward in that it contained glamorous pictures by Pamla Toler, alongside many of Christo's own, but it has nothing new to say, and the tone was almost nostalgic; there was much talk of Daisy and the garden as it used to be, alongside all the month-by-month life of the garden – composting, weedkilling and the rest. The photographs leave an impression that the garden was indeed quieter then, the structural plants more tightly controlled than they would become towards the end of Christo's life, when (rather as in his social life) he enjoyed seeing woody plants, old and picturesque, being used as a foil for the vigorous and colourful.

Christo's intense interest in plants as a child was undoubtedly odd, but his experience was not unique. In 1964 an eleven-year-old boy named Tom Bennett took out the book *Clematis* from his local library to satisfy his fascination with plants and subsequently ordered two clematis plants from Christo. In September 1987 Tom, now an environmental health officer in County Durham, was at a conference in Brighton and, with a spare afternoon, thought he might visit Dixter.

He telephoned, which was an uncertain thing at Dixter; you were just as likely to get someone in the nursery or the office as Christo in the Solar. But there was never any mistaking Christo. 'Hello?' he answered in his usual impatient bark. Rudely, he gave the opening hours. Tom was equally forthright back: a red rag to the bull. Christo said come. When Tom got there Christo was on his knees weeding in the Sunk Garden, rubber-gloved because of the plant allergies he had developed over the years. The garden was in a mess; it was just after the great gale of 1987 and the last of Lutyens' mulberries had been wrecked, as well as a massive wild pear that had stood outside the front door since before the Lloyds came to Dixter.

In the presence of his hero, Tom rambled on the subject of clematis, mentioning Christo's friend and clematis grower John Treasure along the way, and asking when Christo would republish *Clematis* (it was ten years since the last reprint from the publishers Collins). Christo was forever reluctant to revisit old ground and, with another of his leaps of faith, replied, 'I can't be bothered, would you do it with me?'

Perhaps to the surprise of both, Tom said yes. He was asked to leave his name and address and a couple of days later a postcard arrived in Durham confirming the proposal.

It was Tom's precocious interest in gardening, and clematis in particular, that appealed to Christo who, as a fourteen-year-old, had himself been thrilled when, in 1935, Ernest Markham, head gardener to the great writer William Robinson, had brought out his little book *Clematis*, published by *Country Life*. And so, over the next nine months, Tom would periodically abandon his family to spend a couple of days at Dixter; they would discuss a chapter of the old book, and Tom would make notes and go home and bash out a new version. On the next visit they would agree a text and move on to the next chapter. Then captions; 'Ah yes,' remarked Christo impishly, 'Comtesse be Bouchaud prostate on a lawn!' Finally paper proofs were bundled up and Tom took them to the post office in Hawkhurst to be posted.

Dixter was a new world to Tom – the shabby country-house style, the excellent food and wine – and he found himself feeling the odd one out at Christo's artistic weekend gatherings. He felt there was a sexual frisson in the air, as if he was the weekend's bit of Northern rough. Christo, in his usual provocative and sometimes supremely tactless manner, would pit people against each other in conversation, then sit back and watch how they fared. Tom could take so much of being set up, and would then nip outside to smoke a cigarette (on one occasion bumping into Paul McCartney, a neighbour, on his way in to deliver a Christmas card; Christo proudly *never* sent cards).

Like everyone else who visited Dixter regularly, one of Tom's duties as guest included lighting the log fire in the Solar with one-quarter of a firelighter put into his hand by Christo. As boys, Christo and his brothers had competed for weeks to see who could light it most easily, and Christo had once managed it with one match. Another duty was going into the cellar where the billiard table stood, to bring up bottles of Courage for lunch. 'Find anything?' asked Christo disingenuously one day. Tom had found, amongst the chaos down there, that someone had recently fished from some dark recess several square tins of Spillers Plain Flour, which, Christo explained, his 'mother had put down there against rationing in the war. Is it any use still, do you think?' At lunch two months later Christo asked, 'How's the steak pie, Tom, pastry okay?' It *was* okay, and it *was* the wartime flour. Beth Chatto, with some reluctance, had turned it into pastry.

Clematis, by Christopher Lloyd, revised with Tom Bennett appeared in 1989, published by Viking. It contained moments when Tom's ideas were directly credited and others when it was a discussion between the two of them. With it began Christo's enjoyment of dual-authorship books written as dialogue: *Garden Flowers from Seed*, with Graham Rice, appeared in 1991, and *Dear Friend and Gardener*, with Beth Chatto, in 1998. Tom, the lesser partner, was given a generous royalty-split by Christo and the book soon went international.

Clematis proved the spur for a change in Tom's life. A year later he left his job in public health and set up Bennett and Brown Clematis Nursery at Beamish, County Durham, with a small loan from Christo. In the same year Christo came to lecture at Kirkley Hall College in Northumberland, inspected the Gateshead Garden Festival and visited the nursery. He was unimpressed. The business was a struggle, and Tom later bought himself out to go back to his old profession. More recently the nursery has begun to thrive.

In America the word was definitely out that Christopher Lloyd was the man to hear, and in March 1989 he was off again to Georgia, for just two forty-five-minute lectures, to fully booked audiences of 400. He was meeting even more young people, and calling his coevals 'elderly'. To his notebook he confided his wish that men to whom he was attracted, and whom he judged to be in frustrating marriages, should get out of them, for their own sakes; no mention of his own long 'marriage' to Daisy. Adventure was it, now. Travel was it.

And so when an invitation came to speak alongside the great and good of the garden world at a design conference in Melbourne in early October 1989, he couldn't wait. Beth Chatto was becoming as famous for her garden in Essex as Christo was for Dixter and she, too, had important books to her name. *The Dry Garden* had been published in 1978, and a collection of her journalism in the *Daily Telegraph* appeared in 1985. She, too, had received an invitation to speak in Melbourne, but had refused, feeling that she was more a gardener than a writer. Christo persuaded her to go. The trip then expanded to become what he liked to call their World Tour, to New Zealand, Australia and America. And all this was happening for Christo, that year, on top of Georgia and Scotland. He was on a roll, and the faster he rolled, the louder became the colour of his shirts; people wondered who this stooped, pouting, portly old man with twinkling eyes under shrubby eyebrows and in a bright-mauve shirt might possibly be. Christo was spinning plates, out to show what he could do.

To be away from Dixter for a whole month meant writing a stack of articles before he left, which he did with relish, as well as preparing the slides for the different lectures he would give. The Australians were paying for them to travel Business Class, but offering no fee. Beth got to the airport first and waited in the Business Departure Lounge until Christo stumped tweedily in, clutching his peeling black leather bag like a character from *The Importance of Being Earnest*, then proceeded to pull out a paper bag of sandwiches and eat them there amongst 'the rich, bejewelled Arab ladies'. Now to the skies, over Russia and Afghanistan to Bangkok, and finally to Sydney. On arrival their hostess drove them into the city to see the harbour, bridge and opera house, which created no more impact on Christo than Manhattan ('Quite!') and then on to sleep at her house where, out of sync with local time, Christo woke at 5 a.m. on 21st September 1989, cold, on a sofa-bed, and watched Jupiter through the skylight. Never mind: what a trip this would be, what a new world: he had already spotted many eucalyptus, but oh, the tree ferns, the coral trees . . .

Auckland in New Zealand was heaven; he could not get over the number of plants coexisting happily in this climate that might have been expected not to cohabit, and plant cohabitation was, after all, his special subject. His talk to the Rose Society went well and there were piles of books to sign and people who knew him from meetings at Dixter. Assiduously he made diary notes of people's names and addresses, and of the quality of the wines. He and Beth took part in phone-in programmes on the radio and had their pictures taken for the newspapers. 'I sparkle throughout!' Christo chuckled.

Then it was west to Melbourne. Tired from inadequate sleep, Christo was low in patience, and in a phone-in he was cross to be pigeonholed as a clematis-only man. 'Okay, what then? Compost?' suggested the journalist about to host the programme. Christo settled for mixed borders.

They were taken to see the garden of Dame Elisabeth Murdoch (mother of Rupert Murdoch, the media mogul). They romped around the garden together in her four-seater buggy – she was eighty – and plunged down slopes and through bogs, as she showed him the alterations she was making. 'As though she were a girl,' he said afterwards, feeling challenged to be as adventurous.

Beth and Christo now left for Toronto, for the two-yearly Great Gardening Conference, here to speak alongside that great promoter of American gardens, Frank Cabot, and Christo's old friend Allen Paterson, director of the Botanic Garden at Hamilton, Ontario. Finally Minneapolis and more lectures, with a chance to see some real savannah grasslands that might help Christo enrich his meadows at home.

Christo always asked to stay with people rather than be put in a hotel, and with his high reputation, people were thrilled to have him, and generous with their time as well as their hospitality. More often than not, these days, Christo was hosted by gay couples, which he found comfortable, not least because they were always keen gardeners too. It was on this trip that he first properly understood and came to terms with the reality of AIDS, which horrified him. Yes, he was attracted sexually to male beauty, but mostly puzzled by lust. Learning about AIDS made him relieved that his delight in young men was with their minds as much as their bodies, with their *aspirations* and – as simple as this – their shared love of plants. Half of him would have loved a full relationship, which as far as I know he never had, and half of him was happy to sit behind the gauze of age and watch from the sidelines. Dreaming was easier than doing. But why should he not dream? This was *his* life, and Daisy and *l'affaire Piglet* were far behind.

Christo was now sixty-eight, but still ready to take on anything. Hardly had he time to turn round and write a few more articles than he was off on a jaunt to Tokyo in October 1989. This time he came down with a bump.

His travelling companion was Ken Hadley. This was the trip they had proposed the previous year in Vancouver. Ken, who was in charge, was not used to having the minutiae of a holiday completely fixed in advance; Christo was used to being fêted and *managed*.

Christo travelled alone from England and, racing off the plane in Japan to avoid customs queues, rushed to his hotel only to find that the hoped-for visit to the Imperial Gardens had not been organised at all. A bad start. Breakfast the next morning was 'too expensive', so instead he walked off into town. Making notes of the weeds in the gutters and gliding invisible, like a ghost, through the townspeople, he was pleased to be spared the embarrassment of being a foreigner unable to speak the language.

'Soon I am in the thick of a small town,' he noted:

Shops all temptingly displayed on open counters and quite small packets of tiny fish. Nobody *bothers* you or stares or tries to make you buy. It's easy to feel anonymous. Actually, I don't feel so immensely tall. Quite a lot of the young men are not far off my height – much taller, more strapping than the older folk.

I soon get to the temple I can see from my bedroom. It is a large complex of buildings on rising ground, well segmented by paths, areas of coarse gravel, bits of garden, water, fountains. Upright stones with inscriptions, walls of inscribed tablets, tailored bushes, a pool with tortoises and ornamental fish, ferns, a small moss garden from which the public are debarred. A tremendous number of people about, in holiday mood. In front of each Buddhist shrine is holy water, heated, which coloured pebbles are thrown into. You then dab yourself with the water. Up at each shrine, shoes are cast off and a circuit made within. I felt it would be intrusive to join in this. The buildings themselves have a certain panache, but they are excessively heavy, ponderous and elaborate, the decoration often ugly, but seldom tawdry as in Roman Catholicism. There is a certain unity and dignity, totally unappealing to me, but it's there.

I try to find the Naritasan Shinsou temple proper [this turned out to be it], but although I plod on for several miles I fail in this, so return largely by the same route, having done about 12 miles.

That evening Ken arrived from Vancouver and phoned his contact, the Reverend Hagiwara, who, to Christo's huge relief (how he disliked hotels!), said to come and stay. But, on every hand, embarrassment at not knowing what to do shamed Christo. He could not use chopsticks and took some from a restaurant to practise in his bedroom. He failed to remove his shoes on entering the Hagiwaras' house. He soaped himself in the deep hot-water tank in which everyone *soaked*, having first taken a soapy shower. Sleeping on the floor, he found it hard to write up his diary. Ken, by contrast, was an instant mixer, never shy in any company, the sort of person who weighed in whether he knew the language or not.

Hagiwara helped Ken fix the accommodation and programme for the rest of the trip and took them to see the sights, but it did not suit Christo: they stopped too rarely to look at plants, saw a boring rock-garden-cum-nursery at great length, and the place where they expected to see autumn colour was overrun with coach parties. Christo lost his camera by leaving it on the roof of the car as they drove off. No, he would not bathe in a sulphur spring, and nor would he attend his host's church. 'Our host's knowledge of plants,' he concluded, 'is very limited. He likes them best if they are rare and expensive, but that sounds unfair because he is a dear.'

When Christo was in the company of enthusiast plantspeople, as he had been in Hungary, he enjoyed the rough and tumble of sharing ordinary homes, but now the public indignity of youth hostelling in Japan proved to be something else entirely. Their room had eight bunks, the water was cold and the washing communal. Christo had been happy camping in America, assumed Ken, so why not this?

They did get to see Watanabe's famous iris nursery, and Mr Watanabe himself looked after them for fully two days, but Christo distrusted his lack of *enthusiasm* for the plants. In restaurants Christo was humiliated

by difficulty in sitting cross-legged on the floor and admitted, 'I have
come too old to enjoy these very new experiences and have to admit
that I'm less adaptable than I was. Much as I should like this to be,
this is not a relaxed holiday (my bowels and piles tell me that) but then
I never expected it to be. And I'd still rather not be feather-bedded
from the real thing by a package tour.'

By bus, now, to Omorika, for a tour of the Japanese alps. Their host,
when Ken telephoned, wanted to know which hotel they were booked
into. No home hospitality here, then; so a bearable last-minute hotel
was found and Christo was left wondering if Ken was simply tired of
planning ahead. At 2 a.m. there was a fight in the room next door and
Christo asked the manager to find them another room. Ken had a bad
cold and Christo dreaded catching it.

They now took the bullet train to Tokyo, to do the tourist sights and
gardens. 'So much gravel!' he lamented. And what was the pleasure in
rock and gravel raked in circles, and places awash with pesky schoolchildren? At this low point, Ken left Christo alone for a few days, as
they had planned in Vancouver, while he went to see friends.
Unaccustomed to the indignity of getting by without the language,
Christo sulked, finding it easier to get two fruit drinks and a bag of
crisps than buy lunch. In the evenings he consumed his whisky and
Dundee cake in the hotel, before going out to a snack restaurant for
bacon spaghetti. By day he saw *more* dreary temples in the rain, and
he *did* get Ken's dreadful cold. He sat in his room writing postcards and
pieces for *The Guardian* and reading *Death of a Salesman*, which he had
picked up in an English bookshop

When Ken returned, a depressed Christo blamed him for his own
discomforts and they began to go their separate ways. Christo concluded:

> Travelling with a companion puts you both to severe tests, because
> there are many moments of tension, uncertainty and discomfort
> when you are feeling low. It is not for nothing that I live alone,
> but I don't think I've been too difficult on this trip. On many
> occasions I have held my tongue when I could have pointed out
> some unreasonableness. Well, at my age I should be able to do
> that. And anyway the interest of the trip was all of Ken's making.
> At the end of it, however, while recognising his adventurous and
> questing nature, I have to admit that I think less rather than

more highly of him as a person. In a good mood he's the best of companions. The best way to catch him like that is to see him occasionally and for not too long at a time.

Like Daisy, Christo was right whatever his faults.

Chapter 10

The Youth Vote, 1990–2000

In a month there will be purple stars on the clematis, and year after year the green might of its leaves will hold its purple stems. But we never get back our youth.

Lord Henry Wotton in *The Picture of Dorian Gray*,
1890, by Oscar Wilde

Perhaps it was the thought of his forthcoming book *The Cottage Garden* (1990) that was getting Christo down, for it was not to be his finest. This time he was writing for the publisher Dorling Kindersley, which specialised in step-by-step and how-to books, often for beginners – hardly his style – and was working with a co-author Richard Bird. Only a few thousand words, but still getting half the royalty, and with his name big on the cover: how could he afford not to do it? 'I have sold out to Mammon,' he said, shamefaced.

Sentimentality oozes from the book's every page, as an image is drawn of kindly country people – *cottagers* – busying away in a sepia glow amongst their flowers and vegetables and herbs. Even the text is sepia-coloured. You can feel the words being ground out like meat through a fine mincer: 'Steps are normally considered to belong to the grander garden than the humble cottage garden . . . the main reason for including herbs in our gardens is to use them for flavouring food . . . you will require a spade and fork for digging and lifting.' How could he do it? There were pretty-pretty pictures throughout and an ugly, over-complicated layout, with 'instructive' crayon views of putative cottage gardens – 'This cottage gardener has obviously indulged his love of flowers; the whole cottage is immersed in their beauty and fragrance.' It was, in effect, the publisher's book not Christo's.*

A bad holiday, and now a bad book: where was he going wrong? Perhaps he was not surrounding himself with the right company; perhaps he ought to focus on Dixter again, properly. Perhaps Ken Hadley was not too young a companion, but too old, and expected too much from their friendship. The friends of Christo's own age, north and south, were beginning to die (even his ancient Volvo had died), and those old friends who were alive complained that their coevals were dying too. Christo's answer to their laments, invariably, was to tell them to get out and find some young friends, as he did.

There was a touch of the Peter Pan about Christo's passion for youth, an element of escapism. People who ten and fifteen years previously had been his young heroes were beginning to grow up and be less in awe of him. Sometimes, they just fell off the end of his hospitality list: they became boring, even began to go grey. He dropped them in the way that Daisy had dropped people when they ceased to be useful to her tribe. Christo was a man who never liked to indulge in heart-to-hearts and confide intimacies about himself. He felt this to be sentimental. Yet surely one of the benefits of knowing someone well over a long period is to be able to share confidences. In a sense, therefore, long-standing friendships with Christo had nowhere to go. It was understood that Christo liked to have his generosity and expertise appreciated; but equally that loving old friends had to accept, with patience and comprehension, how shy he was. Young people, on the other hand, expected no confidences. They were simply and uncomplicatedly grateful for his generosity and keen to learn from him. And so more interesting for Christo right now were the students from Wye or Wisley who came for day visits as part of their courses, youthful people who could only look forward.

At Dixter, he had created an effective and extraordinarily generous mechanism for meeting young people: his part of the bargain was to offer them time working at Dixter, perhaps even accommodation in an estate cottage or in one of the old servants' rooms on the top floor. These garden enthusiasts were given the opportunity to meet the many

* Yet a good advance found Christo publishing again with Dorling Kindersley in 1993: *Christopher Lloyd's Flower Garden*, a serviceable revamp of Dixter through the year, but without the worst mechanical and sentimental intrusions of *The Cottage Garden*.

influential people from the gardening world who passed through the doors of Dixter, as well as free access to Christo's years of experience. Their part of the deal was to be full of life and of the forwardness Christo had so lacked in his own youth; to share his passion for plants, seriously; to love Dixter and life as it was lived there; and thereafter, in some cases, to become real friends. And one of them was usually the man of the moment.

In the early 1990s Christo found not one, but two new leading men: Fergus Garrett and Ed Flint. Ed lived not far away and came for practical experience after his college days. He was everything that Christo had never been – tall, loose-limbed, physically active, rugby-playingly straight, and given to guffawing at the pleasures and madnesses of the world: a dizzying Labrador pup to Christo's wise dachshund. 'Incandescent,' Christo called him. Very soon Ed was driving Christo to Wester Ross on his annual Scottish trip, because he himself no longer enjoyed driving (to his amazement, Ed *hitch-hiked* home again). Ed looked after Dixter while Christo was away, and even coped with a burglary.

But no sooner was Christo in Scotland than he began to wish himself back at Dixter, *busier*, with the boys and the gardening, with his teaching.

'Letter writing seems to have developed into a second life while I've been away this time,' he wrote:

> particularly here, where I get a distinct feeling of claustrophobia. I love Dundonnell; it's a real home. I'm very comfortable; Alan is a warm and generous friend (for instance he always suspects I might like a drink when I would like one). But there is a kind of déjà vu quality to living which is numbing to the senses. Letter-writing (or dipping into a doze) is my escape while I hear Beth talking for the fifth time at least about how she missed Madge, her oldest member of staff, and while she's spinning the story out, Alan is getting impatient to be able to reel off anecdotes which I've heard so many times that I can anticipate well beforehand when the next repetition is due.
>
> There are few outside stimuli. Alan likes young people and gets on well with them, but he rarely meets them here. He has his set of old friends, neighbours, and exchanges visits with them, but they're hardly stimulating.

When I'm writing to a friend I enter another world in which they become very close and real to me . . . it's almost a case of 'Who can I write to next?'

Returning from Scotland with me, Christo visited the modern, science-inspired garden of Charles Jencks and was delighted by the landform spiral-DNA mounds, but was depressed by the wild, moorside garden of Geoffrey Dutton, which made its mark so minimally on the landscape (Dutton wrote about it in *Some Branch Against the Sky*). 'An old man's garden,' pronounced Christo, not liking the slow pace of change and the degree to which the garden waited for nature to make the first move: at Dixter, man drove plant furiously towards a spectacular display. Everything must be youthful now. How about a quick lecture trip to Seattle and San Francisco in 1990? Fine: plenty of young Americans there. Paul and Linda McCartney to dinner? Fine, let's do it. But 'Apparently I am sharing a box at Covent Garden tonight with Leonard Bernstein. Should I know him?'

1991 saw the publication of the second of Christo's good collaborative books, *Garden Flowers from Seed*, this time with Graham Rice. Once again it had sprung from a chance encounter. Christo happened to read Rice's *Annuals and Bedding Plants* and was much taken with it. He contacted Rice, thirty years his junior, and asked him down to Dixter for the weekend. They got on well, sharing an interest in the detail of propagation and seed varieties, and Christo proposed the idea of a joint book then and there. Such was his desire not to be writing alone on material with which he was already familiar (he was now seventy), but to be able to spar with another writer, to make the book a conversation, as he had in *Clematis* with Tom Bennett. It would be their book too, not a construction of the publishers.

It's a practical book for serious gardeners looking for insight into how to make particular plants grow from seed, often plants that one would normally buy mature in a pot. Like Socrates and his pupil, the two of them swapped paragraphs as they moved through an A–Z of annuals and perennials, sometimes one man having more to say, sometimes the other, not quite answering each other, but with an awareness of the other's attitude to the issue and of the potential for disagreement. It was entertaining as well as useful reading, even if it lacked quite the best Lloydian manner of personally leading the reader by the nose (and occasionally tweaking it). It was brave too, daring to talk not just about old varieties but new seed strains, plants of the moment.

But another book was already brewing, one that would look directly at other people's gardens. With this in mind, Christo went to Dorset and Lincolnshire in May 1991, generously driven by Fergus Garrett, whom he had first met and befriended three years earlier. Eight days with Fergus to himself, and he would be thoroughly looked after! The two of them were now regular correspondents, since Fergus was working in the south of France and correspondence with Christo could be fast and furious – his take on tennis. One got to know his mind and how it worked, and there was pleasure in keeping the volley going. Fergus' letters, so full of life and plants, were music to Christo's ears: 'I have never felt so close to anyone,' he confided to his diary. Staying in Dorset with the author and garden journalist Anna Pavord, they saw gardens aplenty – Abbotsbury, Mapperton, Chilcombe – and then headed north via Stourhead to Lincolnshire and Burleigh Park, finally returning via Alan Caiger-Smith's pottery at Aldermaston to buy six or seven pieces. Christo would talk seamlessly to the gardens' owners and dig his amanuensis Fergus in the ribs when something needed noting; Fergus the Turk was particularly dark and stubbly just then and, as Christo fondly quipped, looked every inch the bandit. 'My hired assassin will do any necessary dirty work!' Christo crowed.

In 1991 Ed Flint moved on, and a twenty-seven-year-old Australian, Michael McCoy, came to Dixter as a volunteer. Christo cleared out the Day Nursery of boxes of junk for him, so that he and his girlfriend could have space. True to form with people he fell for, Christo was irritating and appealing to Michael in equal parts. He excelled himself in his possessiveness, rudeness, provocation and subsequent apologies, especially over Michael's religious convictions. Eventually Michael went back to Australia where he, in his turn, played host to Christo. In 1992 the Victoria Gardens Scheme (the equivalent of the British National Gardens Scheme) was expanding to cover all of Australia under the name the Australian Open Garden Scheme, and there was to be a grand launch backed by the British Council and the Australian Broadcasting Corporation, for which an international speaker was needed. The old curmudgeon's reputation had gone before him, and Michael McCoy was asked to intercede for his blessing. The result was a tour expanded to include several more states than the original Victorian starting point. 'I have lectures, interviews and broadcasts, and am allowed to have Michael as shepherd and chauffeur.' It suited Christo down to the ground, and the fact that Michael was happy to take time to look after him is testament to how much young people valued Christo's help and generosity at Dixter. On free days they saw gardens and nurseries and got out into the bush to see wild plants.

The tour began in Canberra with a speech at the National Press Club to an audience of garden writers, designers and landscape architects. 'What I've written is fairly provocative,' wrote Christo, 'and could lose me my slot on *The Observer*, as I've been rude about the new Sports Editor . . .' That was the least of his provocations. Christo had never had patience with gardens that were on an ecological mission, even when the mission was pursued by as talented a gardener as his friend Beth Chatto. But the 'native' gardens he saw in Australia appalled him by their pointless exclusion of good garden plants for the sake of natives, whether or not the natives looked attractive together. He announced that native gardens were awful, although there was nothing wrong with Australian plants per se. The audience took him to task and the next day the *Canberra Times* bore the headline 'Canberra a Blot on the Landscape'. Christo was rather tickled, and felt backed up in his argument on visiting a garden where unattractive but PC plants were kept in their proper place, in a GULP – a Garden of Un-Loved Plants.

More lectures followed in Canberra and Sydney and then, still with Michael, in Hobart, on 'Tapestry Gardening': 'As these people are clueless on putting plants together in their gardens, I thought I would open their eyes a bit to what they're missing.' From Adelaide they flew in a tiny plane to Port Augusta, to see nurseries, fruit farms and more wild eucalyptus; Christo, in chipper mood, complimented the pilot on his command of the aircraft in wet and windy conditions. 'There are old pilots and bold pilots,' he replied, 'but no old bold pilots.'

At Dunedin in New Zealand he spoke at the university and visited national parks, Mount Cook and the coast, where he finally saw a king albatross with a mighty nine-foot wingspan. In Christchurch hundreds of people packed the halls, and, talking to the Heritage Rose Society, he aired for the first time plans he was making with Fergus Garrett to take out the roses from Lutyens' Rose Garden, a move that won him infamy in Britain. Christo saw the move as a change in *decoration*, not a change to the substance of Lutyens' masculine, but imaginative design.

Back at Dixter, Christo and Quentin were ludicrously still at serious loggerheads over domestic and financial matters, making it all the more embarrassing that Quentin marched through Dixter every Sunday morning to wind all the clocks. No other sibling was around to bang their heads together. There had been bad repairs made to the water supply, resulting in there being no water upstairs and none at all at Little Dixter; Christo was angry. Dixter was burgled and many of the clocks were taken, and twice tiles were stolen from the wagon lodge roof: now it was Quentin's turn to be angry. Christo wanted to install gates at the end of the drive, with a combination lock; but Quentin would only entertain electrically operated gates and at Christo's expense, since Christo was the one living in a house full of valuables; the estimate was £13,000, so nothing happened. The new boiler, which Christo and Quentin had installed in the 1980s, failed suddenly and the house was morgue-cold. The boiler turned out to be of a kind that never should have been installed in the first place, and it was now a write-off. A new one would cost £12,000.

And now Quentin was diagnosed with prostate cancer, which was spreading to the bones. 'I feel less sympathetic than I should,' grumbled Christo.

One morning Christo woke up to see from his bedroom over the porch that one of his father's topiary peacocks in the Lavender Garden was lacking its head. There it was, lying on the ground; and it was not the only peacock that was so abused. Further inspection showed a decapitated yucca (the plant, not the dachshund) in the Exotic Garden and various trees sawn partway through. No one was caught, but the press loved the issue and Christo became sick of grimacing for the camera beside the headless creatures. He wrote about it in his column, and loyal old lady readers threatened to form lynch-mobs; condolences were received, Christo quipped, even from the Vatican (he had an acquaintance there). If it was meant to hurt him, then the perpetrator did not know Christo. He quickly got over it, but within Dixter a silent finger pointed to an agent closer to home.

Quentin's easy-going attitude to maintenance meant that the house itself urgently needed repairs to the timberwork and walls. When the Historic Buildings and Monuments Commission (English Heritage) was formed on April Fool's Day 1984, Christo had become aware that money might be available to help with repairs to Grade I and II* houses, but felt there were too many strings attached to grant-aid for it to be worth pursuing. Meanwhile the barn roofs had been damaged by the 1987 storms and repaired, and help was certainly now needed on house repairs. He contacted English Heritage, which was reluctant to give financial help and suggested that Christo take a loan, since the sum involved was 'such a small part of the value of the house'. Alternatively, they added, he might sell the place.

There was income from the nursery, whose turnover Fergus was increasing by leaps and bounds from the garden visitors, from books and journalism (£400 a week from *The Guardian* at that time), and there was the possibility of television work with the BBC and Channel 4; but it was still a shocking slap in the face to find that Dixter's 60 per cent share of necessary repairs, even when English Heritage had finally agreed to provide the rest, would cost £100,000. In the end the work went ahead, closely specified by English Heritage, and Nathaniel's beloved apricot tree was peeled away from the wall in readiness; it was a disaster, the house leaked at every seam and amid much legal wrangling the work had to be repeated, *twice* – removal of the apricot and all.

As repairs were coped with, the question of what to do after Christo's death rose to the surface. In 1992 there were discussions again with the National Trust about whether they could take Dixter on, and a representative was engaged to discuss the matter with Christo and his co-heirs. These, since the death of Oliver, were only brother Quentin and his niece Olivia. 'Apparently for tax reasons,' wrote Christo, 'it's important that the matter should be settled *before* I die. Otherwise I'd gladly wash my hands of it and leave it to the next generation to do as they pleased. But I must not be irresponsible.' Naïve perhaps he was; for the Trust was not in the business of taking on houses and gardens without a substantial financial endowment for their upkeep, and this Dixter could not provide.

But when it came to money, Christo had never been quite in the real world. 'To be genuinely wealthy,' he said, 'you have to have capital', which, in broad terms, he did not. Yet his generosity with opera tickets was legendary. When he was advised by his dentist in Harley Street that he needed bridge-work costing many thousands of pounds, he found himself offered a better price for cash; Christo accepted, but since he did not relish carrying even a smaller number of thousands into London as cash, he took one of his gardeners, like an Indian bearer, to carry it for him. He was happy to spend thousands on an exact replica of the bench Lutyens had designed for the Long Border, and at the same time was amazed that a new freezer cost £200 rather than £2,000. And still every year he would parsimoniously call in a tradesman to have his ancient, sagging 1950s fridge serviced and its circulating system topped up with coolant. When his crumbling old Volvo needed replacement, he called the dealer and asked him to *bring a few cars* round, from which he might choose.

But Christo was actually beginning, now, to admit that Dixter would create a burden for Olivia when he died, and there was the question of what to do with the Dixter archive. Archive is the wrong word. Better to explain that scattered throughout the house was a hoard of mouldering Lloydian correspondence ancient and modern, some crammed into drawers, some bundled into suitcases at the back of dusty cupboards, some put aside by Daisy (one beloved child per drawer), some put aside by Christo, some by accident. There were Nathaniel's collection of glass plates; plans by Lutyens; designs for Dixter embroideries by Dorothy Buckmaster, Lutyens' draughtswoman; sixty years' worth of Christo's garden slides; and endless curling family snaps. Some papers were stacked, others rolled up in rubber bands, and much of it was quite, quite filthy. Christo's bureau alone, in the Parlour where he worked daily, sported heaps of paper of archaeological texture, descending in one heap from letters of 2005 through 1960s Green Shield Stamps to school clothing lists from the 1930s. To all of it, this otherwise very precise man shut his eyes. The best that can be said is that in 1998 many of his father's architectural glass plates and acetates were given to the National Monuments Record.

Why should Christo want to look at old letters anyway? It was all past now. It was the present – and the more optimistic aspects of life – that commanded his attention. So it was that 1993 turned out to be a joyful turning point for him and for Dixter. He appointed Fergus Garrett to be his head gardener.

Fergus had first met Christo in 1988 when he came to Dixter on a trip from Wye College, where he was doing a degree in horticulture under the lecturer Tom Wright, himself Christo's pupil in the 1950s. Fergus thought Christo a funny old man in a funny old garden; there wasn't even a head gardener.

Fergus came from Brighton, his mother having been born in Istanbul and his father in England. When he was six months old his mother left his father and returned to Turkey with the children, but she wanted Fergus and his older brother to continue their education in England. The two brothers lived an independent, laddish, interesting life in Brighton, staying initially with their grandmother, and thereafter with their mother when she retired and came back to England.

Fergus' school in Hove was a massive comprehensive, but it provided him with little idea about what he might do in life. His geography teacher said why not do something land-based, so he applied to do an agriculture degree at Wye College, secured a place and hated the principles of modern agriculture. The college offered him horticulture instead – a word with which he was totally unfamiliar – so he talked to Tom Wright and was persuaded to accept. Having got some practical experience under his belt with the excellent Brighton Parks Department, he went back to Wye and got his BSc. While he was there, he spent a weekend at Dixter with his friend Neil Ross who was volunteering there, and found Christo more interesting than he'd previously thought. 'I think I like you,' announced Christo. 'Yes, I think I like you,' Fergus replied.

What to do now? Fergus got a job clearing brush for Rosemary Alexander, principal of the English Gardening School, at her house, Stoneacre in Kent, and all the time was busily keeping in touch by letter with the 'funny old man'. He worked for Beth Chatto in Essex, but found himself caught in the crossfire between her principles and Christo's differing ideas, so he left to work in a private garden in the south of France for two years. A close friendship with Christo developed through their correspondence, and Fergus took time out to drive Christo on his garden-research forays around England. Finally Fergus gave up the job in France so that he could see more of his girlfriend, Amanda Ferguson, in England. The garden at Dixter was then good, but drifting; it needed some drive. Christo's garden-designer friend Ken Rawson said: why not ask Fergus to be head gardener? So Christo did, and the answer was yes. At twenty-seven, Fergus knew he could learn much from Christo.

Of course Fergus appealed physically to Christo – the dark eyes, strong brow, sudden winning smile – but there was more to it than that. It was a meeting of minds, a sharing of a can-do attitude to gardening that extended right down to the detail of the planting. Christo loved Fergus like a son (as a Turk, Fergus had been brought up to respect his elders), and Christo fascinated Fergus through and through; but the secret of their success was that Christo could not *tire* of Fergus, because he was forever shaking the coloured rag of the garden in Christo's face and saying: come on, do something with it, what can we do together? How could Christo resist being played at his own game? And on Fergus' part, when this funny old man indulged in one of his childish, Daisy Lloyd fits of pique or rudeness – whether to Fergus or to others – he never reprimanded or shamed Christo publicly. Instead he smiled; disapproving – yes, a little, but seeing the good in Christo's motives and excusing the bad. He was a loyal parent as well as a son to Christo.

Before Fergus started work at Dixter, he went with Christo, Anna Pavord and her husband Trevor Ware to Turkey. Fergus was guide, interpreter and general Mr Fix-It, making quite a car-load. Anna was then researching her bestselling history *The Tulip*, and the point of the trip was for her to see tulips in the wild and consult Turkish botanists and libraries; the PKK Kurdish separatist forces were active in the east and she hoped Fergus might help her manage the trip practically and safely. Well, if *they* were going, Christo wanted to come too: it would be a holiday to see plants in the wild, no lectures, no speeches this time, and his skills as a field botanist would be of help to the others.

In Istanbul, Christo was in heaven, surrounded by dark, aquiline young men, three to every woman, and the almost-as-gorgeous Judas trees. What a shame it was that Turks so easily turned into the fat, middle-aged men who were also everywhere. At the university where Anna was to consult Professor Baytop, a world expert on bulbs, Ferg and Christo idled away the time watching the more liberated female students, and deciding which one Ferg should have as a wife.

Of course they visited the Blue Mosque; and as they came out and retrieved their shoes, a young man approached Christo (he was often taken for a Turk because of his moustache) and pressed him earnestly

177

to visit a stall selling rugs How many rugs have you in your house? asked the man. 'I don't know, ten, twenty? Perhaps sixty,' Christo suggested. 'Well then, you should have one hundred.' At the Topkapi Palace, Christo stepped into a little garden to sniff *Iris germanica* and an old lady appeared, and picked and handed him a bunch of four, heartily shaking his hand. 'I felt I should have embraced her,' he cried, but a soldier with a machine gun shooed him off for being out of bounds. There were so very many delights in this city: stepping over a sleeping dog in the middle of the university entrance; bears being led through the streets by gypsies; going into restaurant kitchens to look in the cooking pots. It was the perfect holiday, especially with Fergus there to provide and explain.

They now flew to Trabzon, where there should have been a hire car waiting; but no luck, so they hung on while Fergus and Anna's husband Trevor got matters sorted, then they were off on rough roads for 190 miles to Erzurum, stopping along the way for rich hauls of plants – peonies, butcher's broom, hellebores. A bunch of youths pointed out that they had a flat tyre and kindly changed it, for which Fergus plied them with toffees. On they went up into the mountains, in the snow, with Christo dozing in his seat, Trevor or Fergus at the wheel, and the others crammed together in the back. Their hotel scored better on food than on hot water.

Next morning, while the leaking tyre was fixed properly, they saw the market in pouring rain – barrows of dried white mulberries and nuts, starved ponies pulling carts, and piles of eremurus tops to be cooked like spinach. Then off to the melting snowy slopes, where the first celandines were in bud and there were indeed tulips, and ornithogalums, scillas, arabis and drabas.

And so the trip continued, Fergus effortlessly chatting to people along the way – sometimes shepherds with their floppy-eared brown sheep – about how they were looking for places where there might be tulips in flower. There were more markets selling baskets, glassware and what Christo called 'beautiful, complex knitting expressed in socks', which he bought for Fergus. They watched unleavened bread being made in wood-fired ovens and ate it fresh with olives. In the restaurants, Anna – tall and pale, and always the only woman – felt stared at and isolated.

Some days the sun shone and Fergus and Christo explored the hill-sides together for dwarf fritillaries, euphorbias and giant fennel, 'enjoying many little things and feeling in total harmony, one with the other'. Once they split up and Christo, having misplaced his stick, sat in the sun, happy, listening to the clunk of copulating tortoises. Another day they met a boy with a weary old donkey carrying home a load of woody verbascum stalks, for fuel. Fergus asked the donkey's name, which was White Lightning, and he and the boy chatted on while the donkey walked ahead, knowing its way home. The boy was thirteen and had left school at eleven, with no money to continue his education. 'So much wasted potential!' lamented Christo. Later, at home at Dixter, an especially good seedling of a perennial verbascum was named 'Christo's Yellow Lightning' in the boy's honour.

There were tulips aplenty near the Iranian border, Anna was told, and they pushed on again, taking care not to travel close to military convoys in case they were attacked, past cold-eyed military checkpoints (what scorn at their contraband of *flowers!*) to a place where local shepherds said there had been two men with tents all summer, digging up the tulips to sell. And on the way back to town, and thence to the airport and home, they were dazzled by sheets of furry brown *Iris gatesii.* 'From a distance they could be taken for scraps of refuse,' wrote Christo. 'I take *far* too many photographs.' He had never been so happy.

Over Christmas 1992 Christo's Irish novelist friend Frank Ronan was staying with him. He was a regular visitor to Dixter and a great admirer of Christo's focus and feistiness, not to mention his wonderful prose style; he was happy in the old man's company (Frank was twenty-nine) and willing to drive him on his trips to Scotland. Christo in his turn admired Frank's novels (today Frank also writes on gardens, in *Gardens Illustrated*). Speaking with a charming drawl, cruelly funny, Frank had moved during his acquaintance with Christo from a difficult relationship with his girlfriend to gay relationships. To Christo this showed a bravery that he himself had never had, and which he wished upon so many of his friends. They cared for each other greatly.

That Christmas, Frank read the manuscript of one of Christo's upcoming pieces for *Country Life*. It struck him as silly that this quality of writing and journalism (Christo saved his best for *Country Life*) should be seen by such a small constituency. *The Well-Tempered Garden* and *The Adventurous Gardener* had, by Christo's own admission, been reworkings, if not total reworkings, of ideas that had first sprung to life in *Country Life*. Frank asked Christo what he thought of a compilation of the work 'unimproved', and Christo was pleased with the idea, but reluctant to do it himself, so Frank obliged. Christo's agent Giles Gordon, a lively and greatly loved power in the literary world, took the proposal to some publishers and drummed up several who were keen to run with the idea, but Bloomsbury won, in May, paying three times over the odds on condition that the copy be supplied in a few weeks' time – to be called *In My Garden*. A more reasonable two *months* was agreed upon, and Frank moved into Dixter, sitting on a sofa opposite Christo and wading through the 1.5 million words he had typed for *Country Life* over the past thirty years and which were restricted, after commandments from Bloomsbury, to a mere eighty-five pieces. Frank was working from the original flimsy, foolscap type-script, not the published versions. It further turned out that *Country Life* owned the copyright to the whole body of work, but kindly (and very sensibly – what better advertisement could they have?) waived a royalty. And how much happier Christo was to have a wordsmith handling his writing than a sub-editor, tired as he was of in-house journalists fiddling unproductively or mistakenly with his copy for the last thirty years. The accuracy and *transparency* of his prose were a matter of huge pride:

> Certainly it is off-putting if you are expected to run to a dictionary or a glossary of botanical terms every time you sit down with a dog on your lap and a cuppa at your side thinking you'll have a nice comfy read from the old glossy [*Country Life*]. If node means joint, why the devil didn't I write joint straightaway and have done with those nodes? Thus I nagged at myself, but then sprang to the nodes' defence. First, node is shorter than joint but second, far more to the point, you can't make an adjective of joint to mean the same thing as nodal. A nodal cutting is one where the cutting is made just below a node. A joint cutting, if it means anything at all, would mean one that you made holding hands with your wife or apprentice. And jointal doesn't exist. . . . Mr Clapham, in a Country Life article [on how some plants root from internodal cuttings] pointed out that fuchsias behave in this way and I had it from the girls at Sissinghurst – I beg their pardons, I mean the joint (or nodal) head lady gardeners (or lady head

gardeners) at Sissinghurst Castle – that bedding verbenas root from internodal cuttings which is a great convenience when you are short of material.

The book has memorable moments by the score, as you would expect from thirty years of Christo's journalism. Of a green film over spring borders, 'Moss doesn't create a situation, it merely expresses one.' Of dead-heading irises, 'Ideally perhaps we should remove every display before it has even begun. Then there'd never be room for disappointment and we could always be making ready for the next non-event. Imagination could take the place of fact and failure.' Of the results of a bad winter:

Many gardeners are debating what course to adopt towards the hideous trail of victims left by winter's little onslaught. I have to write 'little' because it would be lacking in proportion to set recent events on the same level of high tragedy as the misfortunes of Phèdre or the Duchess of Malfi. Yet I note a threatening bulge in the number of garden owners applying for tragedy-queen roles. In some cases it is hard to distinguish whether it is they who are dying (broken hearted) or their plants.

In My Garden is the place, today, to see the finest of Christo's work for *Country Life*. It has a cross-section of his best writing and preoccupations, work which had been produced for his loyal and experienced readership at *Country Life*, so there is no pulling of punches, and Christo was proud of that:

The gardening journalist does not want to resemble those schoolteachers who are always concentrating on the needs of the backward child, with the result that the bright kids are bored to sobs. We hope to be writing for those who, although admittedly a small minority, are committed gardeners and who love the time and trouble given to their plants.

Anyway the bored majority are constantly being catered for. They are numerous and they are a market. No market for long goes unsatisfied. Why, you can furnish a garden entirely with trouble-free, colourful accessories and never even begin to touch the plastic flower trade, if that is your wish.

It seems unnecessary for a small garden to make anyone miserable.

There were times, of course, when even the best journalist will let content overpower style, and Frank excluded from his selection the pieces that, not infrequently, became lists of what Christo had seen and learned. On the other hand, there are thoroughly practical pieces included, because one of Christo's skills (and it is rarer than it sounds) was to make mechanical things simple and clearly understood in a concise and lively way. It is an invisible talent.

With Fergus in post at Dixter, Christo felt able to do anything, and in no time at all the two of them got on with the much-discussed removal of the roses from Lutyens' Rose Garden.* 'Yesterday, we had a grand exhumation of old rose bushes – I contemplate calling this "The Old Rose Garden",' he joked. It was a nice thought, since there is, amongst serious rosarians, a select club who prefer to grow only the old, pre-1900 varieties rather than *brash*, modern varieties.†

'The rending noise of huge old roots reminded me of a hyena devouring a plank of wood,' wrote Christo in *Country Life*, on April Fool's Day 1993, of the removal of the roses. Old lady readers who had wept over his vandalised peacocks threw up their hands in horror, rose growers denounced him for damaging the industry, and the historical garden lobby condemned him for undoing Lutyens' masterly design. But what nonsense it was! Even Christo, who forever confused spatial design with planting design, was clear that he was merely replacing one kind of decoration, one *treatment* of the space, with another. And anyway, the roses had been there too long for their own good health. Even if someone should put them back one day, for now the soil needed a break from roses.

Christo was flattered by all the attention in the press, like a naughty child gleefully getting away with some misdemeanour. The publicity was good for visitor numbers, certainly, but it also blew out of all proportion the removal of the roses. Christo became famous for it; people

---

* In the same way, he had removed Daisy's lavender with Romke.
† In later years, when Fergus did away with the lines of nursery stock in the High Garden and replanted them in artistically arranged blocks, there was thought of re-christening the High Garden the Old Rows Garden.

outside the garden world knew about this delightfully wicked old man who had dared to take on the establishment and remove something so immutably English as a rose garden; it was as if Henry VIII had replaced the heraldic Tudor rose with a chincherinchee.

Where the roses had been, Christo and Fergus eventually made an Exotic Garden. It came to life only after midsummer, with luscious outsize foliage and loud tropical colours, everything that the 'good-taste brigade' abhorred.

An exotic garden was not anything astonishingly new. As long ago as 1873 James Anderson wrote in his *The Practical Gardener*, 'Subtropical gardening is quite a modern idea, capable of being carried out to only a limited extent in the gardens of this country.' The bedding out of subtropical plants for foliage and colour had indeed been a late-Victorian craze, but then, in the spirit of the age, it was most commonly used in island beds in grass, caged in a zoo of curiosities. The significance of Christo's Exotic Garden would be that now you could walk *amongst* the plants, meet the dahlias eye to eye, lurk beneath bananas like a tiger in a painting by Le Douanier Rousseau. Here you were most definitely up close. Some people loved it, others hated it, and still others just saw it as Christo showing off; 'a delightful little kaleidoscope,' Beth Chatto sweetly called it.

Christo's Exotic Garden cemented the popular trend towards exotic planting, and Christo and Fergus, whether intentionally or not, were held aloft as its champions, on both sides of the Atlantic. The great irony is that the popularity of exotic gardening rode the wave of the public's increasing awareness of climate change – the theory being that if Britain was to be hotter and drier, then surely all Christo's heat-loving subtropical plants were *the* way forward. How wrong this was: there is no more thirsty way of gardening than to plant in a sunny enclosure subtropical plants with large leaves – cannas, bananas, ginger lilies. They need moisture just as much as heat, and Christo was always watering the Exotic Garden, not least because there was such competition from the old yew hedges. Finding themselves sharing such a luxurious sauna, the drought-dwelling succulents with architectural foliage that he included – agaves, puya, cotyledon – luxuriated in such opulent conditions.

More significant perhaps is that Christo's loud palette of colours marked an inevitable swing of the pendulum from the pastel good taste

183

of the 1970s and '80s, as exemplified in Rosemary Verey's books. Christo's new style was a palette of colours that found its way at the same time into the commercial cut-flower industry, where plants such as lime-green zinnias, blood-black dahlias and peach and orange gerberas were coming to the fore.

Having seen that he could get away with changes in the Rose Garden, Christo fancied more experiments – on Nathaniel's topiary lawn, perhaps? It was a clean, green rectangle of lawn where large topiary pieces presided in scholarly silence, and even if they populated the space and stopped it feeling empty, the topiary lawn was still the garden's last calm space where people could walk out into the open, other than the stubbled orchard after hay-making. It was also a contrast with all the busier, more intimate, flowerier parts of the garden, and a perfect place from which to see the full span of the house.

Christo had always felt that grass was a waste of space and energy, and so now the topiary lawn was allowed to run to meadow, retaining as mown grass only Lutyens' vista through it, from the 'family pew' to the hovel by the Exotic Garden. To his delight but not his surprise, orchids soon appeared out of the fine, starved grass and he now had one more meadow; like the exotic planting in the Rose Garden, the change did not matter; long grass was just another way of treating the space.

There was no fuss in the national press this time, partly because Christo himself made no big deal of it in print. Who was going to worry about losing some close-mown lawn at a time when lawns were being slated in the eco-sensitive popular press as 'resource-hungry, ecological deserts'? There was no hysteria from lawn-mower manufacturers as there had been from the rose growers. Roses have always had inescapable sentimental associations for gardeners and non-gardeners alike, because of their history as symbols, and when the Dixter roses were removed, all kinds of people were saddened, even if they had no strong feelings about the change to the garden. But most people were unmoved by the change on the topiary lawn. The historical garden lobby, cross about the roses, showed no interest in the change from lawn to meadow; if they thought the replacement of roses with exotic perennials was an issue of altered structure more than decorative style, then the new deco-rative style of the topiary-lawn grass (which, unlike the Rose Garden, actually changed how the space could be used) sailed by them completely. The irony is that both rose beds and meadows could be removed or reinstated in a season, had Christo wished to.

Removing that cleanest, greenest of the garden's spaces also removed a degree of contrast between the garden's various compartments, and most of all it underlined the garden's increasing tendency to be fizzy everywhere, for the peaceful areas to be overruled by more detailed planting. Christo did exactly the same again, later, when he took up the turf from the landings of Lutyens' supremely elegant circular steps and replaced them with bedded-out succulents. Christo wanted summer high-jinks now, and never mind if the steps looked bald in winter and if the pace of the garden was becoming even throughout. He was spinning every plate he could find at top speed, and with Fergus as his hands and feet, he could do it all.

The plate that refused to spin fast enough was money. Talks with the National Trust had made Pam and Quentin nervous about ever seeing their (and therefore their children's) share of Dixter, and there was the threat from Little Dixter that Great Dixter would have to be sold to liquidate their share of its value. It depressed Christo greatly. But now with Quentin ill, it had to be resolved and it was decided to raise funds to buy him out by selling off 40 per cent of the contents of Dixter.

Slowly the contents of the house were examined by valuers, selecting for sale first those items that would raise the most money and leave the house least denuded. It was not a happy business, and arguments with Quentin over whether to sell Nathaniel's old bound copies of *Country Life* were acrimonious indeed.

The sale took place in a marquee on the lower car park, in May 1994, ironically with the National Trust making a considerable number of purchases; and when the dust had settled, the remaining furniture was rearranged to fill the space. As ever, Christo was keen to make light of his losses. 'So over-furnished was it that one hardly noticed the changes within,' he wrote, 'the house doesn't look at all bad for its pruning; better, in some ways, even though there are some obvious gaps. Perhaps I could have a mural or two . . .' All very upbeat. Dixter was indeed cooler after the sale, sparer, but it had not regained that delightful clarity to be seen in Nathaniel's early photographs. It was an old lady losing a petticoat, a first step in the deconstructing of Tan and Daisy's dream home. Pale patches showed on the bare plaster walls where paintings had been removed or furniture had stood for fifty years.

The dust literally settled. With Quentin bought out, Christo and Olivia were the only two with a share in Dixter (40 per cent to him, 60 per cent to her; Angus no longer held a share) and he looked forward to a time of less wrangling and argument. Quentin could now fairly be replaced as house manager and the job put on a more professional footing. There would be a tea-shop at the nursery in the old Garden Cottage, and good tools for sale. Even T-shirts sporting a grinning Christo peeking out from jungle vegetation.

In 1995 Christo published *Other People's Gardens*, through Viking Press, the project he had been working on for several years. He rarely looked at a garden without making notes, often staying with the owners too, or at least being wined and dined by them. Over the years he had amassed a large collection of garden notes – some of gardens he liked, others not, but still worthy in some way. *Other People's Gardens* was his chance to pull twenty-four of the best together in one volume; to be a Celia Fiennes for the twentieth century. He had already written about many of the gardens as a journalist, and the prospect of 'plagiarising himself' troubled him; his excuse to revisit the gardens in book form was that he could be more personal than in magazines.

The chosen gardens were, in effect, a sample of Christo's favourites, selected not just because he liked the gardeners, but because they gardened as seriously as he, with the same sense of urgency and exper-iment. They shared 'the sweet disease'. From a publisher's point of view, the book should have been 'a gift': it came from an internationally revered author, and a quarter of the gardens were outside Britain. Sad to say, the book failed to find an American publisher, so sixteen pages had to come out to reduce costs, which meant losing the last chapter and the index. The marketing department's opinion was that the book should never have been commissioned in the first place and that it would lose £40,000–50,000. They wanted to pay off Christo and ditch the project, but he would not have it. Financially it was a flop.

The charm of *Other People's Gardens* is to see this seventy-four-year-old taking such an open-minded approach to gardens so very different from his own. But what makes the book so *useful* is to be able to share

Christo's appreciation of how and why plants do well in a particular climate, and to draw lessons from it – how celmisias and woolly willow do so well in cool, moist Scotland, despite having the grey leaves usually associated with a hot, dry climate; or how *Canna glauca* does so well planted *in* ponds in Los Angeles.

Christo offered a tour of each garden, but there was rarely any discussion of the design, even if the various features were found more or less appealing: 'The garden's design counts, of course; a flattering presentation of its contents depends largely on that, as also does the way the plants are arranged in relation to one another, but such matters are probably not what I notice first, being a self-confessed plantsman, first and foremost.' That was Christo's position on design in general. In playful mood he would joke about it: 'I am not a designer, I just go along and carp.'

Other People's Gardens is a catalogue of styles and ideas that influenced Christo's gardening. You can see him falling in love (one of his late amours) with well-grown bamboos at Peter Addington's garden. You can see him being sucked into the idea of making an exotic garden; thinking to try his tetrapanax outside one day (he did); admiring the long season of lush flower and foliage that Jimmy Hancock got out of tender perennials at Powis; and being taken with Ruth Bancroft's desert garden of cacti and succulents at San Francisco: 'This is a plant sculpture garden. As you move through it, shapes advance and recede and change their interrelationships. It becomes a mobile sculpture garden of the boldest design.' It could be a description of his own Exotic Garden at Dixter. And of the Bancroft layout: 'You can't call them beds or borders. You are not aware of any overall design; rather of wonderful plant groupings.' This is Christo again not being quite clear of the difference between spatial design and planting design.

You can see him spotting other people removing rose gardens too, and building up steam to his own attempt at Dixter; at Ventnor on the Isle of Wight, Simon Goodenough had been called 'a despoiler of English beauty' when he got rid of hybrid-tea and floribunda roses.

What is odd is that *Other People's Gardens* does not say more about the gardeners. Christo admires their achievements, but the people themselves seem curiously absent. You get the feeling that he did not want to make space for their ideas, their feedback to him – only for their work. Curiously, there are no pictures of his hosts in a book about other people's gardens, no photographs of people at all in fact, except for a comical one of himself: 'Giving scale: Lloyd with *Wachendorfia thyrsiflora*'.

He managed to use his own photographs and, to his credit, they were adequate even at a time when garden photography was starting to become such a sophisticated skill. But it will always remain a mystery why Christo used such a dreadful photograph for the jacket (the rump of Kingston Maurward house, a missing urn, half-clipped hedges, some inappropriately civic paving and summer bedding). This, as much as anything else, must surely have lost sales.

Invitations to speak in America continued to arrive and were never refused. '*How* to garden transcends all national boundaries,' Christo insisted, as he talked enthusiastically to audiences about the hows and whys of Dixter gardening, and the *spirit* of it all.

Increasingly he was smitten by American gardens of cacti and succulents, not least the garden of actor Tim Curry, whom he asked to visit Dixter. He had loved cacti as a child, so why not start again? One lecture tour was made with the grande dame of English gardeners, Rosemary Verey, and each had great admiration for the other. When one of their hosts asked to take formal photographs of the two elder statesmen of English gardening (he seventy-three, she seventy-six) Christo insisted that he be shot in his famous mauve shirt, by a lavender bush that conveniently grew by a lavender table and chairs.

These days he could command a lecture fee of $2,000, and his explanations of what was done at Dixter to make the astonishing Long Border and the Exotic Garden, combined with fabulous photographs, won him ovations. Yet his lectures were not what they used to be. During one talk he actually lost the plot for a moment. It worried him of course, but there were compensations; he was still seeing new gardens, meeting friends he had already made in America, being introduced to new people, and spending time in the company of gay men with whom he could tacitly be one of the boys. In Atlanta, Christo now seventy-four, was taken round a garden by a thirty-one-year-old gardener, boyish, moustachioed:

one of those men who has a natural way of finding occasion to touch you, and makes you (me) tingle when he does. He takes me round the quarry garden etc., all utterly deserted, the light slowly fading. In a short while we are really intimate and he is not slow to accept an invitation to a kiss. It's lovely to find naturally warm men like this. I doubt, however, whether he'll ever come to Dixter. He says he's bisexual. He'll probably stay alone, like me.

In the summer of 1995 a young man by the name of Phillip Morrison came to work in the garden. He was studying landscape architecture at Edinburgh University, had been fascinated by gardens and plants since he was eleven, and wanted more experience; so he wrote to Dixter asking for summer work. He had not read anything by Christo and knew little enough about the place, but it looked promising. Christo replied that he could not pay, but that Phillip might come as a volunteer; Fergus, by swapping round various other volunteers, managed to house him in a room on the top floor of the house where temporary students and trainees were put, normally fending for themselves and living a largely independent life.

This student was to be different. Phillip – Pip – was pensive, dark-eyed, bearded, with long hair that he had to throw regularly from his face, a deep but quiet voice, everything that Christo loved. They met on his first day in the garden and Christo, with the season's last basket of warm apricots on his arm, asked Pip to join him for drinks and supper in the evening. Later, Christo looked in on the kitchen, and Pip, the shy, God-fearing Baptist from rural Monmouthshire who had never drunk spirits before, was told to help himself to Christo's delicious Syndicate malt. They talked and talked and talked – gardens, plants, music (Pip was a talented pianist), families, Pip's parents and their bungalow in Wales, Pip's future career; and every night of that week they ate together, as one long, extraordinary conversation about Pip.

'I have a most delightful young man staying,' wrote Christo to his friend Colin Hamilton in Scotland:

I am quite besotted about him. Well, he is 19, the most natural person you could imagine in the world, although very beautiful. We spent yesterday morning visiting churches on Romney Marsh – four of them – and both enjoyed that hugely. He leaves me in a week's time and will be back in Edinburgh before the end of the month. I'm sure he'll be straight in the long run (though you can't be sure at 19), but he really loves me just the same. You'll be enchanted.

The conversation turned naturally into weekly telephone calls (Pip was not a writer of letters) and for the rest of his time at Edinburgh, he would visit a couple of times a term and be at Dixter for Christmas and Easter.

The next April the two of them were off touring, mentor and acolyte. After hunting down a known field of native fritillaries near Reading, they visited the garden writer and designer Mary Keen, at Cirencester, to see her new garden, set idyllically around an old rectory. They lunched well and she too took to the boy, if rather less to Christo, who perhaps expected a little more hero-worship. 'Cordial but hardly warm,' he described her afterwards. That evening they spent with Rosemary Verey, who flattered Christo with her usual charm, and he found her 'warm and chatty', although he was less pleased when he discovered afterwards that she snapped at his beloved Pip several times when Christo was out of the room (such was her habit with many people whom she considered 'staff'). 'Something of a split personality,' remarked Christo.

Rosemary Verey, along with many other designers, had a hand in designing the Prince of Wales' garden at nearby Highgrove, and that morning the three of them roared off in high spirits to see it, Christo at the wheel and doing 70 mph on the country roads.

Highgrove brought him down to earth. It was the highly polished muddle that so many people find it, but will not admit. Not so Christo. 'There is a pair of potted Ilex underneath the cedar (which has a number of hideous bird feeders hanging from and on it) and looks entirely wrong – like putting a bow window on the Parthenon, to quote Lutyens . . . Basically Prince Charles's tastes are very fussy and the plantings are all, and generally inappropriately, cottage gardening.'

The return trip brought them through Monmouthshire, and they looked in on Pip's family. Christo wanted to bring Pip out of himself, offer him a new life and wider horizons; do what somebody should have done for him sixty years before. And over the next ten years, with much love and heartbreak, he succeeded.

* * *

Having Pip, and of course Fergus, to lighten his days, Christo bore better the pressures of his busy life. For one thing, he was trying to finish another book, *Gardener Cook* (1998), for the publisher Frances Lincoln, and it was to be his first book for them. For Erica Hunningher, then editorial director, it was a long-awaited coup. She had first met Christo in the late 1980s and was keen for him to join Frances Lincoln's list. Knowing he liked intellectual sparring, she suggested that he write *The Provocative Gardener*, and he took offence. 'One does not set out to be provocative!' he snapped.*

Christo had no shame in filling the book with the recipes of others, mostly Daisy's (her recipe books still sat in the kitchen drawer and he used them all the time), but there were also very many by the eminent cookery writer Jane Grigson. His copies of her *English Food*, *Good Things*, *Fish Cookery* and *The Fruit Book* and *The Vegetable Book* were foxed before their time with splashes from his Magimix. He had met her and become friendly when they were both contributing to *The Observer* in the late 1970s. She once came to lunch at Dixter and he had given her brill in a fishy sauce, which was pronounced good – a coup on which Christo dined out for the rest of his life. According to him, she was of the opinion that a recipe, once published, became a kind of common treasure, and he quoted at every turn her words and her recipes, or his adaptations of them, so he was rather put out when asked to pay for their use by Sophie Grigson, Jane's daughter and also a cookery writer.

At least there was no question that Christo knew all these recipes intimately from experience, and he was still, at seventy-six, cooking Christmas dinner for twenty-one people, even if his excellent house-keeper, Anne Jordan, invisibly washed up and saw to the laundry and so on. Jam and marmalade he still made himself, stirring the great pan under his dripping nose-end in that cold great kitchen, with Daisy's recipe open on the oilcloth. So much still remained from her time: the plug for the sink that must go precisely *there*; the steamed-pudding string, which must be washed and hung up to dry, not thrown away.

In a sense *Gardener Cook* was yet another month-by-month description of life in the garden at Dixter, but this time seen through the eyes

* Later, when they had become friends, she told him, 'If I'd known what you were like I would have asked you to write *The Ill-Tempered Gardener*'.

of a vegetable gardener and cook. It was a gentle memoir without the old Lloyd punch, but full of anecdote, and made more romantic still by Howard Sooley's lazy, hazy pictures.*

It's a nostalgic book – how rare for Christo – looking back on how things had been done at Dixter during his lifetime: explaining how the potter Alan Caiger-Smith had made his salad bowl; how his brother Oliver overdosed on artichokes; how Christo bought stem ginger in gallon jars; and how his dachshund once scoffed a bowl of rising, uncooked dough from the fireside and spent 'the most uncomfortable night of her life'; of being taken as a child to dancing lessons by his mother who, every year, would stop outside a particular humble cottage to buy the entire crop of the cottager's quince tree to take home and crystallise. It is a charming picture of Dixter and its social life in the 1990s, which did indeed centre on the kitchen. 'Things have, of course, changed dramatically over the years,' Christo wrote, 'no dressing bell at 7.00. No dinner bell at 7.30. All servants (resident) gone, but I can do what I like, when I like in the kitchen and servants' hall. That's quite something.' And he did. Those rich creamy sauces, fruit fools, artichokes dipped in melted butter, hard Dutch cheeses . . .

There was to be another book in that same year of 1998: *Dear Friend and Gardener*, written with Beth Chatto, also for Frances Lincoln. Beth, Christo and his agent Giles Gordon had been talking in the Parlour one day, and Beth said she did not want to write more gardening books – she was a gardener, not a writer, she did not want to repeat herself. Giles, ever the optimist, the fixer, said: why not do a book purely in letter form? And so it was born: a backward-and-forward correspondence about life in two gardening households – Christo with his busy circle of young friends and gardeners, Beth with her quieter grown-up family and staff. The idea at the start was for it to be a much wider-ranging book, with more about life outside gardening, but the publishers were determined to rein it in to make it more marketable (their established audience was only in gardening), and so it became.

If *Gardener Cook* was nostalgic, *Dear Friend and Gardener* was positively polite, a sweet exchange of letters between (old) old friends,

---

* Sooley had provided the photographs for a book on the garden of film-maker Derek Jarman, Prospect Cottage, on the sea-shore at Dungeness, and Christo had loved both garden and pictures.

sharing their enthusiasms and enjoying times spent together, and all written in a very gentle rhythm, with no illustrations to force the pace. The letters are not highlights of their correspondence over the years, but rather a snapshot of the moment, created from letters written and collected purposefully during the gestation of the book. There is no push, no great wit, not least because Christo was writing to someone he knew to be an equally knowledgeable gardener. But there is regular agreement to disagree; when Beth received her first 'official' letter from Christo, she actually threw it down in disgust, so much did she disagree, although her considered reply was more measured. Still, there is an underlying sense that the publisher was concerned that the book might not be sufficiently *useful*, that it might be an expensive ego-trip, and there is an air of them having been told to *explain* things from time to time, beyond what would be natural in a letter. The result is a book that has a good deal of gardening meat in it, but that is primarily a picture of daily life, particularly at Dixter.

For Christo, his way of life at Dixter felt like an institution in the best sense of the word, long established and rooted in the civilised benefits of the early part of his century, and in *Dear Friend and Gardener* he was out to celebrate it. It was a kind of thank you too, to all the people who were his friends and who played a part in the life of Dixter; names crop up in every other paragraph. Fine in small doses, but here rather richly laid on. At heart it is a bedside book, for keen British gardeners, although it sold moderately well abroad.

In January 1998 Christo had been suffering from pains across his shoulders and was told by his doctor that it was the onset of Parkinson's disease. His vet, Nick Mills, saw how doddery Christo was becoming and told him to get to a specialist, who pronounced the problem to be angina. So off Christo went to hospital, this time for a triple heartbypass operation. Stamina was now a matter of pride and so, only days afterwards, he was sitting up in a hospital bed in London, writing his weekly *Country Life* column and more annoyed by sub-editors who fiddled with his copy than he was by pain. He had made his feelings known and the handling of his copy was taken over directly by the chief sub-editor, Anne Wright, a remarkably kind but emotionally needy, single woman who lived not many miles from Dixter and chose to look after Christo's interests as might a dutiful daughter. Words, for him, had to be *precise*, and that was how *he* delivered them; she would see that they remained that way.

Fergus was keen to make more money to fund more gardeners, to keep the garden spinning ever faster in all its parts. Lucrative tutorial sessions were set up for American groups from *Horticulture* magazine, who would come to stay locally for a week and spend the days at Dixter learning how the place was run and planted. They were pure love-ins arranged by Fergus, and the audiences could not get enough of the dynamic, fast-talking Fergus, with old bad-boy Christo in the cameo roles; some people came back four and five times. *Gardens Illustrated* magazine also held exclusive lecture days there for its readers, laying on a fabulous lunch and tea and a chance to sit at the knee of the master.

Christo made his one permanent* change to Lutyens' design that March. He wanted to take up the central lawn in the Wall Garden and pave it; at present he felt it was just a corridor, a transitional space in which one could not be comfortable enough to enjoy the planting in its peripheral borders. He had seen David Hockney's drawings of dachshunds and fancied a pebble mosaic showing his two dogs Canna and Dahlia curled up together, yin and yang, and he commissioned a professional design, found it too fussy, then asked Miles Johnson, partner of Frank Ronan, to design an alternative. The grande dame of pebble mosaic, Maggie Howarth, was then commissioned to translate the image into pebbles, and the mosaic itself was laid by her New Zealand assistant Mark Davidson. Thus are the Dixter dachshunds immortalised, and thus was another of Dixter's simpler spaces put into its dancing clothes.

The dachshunds have one further memorial; the heavy wooden box at the garden gate was also installed on their behalf, somewhere for the postman to deposit the mail, since he was tired of being eaten alive by free-range dachshunds. Christo found the attitude weak; he suggested to Fergus that they should get up early and put the dogs *in* the post-box, to greet the postman.

Even now, at seventy-seven, Christo could still work on his knees in the garden, with his trug and kneeling mat, and his dogs nearby. Occasionally, if the weather was kind and if travel and his huge writing

---

* His changes to the Rose Garden, the Topiary Lawn and the meadow, were all reversible.

commitments gave him the opportunity, he would spend the whole day working alongside Fergus, as he had alongside Daisy. Time in the garden, the simple hands-on pleasure, was becoming ever more and more precious, and he refused to get up from his knees and break off when it was not warranted:

> A rather nice looking young Dutchman informed me that he had published the translation into Dutch of one of my books and that he was with a group (then in the house) of writers and publishers who would love to meet me if I would give them a quarter hour of my time. I may say that I'd been closeted in the house all morning and had only just emerged. I told him NO, but if they cared to speak to me while I worked, they could. So while I was on my knees, extracting old forget-me-nots and Limnanthes plants, he introduced his boss. I greeted him while looking at his legs from my kneeling position, and said I'd recognise his trousers (khaki drill) anywhere. If I'd looked up or held up a paw, there'd have been endless introductions. So I suppose they won't want to trans-late me again.

By the end of March 1999 he was submitting his copy for another book to Frances Lincoln, *Christopher Lloyd's Gardening Year* – 'over 70,000 words written in just two months, so that's a load off my conscience' – and it appeared in October. In a sense it was an updating of *The Year at Great Dixter*, of 1987, following Dixter month by month. But now the photographs were by the young garden photographer Jonathan Buckley, infinitely better than Christo's own from a decade earlier. Buckley had been coming to the garden to take pictures since 1994 and had a good library of Dixter shots. He suggested to Erica Hunningher at Frances Lincoln that there might be a book in it, and the project gradually materialised. Further bespoke photography followed and gradu-ally Buckley began to spend more and more time at Dixter, in part taking a brief from Fergus on what particular plants or combination of plants Christo would be writing about in *Country Life* and in *The Guardian* during the next couple of weeks, so that he could have pictures ready to hand. Everybody benefited, and most of all the readers.

Christo himself was notoriously difficult to photograph; portraiture was far too close to nostalgia for his liking. But for the book,

Buckley managed to persuade him to repeat the gestures he had been making in the course of a garden tour, standing, purple-shirted and pot-bellied, in his 'pulpit' – an old, hollow-crowned hebe in the High Garden. For once in a professional shot he looked happy, like an amateur conductor finding himself suddenly in charge of a professional orchestra.

Christopher Lloyd's Gardening Year is a nostalgic book, calm and cool, and not especially witty. Once again Christo toured the different areas of the garden, looking at the planting, and it was an excellent review of seasonal plants. But there was nothing new from him, more a kind of farewell, a 'record of an oasis' as he called it: gardeners at Dixter after him must not automatically or slavishly use the plants he used, but must move on.

In 1999 Christo went with Pip Morrison to Brittany, to see Isabelle and Tim Vaughan's gardens at Crech ar Pape, and at Kerdalo, where he suggested Pip should go as head gardener after his degree, to get more experience.

Every couple of weeks Christo and Fergus would drive over to the Royal Horticultural Society's garden at Wisley to take part in judging the plant trials, where Christo had his own very firm views on what did and did not deserve an award. No votes for wishy-washy colours, but he always gave full and sound explanations for his decisions. Graham Stuart Thomas, now retired from his job as Chief Garden Adviser to the National Trust, and hater of the chromatic fortissimo, bristled at his comments. Latterly, as Christo's knees became more troublesome, he drove a buggy through the RHS garden to the trials ground, until the day he careered off into bushes.

At Dixter, where new Williamson furniture seemed to pop up every few months, Pip had got Christo playing Brahms duets, despite his arthritic hands. Christo even took a lightning trip to Truro to see the premiere of our mutual friend Russell Pascoe's opera *The Murder of Charlotte Dymond*, travelling back through the night driven by Fergus and me.

None of this would have been possible without Fergus who worked ridiculously long days on the garden, and Christo was grateful beyond measure, both for the sake of the garden and for his freedom. In 1999 there was a major earthquake in Turkey, its epicentre only thirty miles from Fergus' mother's house, and Fergus was out there immediately, with his brother, to help the rescue teams. His mother was bruised, but the house was still standing, although thousands had been killed just a few miles away. On their return, they raised funds for the victims, and Christo, delighted at Fergus' energy and loyalty, lent money to help fix his mother's house.

To celebrate Christmas, Christo beheaded his very special ten-year-old blue-coned Korean fir to act as Christmas tree in the Great Hall, and planted another to be ready in 2010. 'Well, the millennium will soon be behind us,' he wrote to Dodo Emsworth, 'and I must concentrate on doing some writing – a book on *Colour*, this time. I shall be alright once I get into it but feel daunted ahead of that.' Daisy, he noted, would have been 119 in 2000.

Chapter 11

Last Words, 2000–6

The wonderful thing about Dixter is that I'm just as happy to be returning home as to be leaving it, so there's no end of holiday feeling.
Christopher Lloyd, 1979

In the New Year's Honours List of 2000, Daisy's youngest received an OBE, as had his father. The award had been fostered by Anne Wright at *Country Life*, who, with Fergus, had canvassed worldwide for support via Christo's address book. Christo was tickled to bits to be invited to Buckingham Palace, and mightily relieved that the dress code did not require him to hire morning dress that never fitted properly anyway.

To Colin Hamilton in Pitlochry, he wrote about the delights of his investiture and encounter with royalty:

We were to arrive between 10.00 and 11.00, the ceremony starting at 11.00. Of course we tried to enter by the wrong entrance. Every move we made was the wrong one, but we were gently redirected . . . On reaching the piano nobile, there was a huge gallery and we were in the middle of one side of it. Enquiry as to which award we were there for, then separation of sheep from goats. I take it I was a sheep, as the goats were far more gaily and informally dressed (apart from myself). My lot were, by and large, horribly sober-looking and correct. The two groups were roped off with a space in between for the master of ceremonies, who proceeded to explain the procedure. You are passed from one lackey to another, being asked your name by each of them. Eventually you walk into the reception room (with a throne well behind the Prince, for it was Prince Charles) who stood slightly raised above us supplicants.

You approached him at right angles, turned to face him, bowed, stepped forwards and there he was, his lined moon face very close to mine. While he affixes the decoration on a special hook pinned to your lapel, he talks.

I talked first, saying I had visited his garden – in April – and that it was very pretty (it was). But I have not visited yours, he admitted. I let him off as tactfully as I could. Perhaps he could learn a thing or two by coming – but I didn't SAY that. He was surprised that I hadn't received my OBE a long time back. That was rather a nice observation coming gratis from him, I thought. He was taking a new interest in ferns, he told me, and had been pleased to read me on the subject in Country Life (slight hesitation about which publication; as I couldn't remember myself that was fine. Then a firm goodbye. Retreat by Lloyd (nervously hoping there was nothing behind him). Bow; turn right, proceed out of sight into the next chamber. Hook and decoration removed, the latter put into a box, labelled OBE.

It was not long afterwards that his magnum opus was published: *Christopher Lloyd's Garden Flowers – Perennials, Bulbs, Grasses, Ferns*, from the publishers Cassell. It had taken him three years to write, on and off, a remarkably long time in Christo's terms. 'I'm reeling with the amount of copy I'm turning out,' he had complained ahead of a trip to Scotland. But at last the book arrived, nearly 400 pages long, an A–Z of perennials with inserts of colour photographs by Jonathan Buckley, of such intensity of colour that the pages almost leaped off the book. They were dazzling, like the luminous, exploding orange dahlia on the cover. It was meant to be a book to grab the reader, a basic reference for gardeners without much experience and, for the experienced, something to refer back to for insights.

Certainly those insights and observations are there by the hundred, but it's not amongst Christo's best books. It is written alphabetically, plant by plant, naturally giving more space to some genera than to others, as the number of species and his own interest demanded; Christo could not, therefore, pursue an argument, with plants entering the stage as illustrations along the way, as he had in his great books, *The Well-Tempered Garden* and *Foliage Plants*. Here the plants rule staccato, one after the other, which of course is what an A–Z should do. And yet each entry is written with the usual, discursive Lloydian verve, a personal account of Christo's own insights and experiences. Certainly it is an enjoyable read: of erodiums, for example, 'The storksbills are closely related to the cranesbills. If you can tell the difference between a stork and a crane, you are well away. If not, the leaves of cranesbills are palmate, those of storksbills pinnate . . .' And of *Bupleurum longifolium*, teasing the makers of all-white gardens and all-blue gardens, 'The inflorescence is chocolate-brown. If grown above a bark mulch, this is ideal material for The Invisible Garden.' Wonderful stuff, but somehow it seems frivolous and long-winded here; it is odd to consult an encyclopaedia on a particular plant and be met, cold, with a joke.

In an effort (under pressure from his editor) to be helpful, he included plants that he had no time for; but instead of explaining their few or supposed virtues, he wrote them off with barely a word. Why give space at all to a plant you don't like and have proudly killed twice, without explanation of its needs and preferences, especially when you are making room for jokes elsewhere? Why give any space to such a plant when you could be discussing further varieties of plants you do like? Was this any better than Monty Don using the word 'herbaceous' twenty-eight times? When a reader looks up a plant, only to find it there but undiscussed, it is no help.

Graham Stuart Thomas's *Perennial Garden Plants* had come out twenty-four years previously in 1976, itself nineteen years after Alan Bloom's *Hardy Perennials*, and it was out of date now in so far as names had changed and new varieties had appeared, but Christo's book did not really eclipse Thomas' work ('*That man!*' Thomas used to call Christo). Thomas' work was not remotely chatty or readable, was more tabular, scholarly, crisper, more wide-ranging and faster to consult. It may well be the more likely of the two books to stand the test of time. Certainly there was nothing in Christo's book that he had not said as well, or better, elsewhere. But it was for him a kind of ruling across the page, a summary of his thoughts upon the tools of his trade. It mattered a great deal to him.

Meantime there was another book, *Colour for Adventurous Gardeners*, to finish for the BBC, by May, to be published in 2001. It would be a rewrite of a series of pieces that he wrote for *Horticulture* magazine in 1999, and Christo worked furiously, producing one chapter a week, sequestered in the Parlour and annoyed at himself for eating too much and not taking enough exercise, but that was his life now.

Colour seemed a ridiculous project to him, 'because I don't rate the subject highly' – how ironic, since the use of colour would become the thing for which he was most remembered in the popular imagination – but it would be tied in with a series of four-minute slots on the BBC's prime-time gardening television programme, *Gardeners' World*, and that would bring more visitors to the garden, even if it earned only a location fee rather than a presenting fee. The showman in Christo loved making television, and he had huge admiration for efficient crews. This was the only series of pieces he ever made for television, although he was often interviewed, and he could always say exactly what he wanted in the first take, which then made him childishly impatient when things had to be done again for technical reasons. Ignorant questions could make him very rude to camera, and he regularly strayed away from the subject as a more interesting line of thought struck him. The expression 'herding cats' comes to mind.

But for the time being he had to finish *Colour for Adventurous Gardeners.* Jonathan Buckley and Erica Hunningher would come down to Dixter for day-long sessions finalising which pictures to use and getting him to caption them. The three of them gathered around a large light-box in the Solar, Christo perched on a stool, with the transparencies laid out before them. Around the middle of the day he would nod off on his stool and stop for a sleep (a spinal curvature was giving him shortness of breath), then the work would continue after lunch. A slide would be selected and Christo asked to provide sixty to seventy words to go with it; and there, after a pause, with the low light streaming in through the long windows, he would effortlessly deliver two or three sentences of succinct, perfect prose and immediately be ready for the next.

Location fee only or not, the garden and Dixter needed money; visitor numbers were down and the saga of failed house repairs continued, so Christo was delighted to be asked to write for the website Greenfingers.com, which – as part of a braver, richer new world – paid him £1 a word. He liked that. So now he wrote and Fergus his manager gardened, or rather more often, now, Fergus fed him the subject and structure of what he would write, often leaving work at 9 pm to go home to Hastings and prepare a lecture for Christo or sketch out an article: what was looking good right now, didn't this look good with that, shouldn't we be planting this out? he might suggest. Christo was not truly aware how much help he was getting, even with organising the programme for his work, and yet he bitterly regretted taking Fergus away from the garden. The book itself was a burden, he wrote:

I have got myself, of my own bad judgement, into a pretty stupidly tight corner, with editors and publishers in the usual last minute race to put a book to bed, as they say; while I want to continue with my next project(s). Why do they invariably do this? Can't they work unless there is a time crisis? And then they make the wretched one feel guilty for holding them up for even part of a day, assuming that we have no other commitments than them. How I hate them all.

Too much work and not enough exercise. Christo wanted to work, it was just that it was becoming harder to hang on to the scope of things, the bigger picture. Given his plan by Fergus, he could write wonderfully, but an overall grasp of the bigger picture was leaving him.

And anyway there was life to be lived. Deadlines did not stop him taking a day in London, lunching at the Oxo Tower and going to see a Fritz Lang film at the National Film Theatre. Life must go on, enjoyably, otherwise what was the point? Lecturing began to be more fun than writing, more immediate, something he could do brilliantly off-the-cuff. To Oxford University for example, for the Friends of the Botanic Garden. But Fergus had prepared the lecture, driven him there and sold £400 worth of books, leaving Christo free to absorb the experience: 'I could tell them a thing or two on how to improve their plantings there. They have lately installed an eyesore rock garden – very expensive, the best rock, but oh dear.'

In March 2000 Pip was to be twenty-four and a celebration was called for. Christo and Beth planned to go to Brittany over Easter to see him at Kerdalo, leaving on 28th March. That afternoon Christo, ever the martyr to piles, saw a specialist in Hastings and was diagnosed with bowel cancer, the disease that had killed Ken Stubbs. Christo ate a good meal, and then, with Beth, was driven by his young friend Aaron Bertelsen to Portsmouth, where they spent the night in tip-back seats on the ferry to Caen. Arriving at dawn, they had a further three-hour drive to Kerdalo, where Pip was in the highest spirits. At the first opportunity Christo told Pip of his diagnosis and that he would be having an operation in two weeks; and thereafter he spent the trip in a kind of bliss, freed of responsibility for himself, but glad that his beloved Pip was a year older, strong and thriving. There was no more talk of illness and he was fêted all the way, insisting on buying all the drinks, which had to be champagne. He didn't shave, only talked to and of Pip, listened to him play the piano and speak of how he wanted to learn to play jazz; watched him making an independent life for himself, speaking in easy French to his new friends and serving long seafood lunches at a perplexing 3 pm. In quiet moments Christo wrote pieces for *Country Life*, slowed only by the cramp in his hand, which he treated with quinine. The holiday was a kind of dream, a pause, uncertain which way the music would go.

A fortnight later the operation went ahead, and Christo was pronounced fit. The music started again with a new vigour, and having Pip to think about kept him bright. Never one to telephone when a letter would do, now he was forever ringing Pip in France to see what he was doing, and when Pip was home on holiday he would drive Christo on his British trips, serenaded by the old man reading aloud from *Hamlet* or *Pride and Prejudice* until the road got too bouncy to concentrate. How proud Christo was of his capable young man, who five years before had been a shy, gauche country boy; and how much, when looking at other people's gardens or being lunched by their owners in grand style, he wanted simply to be elsewhere, able to talk with Pip alone. Pip was his success, Christo was giving him the outside world, as Daisy never did to him.

Christo went to Scotland, where the car broke down and Frank Ronan had to get him back to Dixter in the middle of the night. He packed in plenty of Glyndebourne, visits to Covent Garden, concerts at the Wigmore Hall and films at the NFT. At Glyndebourne he was smitten by the soprano Anya Silya singing in *The Macropoulos Case*, as he often was by powerful women. He invited her to Dixter, where they talked Wagner and he asked if she knew Wieland Wagner; yes, she did, she had been his mistress for twenty years, he was a 'difficult man but she was young and could manage him'. Christo was delighted by the gossip, although rather nonplussed that she loved Rupert Williamson's furniture, but showed no interest in Dixter itself. In the kitchen he continued to do the creative parts of cooking and, despite warnings about his high cholesterol level, he still loved Stilton to accompany his Madeira. The best Aberdeen Angus steak was shipped specially from Scotland, and Fergus would call at their favourite fish stall in Hastings for, say, £60 worth of turbot. Well fed and watered, Christo would now to his embarrassment fall asleep at the table, sometimes even over the main course – 'like a hamster going into hibernation' – and even if he was cut off from some of the conversation by intransigent deaf-aids, at least his table was full and lively. In the little porch bedroom he dreamed of Queen Mary once more making a surprise visit to an unprepared Dixter and of there being maggots in the cheese.

There were quiet times too, when he felt his age, nights spent at home by the Solar fire, in his official seat on the sofa under his designer standard lamps, dogs at his side, writing letters or catching up on the classics, perhaps Sassoon or Dickens ('one should always skip the tiresome bits of Dickens'). On warm nights he would take a stroll in the garden alone, with 'the girls', of course, and leaning on his stick; his gardening days were pretty well over because he could get down to his knees, but not up again. There would be quiet little lunches with Vita Sackville-West's son Nigel Nicolson, over from Sissinghurst, and Betty Hussey from Scotney, when they could gossip about 'the past'; sometimes he would sit on Lutyens' bench at the top of the Long Border and chat amiably to a visitor.

The Guardian had been running his columns for more than ten years now and Christo was wearying of the tyranny of regular journalism. 'The Guardian,' he complained, 'now say that with this new magazine, they'll need my (truncated) pieces three days earlier. Such a bore. I shan't try too hard. 3½ weeks ahead seems distinctly over the odds, especially when they know they can usually lean on Jonathan [Buckley, for photographs].' Each column was only 450 words, and with some pointers and headings from Fergus, he dashed them off with a good deal of repetition.

The garden itself was far from boring and, under Fergus' management, it grew ever better and busier. Feathery grasses came to play a more important role; a spiky, silver astelia stood guard at the end of the Long Border, and in the orchard tall young clumps of bamboo began to wave. Student gardeners came and went, glad just to be there; the quality of the craft skills was exemplary; the bedding, often replaced three times a year, shone with new plant combinations; and the Exotic Garden drew ever more popular attention. Christo was becoming the *trademark* as much as the creator of the Dixter brand, while Fergus was the MD making things happen, but with quite extraordinary self-effacement never taking credit for it, always letting it be Christo's.

Others recognised Fergus' unsung talents. A place was offered to him on the RHS's Floral A Committee, which met in London to assess garden plants for awards. At Dixter itself, he was turning the High Garden from rows of stock plants (from which to propagate) into a great rolling garden, grasses and perennials combined, which would look good together as well as serve their commercial purpose for propagation.

And Fergus, together with Christo's friends, began once again to try to persuade Christo that he must do something at least to plan for the future of Dixter after his death; he must take some responsibility. It was unlikely that Olivia, who owned 60 per cent, would want to up sticks with her (second) husband from Strasbourg and live at Dixter, and if it was not to go to the National Trust, then perhaps it should have its own charitable trust. Gradually Christo began to see the need to comply with the good advice of others. And if Dixter became a trust, it could stay open to the public, which with luck would give him the two things he wanted most in life – that Fergus could continue to garden here and develop his ideas, and that Pip could have Dixter as his base and live in a part of it. It made sense now.

Christo's many friends were determined that his eightieth birthday would be special. There was a party for eighty guests on 1st March 2001, with a concert of his favourite pieces in the Great Hall. The nurseryman Graham Gough, who had worked with Elizabeth Strangman at the celebrated Washfield Nursery nearby, was a singer, and he performed Schumann's *Dichterliebe*, accompanied by Pip on the Bösendorfer supplied long ago by Ken Stubbs. A string quartet from the Royal College of Music played Brahms. Christo was thrilled beyond words. *Country Life* gave him a large dish by his favourite potter Alan Caiger-Smith, and there was a collection of £8,000 from his personal friends, organised by his indefatigable friend and sub-editor Anne Wright, to buy him a table and lamp from Rupert Williamson.

A few weeks after the party he was due to speak at a National Trust conference in the Assembly Rooms at Bath: 'Garden Culture in the 21st Century'. It was to be a major event. Christo had been asked to be guest of honour and he accepted, not realising that he would be expected to make a speech, which troubled him. He refused to read a script as he hated stilted delivery, and decided it would be better to use only prompt cards (his memory was no longer sufficiently reliable to do it all off-the-cuff; he was much older than all the other speakers at the conference). To smarten him up for the event, Fergus sat him on a stool on the terrace with a sheet around him, and cut his hair and eyebrows, and off they went.

In Bath, a string of heavyweight lecturers filled the programme. Tim Smit, in his forties, the man responsible for developing the hugely popular Lost Gardens of Heligan and the Eden Project, spoke as powerfully and charismatically as ever; but his pushy, chatty, on-the-hoof delivery was anathema to Christo, who, showing his age, called him 'a caged tiger – totally without charm – one has no wish to know him'.

During the afternoon of the second day Christo polished up his speech with Fergus, in the light of what had been said so far by other speakers, and he was confident when the time came for him to speak. But it was a disaster. By the time the long conference dinner was over he was tired, and because he was being fitted with a microphone he could not listen to Anna Pavord's introduction. He did not know for how long he was supposed to speak, but 'he found the audience on his side' and by his own admission he became prolix, talking in disparaging terms about the National Trust's gardens and their management, and enthusing rather stiffly about successes in private gardens. On and on he went, losing the thread, until, in the end and before he had had time to wind up and summarise his thoughts on the conference, Anna Pavord had to step onto the stage and point out that, sadly, it was time to draw the evening to a close. 'A bit of a show really,' he wrote, 'but no doubt I deserved it. Anyway, Fergus was pleased with me [he was not] and so, on the whole, were the rest. I never thought I could do it, with so little reference to note headings or cards – though they were essential. My ego was greatly boosted! Oh dear!' Truth to tell, there was a widespread feeling that the grand old man of English gardening had lost it.

Three days later he was heading for safer ground, to lecture in New York, Philadelphia and Toronto, this time to enthusiastic gardeners rather than professionals. 'Aren't *guitars* small these days,' said Christo blissfully to Fergus as they got on the plane, of a boy with a tennis racket over his shoulder. He sat in Business Class writing up his ideas about the conference while, back in Economy, Fergus was drawing up a plan for a border at White Flower Farm Nursery in Connecticut. The border – even longer than the Long Border at Dixter – would demonstrate the potential of the nursery's wares and be written up in Tom Cooper's new American magazine *The Gardener* (published by White Flower Farm). Accompanying it would be illustrations by the English gardener and artist Simon Dorrell.

In Philadelphia, Christo gleefully donned his favourite Lucy Goffin tie, made in the colours of his own Long Border, and sat down to address his audience, using a microphone, with Fergus by his side and close enough to be nudged when the slide needed changing or a plant needed pointing out onscreen. 'It works well,' Christo thought, but twice he overran his allotted time; those with baby-sitters got up and left. And yet the audiences loved him – this witty, wicked old man who was making the garden they could see before them, so lush, wanton, so liberating to the imagination of an American gardener used to seeing less sophisticated gardening. He was just how *they* wanted to be when they got to eighty.

From New York Christo and Fergus flew to Toronto, where they stayed with Susan and Geoffrey Dyer, he a generous, easy-spoken, garden-loving inheritance-tax lawyer who would become a good friend, and after Christo's death a Dixter trustee; she just the kind of little, outspoken, independent woman in the Beth Chatto mould that Christo loved. 'I told Susan as we left that I'd known from the first minute of meeting her that she was BAD.' The lecture here overran again, but Christo's own opinion of the trip was optimistic. 'I have had quite sufficient energy,' he stated, 'while husbanding it.'

It was not so on his next trip three years later, when he, Fergus and his deputy Matt Rees went over to make adjustments to the White Flower Farm border. 'Lovely!' cried Christo, as he took a last look at his own Long Border at Dixter, then said farewell to the dogs. 'Canna suitably tragic but resigned. I shut her and old Dahlia (16½) into the servants' hall.' But even with two helpers and wheelchairs, the effort of flying and a final taxi to his hosts, Tom and Emily Cooper, exhausted him.

Fergus and Matt spent a whole day planting until 8 pm, while Christo rested and read, or watched, or signed copies of his latest books in the shop, glad to be doing something at least, but, because of his deafness, feeling useless and a dummy when others laughed and chatted. It was more cheering when *House & Garden* came to write a feature on them and they were photographed together. As part of a special opening at the nursery there were to be lectures and demonstrations, with speakers from Europe and America. Fergus spoke on 'Succession', and Christo, with an air of closure, on 'My Life at Great Dixter', using for once a mere fifty slides. Bed at 9.45, and it felt very, very late. In Philadelphia on the way home, Christo stayed with his old friends Joe Henderson and Jeff Jabco (assistant director of the Scott Arboretum), and while Fergus and Matt again went off lecturing, Joe played the piano to him and helped Christo hobble round their garden with a stick. 'I am TIRED,' he complained, but would not have been anywhere else.

For Fergus and Christo, America had become their last waltz. Fergus was determined to give Christo every last bit of stimulation that he could cope with, knowing that Christo would never wish to take it easy. And Christo was determined to stand the pace, knowing that such trips gave Fergus pleasure too, and opportunities to show his gardening talents to the world. They amazed each other, and it made them happy.

Colour for Adventurous Gardeners was published in May 2001. As a publisher, Frances Lincoln had served him well, but now, with BBC Books and with Erica Hunningher working for him as a freelance editor, Christo was in much more commercial hands; the BBC had a heavy publicity machine and he would benefit from his television tie-ins. The book read easily, but less conspiratorially than in the past – not patronising, but keeping things very clear for a mass audience. Colour-by-colour he went though his favourite plants, and Jonathan Buckley's vibrant and crisply printed photographs made Christo's ideas leap off the page. For the first time he had double-page spreads of plant portraits demonstrating a particular colour, with long, extended captions to explain their significance in full detail. And yet as usual Christo was determined not to let people fall into the sticky pit of good taste, where they timidly followed the timid colours of timid fashions. Choosing to ignore the received wisdom of the colour wheel, the principle by which harmonious colours are traditionally chosen, Christo proclaimed that every colour can be successfully used with any other, so long as it is not done indiscriminately. The time was right for this attitude: the loud oranges, reds, purples and limes of his Exotic Garden were becoming popular fare, and in the supermarkets pre-selected bunches of flowers echoed his tastes with bright gazanias, zinnias and eustomas. On television, Christo's series of short pieces showed him as the wicked old wizard (or was it gnome?) pointing the way.

Television bred more television, and Dixter was featured in a quirky series on gardens called *The Curious Gardeners*. It was introduced, said Christo, 'by two men who have made a name for themselves in a comic programme where they travel around in an ancient motor car. They were put out because I didn't know them.' He also decided that their preparation for the interview was inadequate and said so, rudely.

Accolades were piling up: an Honorary Doctorate from the Open University; a Lifetime Achievement Award from the Garden Writers' Guild; and now the photographer Tessa Traeger was asked to take photographs of Christo for a projected exhibition of gardening personalities and luminaries in the National Portrait Gallery. 'I said I wouldn't be taken if Fergus wasn't included. She wanted to have me sitting and Fergus standing by my side but I wouldn't have any of that and we're both standing each with an arm round the other.' To Christo it was an important picture, for it recognised publicly his love and debt to Fergus; and the pictures were black-and-whites taken on a plate camera, very reminiscent of the one his father had used.

Christo was featured on the radio programme *Desert Island Discs* (it had been fixed by Erica Hunningher, who had been at university with the presenter Sue Lawley). What a chance for Christo, to think through all the music that had meant so much to him over eight decades – German lieder, his beloved Brahms that he played with Ken Stubbs and with Pip. When it was broadcast he listened to it on a transistor radio, on the 'family pew' by his father's topiary lawn, and wept all the way through.

There has always been a feeling in the gardening world that gardeners and plantsmen know too little about design, and that designers and landscape architects know too little about plants. What Christo recognised and admired in Pip was that, as a qualified landscape architect, he was still passionate about plants and had been keen to get experience of gardening. Since getting his degree he had acquired several years' practical experience in France and Holland, and by 2002 he was back at Dixter, his home now more or less, deciding what to do next. The designer Mary Keen had known him for some years and, taking on a project at Chilham Castle in Kent, asked him if he would join her on the project, as a designer, but also seeing to the implementation of it for the first year. This appealed to Pip, and it could be done from Dixter, which suited both him and Christo.

The difficulty in having protégés is that some day they must go out into the world and stand free on their own feet. Fergus was doing very well at that – lectures, judging, a little writing under his own name – but still managing to remain at Dixter. When groups, photographers and media people came to the garden, it was Fergus and Perry Rodriguez, the kind and indefatigable business manager, who briefed them on what they needed to know, giving Christo time free to write or spend with Pip.

Now Pip too, as was inevitable, was putting a toe out into a more professional world. He must have more space on the top floor, decided Christo, and his own telephone there, and if he lived in an un-Dixterly chaos of clothes and possessions, well, that was his way. What mattered was that he was there.

It was a curious relationship, and one that put huge pressures on Pip. It was undoubtedly a kind of love on both their parts, unphysical on Pip's part and physical – in the sense of adoration – on Christo's. He was jealous of Pip's time, his friends, and, while he was at Edinburgh, his girlfriend. And adoration is delightful and flattering; but Pip did indeed need time to himself, to enjoy life physically – riding, swimming, walking – and Christo could not begin to keep up. They toured the gardens of the Dingle peninsula and Christo was painfully aware how much excitement his company failed to provide. Stopping one day on a country road for a picnic, he sent Pip racing up a hillside to see the view, watching his figure as it shrank all the way to the top. 'He is so lovely,' confided Christo to his diary, 'that I find it hard to take my eyes off or keep my hands off him – but I do.' At Dixter, Pip would 'do his disappearing trick' for hours at a time, to walk or write letters; he was too young to be amused when Christo asked boring people to lunch at Dixter, then fell asleep leaving Pip to entertain them, or when Christo could not see that some people took advantage of his hospitality. At least once a month there would be a steaming row between them, and Pip would shout and go red in the face, creating a difficult atmosphere for everybody at Dixter. Soon afterwards Pip had forgotten it, but that was not Christo's way – the Lloyds had such a burden of self-respect; steaming rows were not things they did, tortured criticism being more their line. The quarrels came as a shock to Christo. And as a result he did, occasionally, see that he was not always right, that he could have shortcomings himself and be a naughty boy: 'even at my age,' he recognised, 'it is possible to become a better person'. In Pip's words, it was a relationship 'full of silent understanding and misunderstanding'.

Despite the fact that Dixter was now infamous in the popular press for its Exotic Garden, in the serious gardening world it was just as valued for its orchid- and crocus-spangled flower meadows. Christo had grown flowers in grass all his life and not thought anything unusual about it (it had been Daisy's passion). But gradually it had become apparent to him that the 'new perennials' movement, heavily mixing ornamental grasses and perennials, was developing a genuine sister movement in the wilder process of meadow gardening. Time at last to write about meadow gardening himself.

Over the years he had gained rich and personal experience at home and he had learned much from his visits to the Alps, the Burren and Braunton Burrows, but the plant communities in the different kinds of grassland varied enormously. He would need to do some research.

Fergus took him to see meadows in the Peak District where, in his Buxton hotel bedroom, his keen eye recognised the same bedroom wallpaper as when he stayed with Oliver so many years ago. I joined Fergus and Christo at a conference at Sheffield University on flower meadows, organised by the pioneer James Hitchmough, and on Christo's visit to Bath, Fergus took him to Emorsgate Seeds, a small company with great experience of creating and maintaining wild-flower (hay) meadows.

There was a jaunt to Germany with Romke, Fergus and me, to see the ecologically compatible plantings of grasses and perennials at Grugapark, Weihanstephan, West Park and the Hermannshof ('very Piet Oudolf – a tasteful haze,' sniped Christo) and to see meadows in the foothills of the Alps, near Innsbruck.

Christo went to Hungary again, this time taking up an offer to be shown meadows by Géza Kósa of the Budapest Botanical Garden and arboretum, whose seed list Christo had used. It was a lightning trip with lots of roadside stops and, despite being embarrassed by his failing energy,

Christo got to see national parks and nature reserves of wet meadows, sand dunes and acidic grasslands. (With the arboretum itself, he was unimpressed: 'Too many trees, as usual . . .')

There was even a three-week trip to Cape Province with Tom Cooper, editor of *Horticulture* magazine, where Christo saw the sandy veldt, many a nature reserve, and aloes to die for, although not the great annual flowerings of daisies when the rains come in Namaqualand. He and Tom lectured to a small packed house, after which: 'Tom and I are each presented with a useless, glossy book on Namaqualand, which I shall leave behind. Awkward, square shape. Nice thought, of course.' They were ferried round with extraordinary kindness by their hosts, always stopping when someone spotted something promising from the car – an anemone perhaps, fifty yards away up a steep bank of burned-out proteas, or wild gladioli by the side of a road where traffic was hammering by. Black children looked on bemused at the two Brits poking about in the scrub . . .

By 2001 his *Meadows* book was commissioned and ready to be written, but for all his enthusiasm for the subject, Christo was deeply uncomfortable about it. On his travels he had seen academic and scientific work being done, in habitat re-creation and the creation of annual or seed-sown meadows; he knew he must include the science, if *Meadows* was to be a worthwhile book. 'I have never felt so lost and confused,' wrote the eighty-year-old Christo, 'if I can only get started . . .'

By the time he finished writing the book he was glad to be shot of it. When his copy reached the editor Erica Hunningher, it was found to be much shorter than its commissioned length and – astonishingly for Christo – appeared to need a great deal of editing and reordering. He had worked with partners before (Graham Rice, Tom Bennett, Beth Chatto), but this time the book came out wholly under his name, despite the fact that great chunks of its wisdom were culled and quoted from others. It was cobbled together. There was no humour in it, no fun. Undeniably *Meadows* is invaluable to a meadow gardener, and it is probably a better reference book than his 'magnum opus', *Christopher Lloyd's Garden Flowers*. There is even a bibliography in it, for goodness' sake; when did Christo do *that*? But it just does not read like Lloyd.

* * *

With the Exotic Garden now up and running, the famous subtropical coda of every season, Christo and Fergus were able to concentrate again on other parts of the garden. The High Garden – Fergus' baby – was a basket of autumn golds and grasses. There had always been an L-shaped bed outside the Parlour where Christo wrote, and, even since Daisy's time, it had been an area for summer bedding, with at least one scheme per year. In different hands it might have been a dreary slab of Parks Department colour, but in their hands it was now always a delightful experiment in looser, mixed planting, trying new varieties and combinations. They were intent on enriching the planting in the Long Border and the Sunk Garden too, with slot-in planting, so that wave upon wave of colour would succeed each other: between the more permanent groups of shrubs and perennials, they would find spaces to stack up several phases of seasonal planting on the same spot. Not just two phases, but three and four: bulbs under spring bedding, followed by bedded-out perennials, followed by bedded-out autumn perennials. There was never a dull moment, never a tired gap in a border. Every tune was being given alto, tenor and bass lines too, to make a work of extraordinarily and continuously rich texture.

There was an ever-growing supply of dramatic plants in pots – succulents, large-leafed begonias, lilies, ferns and many more disparate and unusual species – which were bought by Fergus to stand by the porch door where Daisy had sat to welcome visitors, built into great pyramids of dazzling texture and colour, flourishes of sheer bravado. Why not do it, for the fun of it? Fergus loved growing plants to such perfection, and the pleasure it gave Christo to see them piled so ebulliently high; Christo loved to see Fergus so excited. Pot collections began to spring up all over the garden like baroque molehills, in the Wall Garden, beside the steps leading to the topiary lawn, every one beautifully arranged and maintained daily; the craftsmanship was superb. And on Lutyens' constellation of round steps leading from the Long Border to the orchard, there appeared those extraordinary lunar landscapes of bedded-out cacti and succulents. The garden's season of interest grew ever longer as new plants succeeded old and Dixter became more hectic. The gardening world worshipped at Fergus' and Christo's feet.

Planting for a constant succession of colour was nothing intrinsically new to Christo. To some degree he had been doing it all his life, but never as well and spectacularly as with Fergus' help. Not surprisingly, he now got down to writing about it, in *Succession Planting for Adventurous Gardeners* (2005). It was not a particularly long book, but it was Christo at his height – witty, immediate, and talking (that's the right word) about what he did best. *Having it all.*

Fergus helped to organise his structure of the book and provided Christo with aides-memoires, but nonetheless he was writing with authority again here, on his own terms, because it was the subject he wanted to pass on to the reader more than anything: the spectacular, labour-intensive gardening that he and Fergus had brought to a peak. 'The great game', as he called it.

It was indeed the kind of photography of which garden writers dream – shots of the same place taken through successive seasons – and even the captions are extraordinarily informative. This book, along with *Colour* and *Meadows*, formed the trio of important books that would end his career as an author, and they complemented, in a very different style, the three that kicked it off: *The Well-Tempered Garden*, *Foliage Plants* and *The Adventurous Gardener*.

Dixter's present success was not just because Fergus and Christo thought the same way and had the same high ambitions and standards of craftsmanship, but because Fergus was so much better a manager of people than Christo or Quentin ever had been. There was no Cromwellian or moneyed background in Fergus, no distance kept between him and the staff, and he was loved for it. In his hands, the staff became one great family all pulling together and, as might be expected from a Turk, Christo the patriarch was correctly revered in his old age, whatever his foibles, and allowed all the credit for his family's efforts. Never did Dixter run more smoothly. And since the young friends Christo had deliberately cultivated were there to help him, there might be one more book, on *exotic* gardening perhaps, if he could manage it, and if his painful arthritic knees would let him concentrate. It was the obvious thing to do, it was Dixter's trademark and played with a range of plants that he had loved all his life. If it did not happen, well, he had Fergus his closest friend always to hand, and an understanding beloved in Pip.

Or he thought he did. Pip had been around Christo for nine years and was now twenty-eight. Christo must surely have realised that at some point Pip was bound to – *ought to* – move on, and that he would not – or could not – remain quietly on the top floor as heir apparent for ever. Mary Keen had been pleased with the work Pip had done for her, but felt he ought to move on from her too, to find experience working with greater scope. With this in mind she introduced him to a serious, rather suave young landscape architect, whose sinuous land-form designs had attracted high praise. They fell immediately in love, and that was that. Pip had to recognise he was gay now, not simply in some kind of loving communion with dear old Christo. He knew he had to leave Dixter and start a life of his own. It was messy, as only such things can be. Christo was desperately hurt. It was Frank Ronan who nursed him along (just as he had encouraged Pip to come out), coaxing Christo to come to terms with this inevitable outcome.

What should Christo do now? He had spent the last thirty years trying to help young men as shy as he had been, to sort themselves out at an early age and to be able to make something of their emotional lives, not wait until they were fifty, as he had. He had raised up Pip, given him confidence and watched him take a place in the world, with a job and self-respect, as he himself had found through his teaching at Wye. But now he must do what Daisy had never been prepared to do for him – he must let Pip go, generously, and with his best interest at heart.

In his turn, Pip did not abandon Christo, but stayed at Dixter one night a week until Christo died.

There had been a time when having young people around him had made Christo more comfortable about himself, feeling that he was on the sidelines, but still there at the match. Now he was of an age when infirmity made the age gap seem cruelly conspicuous. He hated being fat (not that he would have considered eating any less well) and his arthritic knees were continuously painful, despite silicone injections. His specialist said he should have a new knee cap, with a view to replacing the other one if the operation was a success. So be it: in March 2005 he was at Hastings getting it done, with plans to go by train and cab to Covent Garden ten days later. In the interim he worked madly to deliver his journalistic copy in advance; but however much everybody at Dixter contrived to give him time in which to concentrate on writing, he felt increasingly confused and slow. It didn't help that electricians had been in the house for months, disturbing the peace.

But the operation went well and a professional carer came in twice a day to help him wash and dress (he had fallen out with and sacked his long-standing housekeeper). During the day he lived in the Yeoman's Hall, Daisy's original ground-floor bedroom, and could be helped to the bathroom next door. But still it wasn't easy. What he needed was a young friend to live in and be permanently on hand for him. And so Aaron Bertelsen, then working at the Jerusalem Botanical Garden, stepped into the breach, to care for him, bath him, cook for him. Aaron's raw Kiwi bonhomie was just what Christo needed. No shred of sentimentality here to embarrass either of them.

Christo could take some comfort in the fact that he had at last agreed to have set up the Great Dixter Charitable Trust, to which he might leave his share of Dixter and which might work to keep the place together after his death. Even this was a most uninstitutionalised enterprise, with Trustees who were valued for their sympathy with the spirit of life at Dixter rather than for their rich City connections. 'I'm hopelessly ignorant about it,' he confessed, but at least it was done and a load off his mind. He could let go a little.

That same March Christo received a letter from Clive Aslet, then editor of *Country Life*, offering him birthday greetings for the 3rd. Christo was touched and wrote back on 16th April, thanking Clive warmly for his kind wishes and commiserating with him on the pressures of working for the magazine's 'greedy and insatiable' American owners. 'So I salute you and the magazine,' ran his final, brief paragraph, 'I hope I may continue to be able to support you till I am 85 – less than a year to go, now! All the very best, from Christo.'

If happiness promotes healing, even of knees, then Fergus supplied Christo with the very best, for that July his wife Amanda gave birth to a baby girl, Ayşegül. She was the nearest Christo could have to a grandchild and he told everybody what a wonderful father Fergus would make. So much warmer than his own cool, gentlemanly father, so much less complicated and demanding than his mother. He saw a lot of Ayşegül – they made sure he did – and it was a tonic for him to have a child in the house; better even than 'the girls'.

Progress on the first knee was good until, to his shame, Christo stood up too suddenly from a chair on the terrace where he had been asleep, and tore it. But still it healed, and Christo decided he was game to have the other knee done: September saw him in hospital in Hastings once more, in a positive mood. When he came home this time, there was a letter from Clive Aslet at *Country Life*, replying to his own letter of 16th April:

> I have been thinking of your letter to me of April 16th, suggesting that you would quite like to wrap up your *In My Garden* column in the coming months. I thought it would be a good plan if we started to wean our readers gently and help them get used to the idea of your retirement after all these wonderfully productive years.
>
> Consequently I thought you might like to reduce your contributions to twice a month from, say, the November 3 issue, with a view to concluding the column some months later.
>
> This will be an extraordinary event in the life of the magazine after all these years, and you will of course plunge the readers into a state of mourning. There are few things that have gone on longer than my own period on *Country Life* and so you can imagine the gap it will leave in my own life. However, I couldn't help sympathising with your letter: a column written week in and week out is, inevitably, a burden, and one that has to be laid down at some point.

Christo was devastated, having no memory of having expressed such a sentiment, and if he had given such an impression, why had Clive Aslet taken six months to acknowledge the resignation of a columnist of Christo's stature and longevity? Christo, rightly or wrongly, did not clear up the matter on the telephone. Frank Ronan asked *Country Life* to produce Christo's so-called letter of resignation and they prevaricated until Christo's agent put on pressure, at which point they admitted that they thought the time had come for Christo to let go. Frank suggested Christo should take the initiative and resign, which he did straight away by email: 'Dear Clive, With reference to your letter date 27/09/05 I wish to inform you that my copy CL271005 is the last I will submit to *Country Life*. I look forward to receiving any outstanding payments forthwith. Yours faithfully, Christopher Lloyd.' He was furious, full of curses and deeply hurt by the stealth of his dismissal. Aslet acknowledged the email, again not picking up the telephone, but regretfully accepting the resignation. What a sorry ending to such an extraordinary career.

Of course Christo was tired, but there was no question of the column having been a burden that was unwelcome. It was the part of his output that gave him most pleasure, since he was writing for his own familiar audience. It brought him self-respect. If there was repetition of ideas, well, perhaps that was inevitable over such a long time; but there was generally no lack of sparkle.

Changes were afoot at the magazine anyway: soon afterwards the contributions of wildlife columnist David Tomlinson ended, and Tony Venison, the magazine's long-standing horticultural columnist, finished also. Clive Aslet too found himself laying down his own burden to become editor-at-large. Fortunately, the monthly magazine *Gardens Illustrated* was tipped off, by Perry Rodriguez, Dixter's office manager, that Christo had time and space for a column, and the editor Juliet Roberts scooped him up at once. A few months later, as his dignity began to heal, Christo was saying that the loss of *Country Life* suited him quite well, although he would miss the money.

Times at *Country Life* had in any case become tricky. Anne Wright, whose mission it had been to handle Christo's copy and save him from the clutches of sub-editors in general, was away from work and ill with cancer. Christo had also written to her, to put *her* at arm's length from Dixter, where, however kindly meant, her close and desperately loyal attentions were beginning to irritate him. Nonetheless when Clive Aslet came to visit her in hospital, even this latter rejection did not stop her from telling him precisely what she thought of the way the magazine had handled Christo's departure.

So: no more *Country Life*, but there was his book on exotic gardening to write, even if it was from the confines of the Yeoman's Hall. Aaron kept Christo in order indoors, and pushed him round the garden in a chair if he felt like it. Christo did his exercises, as his physiotherapist had ordered, to make sure he got better. And now, doing those exercises in the bathroom, he fell and wrenched the knee from the second operation. This time the tear refused to heal, and in January 2006 Christo was in hospital for the third time, to refix the operation to the second knee with a metal bar. The procedure itself went well enough, but, as can happen when breaking into large bones, a fat embolism from the operation appeared in his brain and he was put into intensive care, where his fighting spirit ebbed at last. 'I don't mind if I die now,' he wept, 'I'm so tired, and the last fifteen years have been the happiest of

my life.' With this off his chest, he stopped eating and refused medi-
cines, and then, tough as ever – ashamed perhaps – he rallied, picked
himself up and with Lloydian discipline began to eat again. Visitors
came four times a day – Olivia of course, and Fergus, Perry, Frank, Pip,
Matt, Aaron: the young men who were his family. The nurses had never
seen such attention.

One snowy day Fergus had to be at the Royal Horticultural Society
offices in London, and when in the late afternoon he came to take his
turn at visiting Christo, propped up on pillows in his own private room,
he noticed that his speech was slurred. It was the nurses' opinion that
Christo might have been given a celebratory nip too many of his beloved
malt whisky (it was never far away in the hospital locker), but it turned
out to be a stroke. For ten more days Christo shuddered on, struggling
to communicate. Then words left him, and he slept, and then he died.

Post-Mortem Dixter

On Christo's death, he owned a 40 per cent share of the Dixter estate, and this passed to the Great Dixter Charitable Trust. His niece Olivia, by process of his brothers' and sister's legacies, owned the remaining 60 per cent. She proposed to allow the Trust to buy out her share at an advantageous rate, as soon as the money could be raised. The purchase has now been achieved and the Trust holds the entire estate, securing Dixter's future as a truly remarkable house and garden, and able to keep it open to the public.

The Friends of Great Dixter was set up to raise funds when Christo died. Major funding came on 18th March 2008, from the Heritage Lottery Fund, with a pledge of £4 million towards an ambitious programme of work, which includes vital repairs to the house and barns, improved facilities for the public and staff, the cataloguing and conservation of the Dixter archive, and a continuing programme of public education.

The Lottery grant is entirely dependent on Dixter itself raising 40 per cent match-funding; the appeal for this continues.

*

Exotic Planting for Adventurous Gardeners was incomplete on Christo's death, but was published in October 2007 with the incorporation of further chapters written by his friends.

If one were to ask what made Christo important in the grander scheme of things and in the gardening world in particular, the answer might be focus. Not only did he spend his whole life, from early child-hood until his death at eighty-five, working on the same garden, but he also wrote about it. His legacy is in the brilliance and liveliness of his books and journalism, and in the sheer size of the corpus of his writing. There had been other astonishingly prolific garden writers in the nineteenth-century – William Robinson, J. C. Loudon – but none who had been able to speak so closely and engagingly about the growing and using of individual plants, nor in such witty and beautifully crafted prose. Christo's whole career of writing was focused tightly upon Dixter, at a time when garden photography had reached a peak of excellence. His picture of the life of one garden is a unique and utterly remarkable resource unlikely ever to be eclipsed. If one includes the contents of the Dixter archive, this picture covers almost a hundred years – most of the twentieth century. It is an intimate picture – yet at the same time the qualities of Christo's writing were such that he managed to make a (not always very happy) family house and garden in East Sussex an internationally loved and respected beacon of artistic and horticultural husbandry.

*

Christo had done all he could, or wished to do, with Dixter. Asked in an interview with Frank Ronan in *Country Life*, shortly before he died, if there was another style of gardening that he hankered to try, his answer was a resounding NO. For him, the point of gardening was the doing and the thinking, and the doing well. 'To get the most out of gardening,' he wrote in *Other People's Gardens*, 'it is important to have a like-minded and equally committed friend or relation on whom to draw for ideas and off whom to bounce your own.' Christo had this in his first life, with Daisy, and found it again with Fergus in his second.

*

His obituaries made much of his constant desire to see change in a garden, which is to misinterpret him. What Christo wanted to root out was stagnation, and to encourage people to be imaginative, free-thinking and ambitious in their gardening. In handing Dixter to a trust, he was making space for other people to experiment on the garden as he had done himself; to make it sing. Fergus Garrett understands well enough that Christo had no love of change for change's sake. 'Change should be natural,' says Fergus, 'no more than the thoughtful gardener would ever make. But that might mean making a gravel garden over the topiary lawn. Christo's legacy is his writing.'

221

Acknowledgements

There are so many people to thank for their help during the making of this book; but my greatest debts are to the Lloyd family and the Trustees of the Great Dixter Trust, who were outstandingly generous with their memories and their time, and also made available the treasure-trove of Dixter's papers. I am grateful to the Trustees of the Great Dixter Trust for permission to reproduce private photographs and to quote from letters, diaries and other documents relating to the house, garden and family. I would also like to thank especially:

Clive Aslet, Thomasina Beck, Tom Bennett, Aaron Bertelsen, Jonathan Buckley, Beth Chatto, Mary Christie, Tom Cooper, *Country Life*, Kulgin Duval, Olivia Eller (née Lind), Elizabeth Ennion (King's College, Cambridge), Edward Flint, Fergus Garrett, Mandy Greenfield, Colin Hamilton, Carol Heaton, Roger Highfield, Charles Hind, James Hitchmough, Erica Hunningher, Anne Jordan, Romke van de Kaa, Mary Keen, Angus Lloyd, Pamela Lloyd, Rusty MacLean (Rugby School), Michael McCoy, Nick Mills, Phillip Morrison, Anna Pavord, Audrey Pharo, Peter Roberts (Bradfield College), Graham Rice, Perry Rodriguez, Frank Ronan, Dorothea Rose (née Emsworth), Michael Schuster, Robert Seeley, Alan Titchmarsh, Pamla Toler, Raymond Treasure, Royal Horticultural Society, Tony Venison, Rupert Williamson, Tom Wright, and my editor at Chatto and Windus, Penelope Hoare.

The Great Dixter Charitable Trust

The Great Dixter Charitable Trust needs funds to ensure the continuation of Christopher Lloyd's inspirational style of gardening, creative plant combinations and high-maintenance horticulture. This will be achieved alongside investment in conservation of the buildings, historic archives and house collections, as well as in providing facilities for training in intensive and experimental horticulture and extending educational opportunities. If you would like to make a donation please contact the Fundraising Office, Great Dixter House, Garden and Nurseries, Northiam, Rye, East Sussex, TN31 6PH, Tel: 01797 254048, or email friends@greatdixter.co.uk

Index

Index